MEDIEVAL STUDIES AT MINNESOTA 2

The Medieval Monastery

Edited by Andrew MacLeish

MEDIEVAL STUDIES at MINNESOTA 2
The Medieval Monastery

MEDIEVAL STUDIES at MINNESOTA 2

The Medieval Monastery

Edited by Andrew MacLeish

NORTH STAR PRESS OF ST. CLOUD, INC.
St. Cloud, Minnesota

Contributors

Bernard S. Bachrach, Department of History, University of Minnesota

Helen T. Bennett, Department of English, Eastern Kentucky University

Constance H. Berman, Department of History, University of Iowa

Hugh Feiss, OSB, Mt. Angel Seminary, St. Benedict, Oregon

Thomas Head, School of Theology at Claremont, Claremont, California

Geoffrey Koziol, Department of History, Harvard University

Jerome L. Kroll, Department of Psychiatry, University of Minnesota

Stanford E. Lehmberg, Department of History, University of Minnesota

Kathryn L. Reyerson, Department of History, University of Minnesota

Linda Seidel, Department of Art, University of Chicago

Alan M. Stahl, American Numismatic Society, New York, New York

Emero Stiegman, Department of Religious Studies, St. Mary's University, Halifax, Nova Scotia, Canada

Library of Congress Cataloging-in-Publication Data
The Medieval monastery.
    (Medieval studies at Minnesota; 2)
    Selected papers from Conference on the Medieval Monastery held 14-16 May, 1985, at University of Minnesota and St. John's Abbey in Collegeville, Minn., and sponsored by the Medieval Studies Committee of the University of Minnesota.
    1. Monasteries—Europe—History—Congresses. 2. Monasticism and religious orders—Europe—History—Congresses. 3. Europe—Church history—Middle Ages, 600-1500—Congresses. I. MacLeish, Andrew. II. Conference on the Medieval Monastery (1985: University of Minnesota and St. John's Abbey, Collegeville, Minn.) III. University of Minnesota. Medieval Studies Committee. IV. Series.
BX2470.M43 1988   271'.009'02   88-19608
ISBN 087839-048-0

Printed in the United States of America by Park Press, Inc., Waite Park, Minnesota. All rights reserved.

Published by:
    North Star Press of St. Cloud, Inc.
    P.O. Box 451
    St. Cloud, Minnesota 56302

Contents

Preface vii

Art and Architecture

Medieval Cloister Carving and Monastic
Mentalité
    Linda Seidel 1

Analogues of the Cistercian Abbey Church
    Emero Stiegman 17

In the Monastic Community

The Way of Mary of That of Martha:
Conceptions of Monastic Life at Savigny,
1112-1180
    Kathryn L. Reyerson 34

Men's Houses, Women's Houses:
The Relationship Between the Sexes
in Twelfth-Century Monasticism
    Constance H. Berman 43

Circatores in the *Ordo* of St. Victor
    Hugh Feiss, OSB 53

Monastic Medicine in Pre-Crusade
Europe: The Care of Sick Children
    Bernard S. Bachrach and Jerome Kroll . 59

Coins and Justice

Monastic Minting in the Middle Ages
    Alan M. Stahl 64

The Monastic Idea of Justice in the
Eleventh Century
    Geoffrey Koziol 70

Of Books

Deconstructing the Monastery in
Umberto Eco's *The Name of the Rose*
    Helen T. Bennett 77

Fideli famae adscribendum iudicantes:
Four Monks in Search of a Hagiographic
Method, 980-1125
    Thomas Head 83

The Reformation

English Cathedral Monasteries and the
Reformation
    Stanford E. Lehmberg 90

PREFACE

The papers in this book have been selected from among those delivered at the Conference on the Medieval Monastery held 14-16 May, 1985 at the University of Minnesota and at St. John's Abbey in Collegeville, Minnesota.

This collection seeks to explore the monastery and its place in medieval European society, economy, and the arts. The monastery played a key role in this society from the sixth through the sixteenth centuries, monks having long been heralded as the guardians and transmitters of the heritage of the Graeco-Roman world. Thus, in defining this role, one must consider the artistic and literary productions of the monastic ateliers and scriptoria as well as the impact of monastic culture through education on the broader community. Monasteries were major landowners, their dependent peasantry numerous, their agricultural production often substantial. The influence of abbots on local and royal politics was frequent as well as pervasive. Related to this pragmatic aspect of medieval monasticism, the enthusiasm of the medieval population for genuine monastic piety, and the dangers of corruption inherent in such popular success in the secular world created a tension in monastic existence. And this tension changed a number of concepts of the monastic experience.

Accordingly, these papers examine monastic life from a variety of perspectives. And they employ a variety of methodologies reflecting use of a wide range of sources. For example, the artistic, visual splendors of cloistral carvings can serve as records of ideas and suggest ways of reading the Scriptures. Another empirical approach interprets the design of churches against the background of the reform of the canons regular.

Several interpretations of monastic life are based upon a variety of written records. An examination of the English monastic cathedral priories at the time of Henry VIII's dissolution of the monasteries depends upon evidence from public records, library catalogs, and financial records. Reading saints' lives "on the level of fact" is a means toward an interpretation of twelfth-century monastic life. Hitherto unnoticed relationships between male and female religious and their communities emerge when records of both kinds of houses are examined. A view of attitudes toward, and behavior concerning, illness in pre-Crusade England and Europe comes from a search through medical tracts and herbals, and a reading of a book of twelfth-century customary laws, the *Liber ordinis*, enables an understanding of the office of *circator* and its development in early Benedictine communities. Legal records such as cartularies yield evidence of a frequent tension between monastic and secular life; Cistercians and Premonstratensians saw litigation as an attempt to restore reason to their disputes with their enemies. Early documents plus the empirical evidence of coins suggest the vicissitudes of monastic minting in France and in the Empire from the eleventh through the fourteenth centuries.

Finally, two papers in our volume use literary sources as means of gaining perspective on medieval monastic life. The hagiographic method and "the cult of the saints" in the Orléanais are analyzed by reading saints' lives by three eleventh- and twelfth-century hagiographers recomposing the sacred history of their foundations. And a critical reading of a contemporary novel, *The Name of the Rose*, demonstrates the appropriateness of a medieval monastic setting to the aims and methods of deconstructionist analysis.

Thus it is that medievalists of diverse disciplines and interests confront, at some point in their research, the omnipresence of the medieval monastery. In presenting these papers to a wider audience, we recognize a well-spring of response among the contemporary public for the ideals which the monastery incarnates. This response was evident in the large and steady attendance of this public at the 1985 Conference on the Medieval Monastery despite the fact that monasteries are no longer in the mainstream of twentieth-century life. Serenity, meditation, retreat, and scholarship are some of the values which we associate with the monastery today. In medieval times, on the other hand, the residents of monasteries were often in the forefront of intellectual advances, thus, of controversies, which role is today filled by the universities. Architecturally, the appeal of the cloister as an element of design for homes and public buildings remains strong. The architectural impact of the monastery goes beyond what might be associated with church or parochial school.

So the existence and influence of monasteries today extend their medieval reality to the present time, stimulating the contemporary imagination. The year 1980, for example, saw several specialized conferences for students of monastic history celebrating the birth of St. Benedict. Recent products of this activity in this decade include the publication in 1983 of *Monasticism and the Arts* by Syracuse University Press. The interest of the general public in monasticism and the Middle Ages has been further demonstrated in the success of such books as Emmanuel Leroy Ladurie's *Montaillou*, Barbara Tuchman's *The Fourteenth Century: A Distant Mirror*, C.H. Lawrence's *Medieval Monasticism*, and the beautifully illustrated *Monastery* by M. Basil Pennington. William Weaver's translation of Umberto Eco's *The Name of the Rose*, a novel based on many aspects of monastic life, has been a bestseller in the United States.

The Conference on the Medieval Monastery was organized and sponsored by the Medieval Studies Committee of the University of Minnesota. The Minnesota Humanities Commission provided major financial support for this conference. The editor owes a debt of gratitude to members of the Medieval Studies Committee for intellectual, moral, and financial support in the publication of this book. Gratitude for generous financial support of this publication is also due to the College of Liberal Arts of the University of Minnesota and the benefactors of The Carl D. Sheppard Publication Fund.

Medieval Cloister Carving
and Monastic Mentalité

Linda Seidel

The physical heart of the twelfth-century monastery was the cloister, a richly articulated and often remarkably decorated set of corridors that provided passage for the religious as they made their daily rounds. Yet scholars have not been able to account satisfactorily for the enclosure's visual splendor; like St. Bernard, some have wondered at the purpose there of "*curiosas depictiones*, which divert the attention of those who are praying and impede devotion."[1] I shall, in this paper, be posing Bernard's question: what function did images serve in the cloister "where there are brethren reading?" I shall try to find clues to the answers in the art itself, in part because extra-artistic evidence is not forthcoming. Texts, such as Bernard's, do not tell us how images functioned in monastic life; rather, a remarkable silence cloaks the issue.[2]

The material I shall examine in my search for an answer comes from two Toulousain cloisters, one Benedictine, one Augustinian. Through a careful study of the imagery and internal organization of a few of their sculptures, I shall attempt to generate suggestions about the attitudes and practices of those for whom the works were made; if we can understand what was seen in the cloister carvings, we may gain insight into why the works were put there. I shall, throughout, be treating the sculptures like documents, that is as records of ideas rather than as objects of beauty. First I shall describe formal properties and thematic elements along with the syntax of their organization; then I shall attempt to elucidate how these aspects, in the context of particular historic, social and spiritual circumstances, might have stimulated, in their viewers, certain kinds of responses. Through an interaction of objects in a particular setting with a specific audience meaning, I believe, was constructed.[3] My study thus compresses concerns of form, style, content and function, traditionally distinguished by art historians and held apart by them, into an indivisible entity. By keeping

several issues deliberately in suspension, as the monk or canon would have done less self-consciously, we approach an understanding of the complex role carvings played in the life of the cloister. Sculptures neither had single sources nor served solitary goals. If they are regarded as texts and are approached in that way—as bearers of different sorts of meaning—they yield varied and alternative readings. Their presence in the cloister ceases to be hard to explain and the threat that Bernard saw in them becomes readily understandable.

The two cloisters I shall be discussing, that of the Benedictine house of Notre-Dame La Daurade in the *cité* of Toulouse, and the one built at the nearby Cathedral of St-Etienne, no longer survive. Victims of the disdain for ecclesiastical relics that characterized the aftermath of the French Revolution, they surrendered a portion of their sculptures to the local museums around 1812. Because we have little incontrovertible evidence about the disposition of either cloister before its demolition, the sculptures, as cycles or sequences, have never received the attention they deserve. Deprived of the sense of place that so distinguishes the carvings at the cloister of Moissac not far to the north, the Toulouse capitals give, not inappropriately, the appearance of a somewhat random collection of fragments.[4]

The earlier cloister, but not by much, is the one for the Benedictines. Here, probably sometime in the 1120s, a decision was made to enlarge or expand a cloister which had been begun a decade or two before by carvers who had worked at Moissac. Eight capitals, single and double, had been carved when a halt was called to that project;[5] the pieces were probably installed in a single walkway to which the additional series was added in some fashion. The capitals produced in the second campaign present an unprecedented illustration in stone of the Passion of Christ. Carved on six single, four double and two triple drums, the remarkable manner in which the scenes are presented, the particular detail that characterizes the figures and the props, and the innovative use of architectural superstructures distinguish these works from capital carvings which had preceded them. The aura of immediacy that marks the Passion narrative was pointed out by Kingsley Porter more than half a century ago and has, of late, attracted interest.[6] While the massing of figures and the continuity of their action contribute to this impression, it is, I believe, the arcaded framing that plays the biggest part in creating this effect; it simulates a variety of miniature interiors on the capitals, concrete spaces within which events appear to occur. This quality would have been complemented, I believe, by another feature: a sequential arrangement of the capitals in their original installation. Such an arrangement of the La Daurade Passion narrative has much to suggest about the meaning of this program in a monastic enclosure. Further, it modifies notions of what the cloister might have looked like and enhances our understanding of how the space may have been used.[7]

The Passion story begins with the Washing of the Feet and is continued by scenes of the Last Supper and the Agony in the Garden (see Figs. 1, 2. For another illustration of this capital, see Kathryne Horste, "The Passion Series from La Daurade and Problems of Narrative Composition in the Cloister Capital," *Gesta* 21 [1982], pp. 34-37.).

Fig. 1. The Washing of the Feet, single capital formerly in the Cloister at Notre-Dame-la-Daurade, Toulouse.
James Austin

Arrest, Flagellation and the Carrying of the Cross, displayed around the three connected drums that make up one of two exceptional triple capitals, are followed by the Descent into Limbo, Christ's Deposition from the Cross, and his Resurrection (see Figs. 3-6). The latter three events, like the first three, are presented on single capitals. When placed in narrative order then, all the single capitals from the Passion series are disposed symmetrically around

Fig. 2. The Last Supper, single capital formerly in the Cloister at Notre-Dame-la-Daurade, Toulouse.

one of the two triple ones; broad, monolithic drums serve as the primary vehicle for this poignant depiction of Christ's last days. This sequence of seven sculptures is punctuated by the clustering of arcaded frames at either end and in the middle. The two capitals with which the story begins utilize especially detailed architectural settings for those events that were described by Crusaders as having occurred in different parts of the same building (see Figs. 1-2). These events, the *mandatum* and the Eucharistic meal, are, following the Rule, re-enacted within the cloister setting. Perhaps that is why the narrative strategy used in their design treats the drum as a continuously decorated surface on which all figures are to be understood as existing under the vault of a miniature canopy.[8] The two non-arcaded single capitals in this sequence, which display separate scenes on each face, use the narrative constraints of their settings and subjects to aesthetic advantage (See Fig. 4, and above reference to Horste.). In the arrangement I propose, they would frame the central composite capital, differentiating non-architectural locales from interiors and introducing, thereby, spatial and visual relief into the sequencing. Together with the triple capital that they enclose, they

Fig. 3. The Flagellation, front face of a triple capital formerly in the Cloister at Notre-Dame-la-Daurade, Toulouse.

Fig. 4. The Descent into Limbo, single capital formerly in the Cloister at Notre-Dame-la-Daurade, Toulouse. *James Austin*

are crammed with figures of soldiers, apostles and the blessed who both interact with Christ and do things on their own. These two carvings stand in contrast to the arcaded capitals I have placed to either side on which Christ appears as the undisputed protagonist.

The Crucifixion occurs at this point in the Passion story but there is no representation of it in this cycle. It is conceivable that such a carving was lost, since the cloister suffered destruction at the time of the French Revolution. But it is also possible that the event was not planned to be part of this presentation. In the twelfth century, the Descent from the Cross was understood as standing for the Crucifixion in liturgical enactments;[9] if this event, so exquisitely depicted on one of the La Daurade capitals (see Fig. 5), had been intended to fulfill that role in the arrangement then it would follow the triple capital in placement. It may indeed have done so. I would suggest, however, that Christ's Descent into Limbo would have been a more plausible stand-in in this narrative configuration; that is why I have placed it after the Flagellation. Matthew's Gospel identified the moment of Christ's corporeal death on the Cross with the salvation of souls, an association that was

Fig. 5. The Descent from the Cross, single capital formerly in the Cloister at Notre-Dame-la-Daurade, Toulouse. *James Austin*

made as well by Ordericus Vitalis in a conflated account of the Passion written in the 1130s.[10] The substitution of the Descent into Limbo for the Crucifixion could be understood in this way if it were seen as part of a sequentially arranged story; meaning, in other words, would relate to association with other scenes and would not be a function of subject matter alone. In this location, between the Flagellation and the Descent from the Cross, the Limbo scene would allow the viewer to experience the victorious message of Christ's death without presenting him with a representation of that event: Christ's sacrifice on the Cross.

Fig. 6. The Resurrection, single capital formerly in the Cloister at Notre-Dame-la-Daurade, Toulouse.

On the last two capitals in this reconstruction of seven, "hanging arcades" are to be found (see Figs. 5, 6). In addition, these two La Daurade sculptures utilize opposing ends of the drums as the exclusive fields of representation. Although only half of the "action" on the capital can be seen at any one moment, the scenes that are juxtaposed on a single carving are chronologically so intimate in their relationship that they can act as alternatives for one another. Either the Deposition or the Entombment on the same capital addresses Christ's death as a man; both the Resurrection and the Three Marys on the other capital provide the first tangible evidence of Christ's own triumph over death, the former by emphasizing presence, the latter by stressing absence. Indeed, since this is the point at which Christ's life begins to surpass human dimension, this disposition of events may have been

conceived in order to provide the cloister viewer with opportunities to contemplate the culminating events in Christ's Passion from more than one point of view, i.e., both the cloister walk and the garden. Moreover, the post-Crucifixion events shift the emphasis from Christ to his friends and followers who are now entrusted with his memory. Thus, the repeated use of an unsupported arcade on these and on the remaining double capitals in the series, combined with the intensification of the narrative— the presentation of multiple moments of a single event—demonstrate, at once, heightened attention to the nature of this particular portion of the story and the desire for expanded participation at this place in the drama.[11]

There is a further observation that can be made about my "ordering" of the La Daurade sculptures; in many ways, it seems to me to be the most significant. One of the faces of each of these seven capitals presents a specific and distinctly different image of Christ. These were, in each case, the main faces of the capitals, the portions of the sculpture that would have been visible head on from the cloister walk, opposite the benches where, as Professor Meyvaert has noted, the *pueri* would have sat.[12] Imagine then the powerful impact on the monastic viewer of a thoroughly Christological sequence that would have commenced with representations of Christ's humility and piety by showing him washing Peter's feet, feeding the sop to Judas while John sleeps on his breast, and then praying in the garden. Central place in this sequence of seven scenes is occupied by the Flagellation, around which Christ's physical torments are amassed.[13] On the other side of this axis, Christ's spiritual triumphs for mankind—the Descent into Limbo and the Resurrection —would have enclosed a representation of his attachment to a splendid jewelled Cross. Such an arrangement transforms the historic narrative of Christ's Passion into an explicit model for monastic emulation. The images would present the viewer with a compelling visual program for meditation and imitation; they would offer the monk inspiration for his own life. The depiction of the Passion sequence on a series of capitals in the cloister of La Daurade could be perceived then as a representation, for the Benedictine residents in that place, of Christ's command to take up his Cross daily, in the words of Luke 9:23 which were understood in the twelfth century as applying specifically to monastic routine.[14] Such an ordered installation of the La Daurade capitals would give visual reality to what we read of monastic spirituality during the second quarter of the twelfth century, providing us with evidence of the practice that is not known so concretely from contemporary texts.

The capitals, with their "realistic" representations of events and places, may have served the community in another way. By making the Passion appear to be occurring in this place, the sculptures would have suggested to the monks that there was no need to go off to Jerusalem to see where it had actually happened. The place of the monk, the carvings may be stating, is not on the Crusade, but in the cloister for it is there that he does Christ's work best. This interpretation, stimulated by the varied characterizations given to the places of Christ's Passion on the capitals, again confirms what we read in texts of the time, most especially in the work of Bernard: monks should make the pilgrimage, he argues, "with feelings not with feet."[15]

My second examples, from the Augustinian canons' cloister at St-Etienne, are in certain ways very similar (Figs. 7-14). They look, stylistically, like the capitals from La Daurade, a fact that has drawn art historical attention to these pieces for it allows us to hypothesize that a single workshop carved both the Passion series and the fewer surviving figured sculptures from the cathedral complex.[16] Within that similarity, which includes figure types, gestures and handling of drapery, lie significant differences. On the Passion capitals, the dramatic activities of the players absorb barely two-thirds of the vertical surface of the sculpture; above, as we have seen, loom continuous architectural and natural elements that re-create the environment within which the activities of Holy Week are seen as taking place. The capitals from St-Etienne, while using similarly active figures, avoid the use of any non-figural elements in such a way. In this unscenic approach, patterns of elegant, ornamental figures appear as the solitary elements in the re-creation of a story. I believe that the appearance of this kind of representation at St-Etienne, alongside another at La Daurade, demonstrates awareness, on the part of a single group of sculptors, of different genres of visual narration. The Passion sculptures from La Daurade present the viewer with an unambiguous re-enactment that appears to occur in a proximate, plausible manner. In contrast, the St-Etienne capitals organize similar figures into units which lack rational spatial context. This later format invites the viewer's intellectual involvement in the analysis or explanation of the figures' activities in ways that the La Daurade conception does not.[17]

These two approaches to the visualization of a story are analogous to the different ways of reading Scripture that are distinguished in twelfth-century

commentary. First, there is the historical meaning that is often seen as a primary level of understanding; it is the goal of monastic studies. This reading of Scripture corresponds to the clear-cut illustration of Biblical episodes, verse by verse, scene by scene, with one figure carefully framed and set off from another and specific actions and settings carefully differentiated. It is a literal approach to texts which resembles the presentation on the La Daurade; such

Fig. 7. Herod and Salome, left side of an engaged capital formerly in the cloister area at the Cathedral of Saint-Etienne, Toulouse.

an understanding of Scripture was espoused in Benedictine monasteries.[18] It is appropriate, therefore, to note that La Daurade had been attached to the mother house of Cluny in 1077 when monks from the abbey of Moissac were invited to reform the Toulousain establishment.[19] Distinct from, although in no way in conflict with, this *lectio divina* is a manner of reading that understands texts allegorically or tropologically, that is spiritually or morally. Hugh of St. Victor noted that whereas "history follows the order of time, to allegory belongs more the order of knowledge." He argued that this kind of understanding followed the historic reading; "Nor do I think that you will be able to become perfectly sensitive to allegory unless you have first been grounded in history," he observed.[20] The Gospel of Matthew was picked out by Hugh as a particularly good text for the study of allegory.

And it is in the Gospel of Matthew that the texts for three of the figured capitals that survive from St-Etienne are found. The sculptures of the death of Saint John the Baptist and the Parable of the Wise and Foolish Virgins, of which there are two versions, explore, in their closely packed, rhythmic and repetitive arrangements, the allusiveness of Scripture; like the texts, they make veiled references to hidden meanings through the choice and manipulation of particular elements.[21] The presentations are full of the sorts of ambivalences and seeming paradoxes for which allegorical writing is celebrated. For example, the martyrdom of John seems to be more of Salome's story (see Figs. 8, 9). The head that is sacrificed off-axis is presented on the main face of the capital by a young girl; the end of life that is represented by John's beheading becomes the ongoing offering at a ceremonial feast. John stands for the renunciation of wordly pleasures; Salome, the indirect agent of his death and the celebrant of his immortality, testifies to their exploration. The extraordinary and the ordinary mingle here, in such a way as to make the viewer alert to the possibility that something special is going on. In

Fig. 9. The Beheading of John the Baptist, right side of an engaged capital formerly in the cloister area at the Cathedral of Saint-Etienne, Toulouse.

Fig. 8. The Transmission of John's Head to Salome and its Presentation to Herodias at a Banquet, front face of an engaged capital formerly in the cloister area at the Cathedral of Saint-Etienne, Toulouse.

Fig. 10. Christ as Bridegroom, *Sponsa* crowned and a Wise Virgin, end face of a broken double capital formerly in the cloister area of the Cathedral of Saint-Etienne, Toulouse.

the most unforgettable scene on the capital (see Fig. 7), Salome appeals to our visual senses to become engaged in her activity, to contemplate her as Herod is so acutely doing. Indeed looking is the major activity of this scene and the image seems to instruct the viewer to do the same.

Neither contemplation nor the learning that flowed from it would have been strangers to the routine of an Augustinian cloister. In St. Augustine's writing, the metaphor of physical vision, initiated by the viewer and then applied selectively and with effort, is used as a model for spiritual vision.[22] Hugh of St. Victor, in his treatise *De Sacramentis*, characterized the eye as the central faculty for knowledge of the world, of the self and of God. But since the first of these alone remained fully intact, he argued, it was through contemplation that the soul could

regain its capacity for perception of the others. Imagination, he wrote elsewhere, is sensuous memory made up of the traces of corporeal objects inhering in the mind.[23] The intense activity through which the outer eye could be linked with the inner one may be what the image of Salome and Herod, on the St-Etienne capital, intends the viewer to replicate.

The Augustinian canons, the patrons of the St-Etienne cloister, were exhorted in their texts to teach through moral example. Caroline Bynum's study of treatises by various twelfth-century canons has emphasized the concern for edification and the dedication to teach by word and example that distinguished this group from contemporary monks. Behavior, for the canons, was a pattern that would excite desire to copy; it was thus an effective way of teaching morality. In the writing of one mid-century canon, Philip of Harvengt, John the Baptist is identified as an example of someone whose reputation moves men to copy his life, to follow his example, "to acquire a pattern of living."[24]

Analogy, the method by which I have compared what goes on in sculpture with what can be found in contemporary texts, was, in itself, a newly popular method of oral commentary used by both Anselm and Bernard. In it, familiar examples or stories, suited to their listeners' circumstances, were employed to create apt illustrations of the speaker's ideas. These *similitudines*, which matched point by point the lesson with which they were compared, emphasized, not speculative theological matters, but rather practical and pastoral ones.[25] The method then of using a more immediate format to drive home a point about a related, but of itself less available, nature can be observed, flourishing, in twelfth-century preaching. It may be that analogy is what the art of sculpture is, in part and at this moment, about.

Fig. 11. Christ as Bridegroom and *Sponsa* veiled, end face of a double capital formerly in the cloister area of the Cathedral of Saint-Etienne, Toulouse. *James Austin*

Fig. 12. The Wise Virgins, side view, detail of capital in Fig. 11. *James Austin*

Fig. 13. The Foolish Virgins, side view, detail of capital in Fig. 11. *James Austin*

If the John the Baptist martyrdom is intended to serve as an analogy, what more abstract yet practical idea might it illustrate? I have suggested elsewhere that sexual stimulation is an explicit issue on the capital, both in the encounter of Herod with Salome and in the combination of the motifs of dance and feast; the latter are associated with Luxuria in earlier and in contemporary manuscript illuminations of the *Psychomachia*.[26] On the St-Etienne carving, youthful Salome is shown approaching the table.

Fig. 14. Wise Virgin and Tree, end face, detail of capital in Fig. 11. *James Austin*

She is the center of attention between Herod who is off to the left and John, to the right. She is responsible for both their fates and the fact that she is portrayed as neither wicked nor lascivious is important. The pleasure that Herod takes in admiring the alluring maiden is "objectively" understandable in so far as it can be perceived and is shared by the viewer. And in sharing it, we participate in it.

Such participation in an erotic encounter was specifically proscribed for members of religious orders by two Lateran Councils that were held in the 1120s, just a few years at most before the capital was carved. Heterosexual activity by monks and canons, vigorously condemned in the Councils' decrees,[27] is addressed in a distinct yet complementary way in the private image of the sculpture. The St. John capital, in its deliberate arrangement of figures, particularly the pairing of Herod and Salome, implies that relations between a man and a woman were not strange to the thoughts of the clerics of the cathedral. The canons must have understood

such provocative gestures; why else would an image of this sort have been carved for them?[28] The capital presents the story of John the Baptist and Herod as a lesson on the risks of sexual arousal. Although Salome is seen to be within grasp of the Roman ruler, she arrests his advances and keeps him at arm's length from her. In contrast, the martyr John surrenders to the tender, full embrace of the arms of God. The sculptured imagery makes an unforgettable statement about an intimate human experience; it acknowledges physical desire, fleeting—even forgotten—pleasure, by presenting it so tangibly. But evocation of such experience is not an end in itself. The sculpture stimulates reflection on encounters of this kind in the service of a higher good. It is, in itself, as controlling as are the Councils' published Canons.

Two other capitals from the Augustinians' cloister present variations on the Parable of the Wise and Foolish Virgins; both are double: one is broken and one appears to have been unfinished (see Figs. 10-14). They resemble the Salome capital in their treatment of figures and can be shown to present their subjects in analogous ways.[29] On each capital, two rows of female figures proceed across the cylindrical twin drums of the long sides, toward a seated couple shown on one of the short faces. On the broken sculpture, the two surviving wise Virgins hold their lamps aloft and approach the long-haired, beardless figure who wears a cruciform nimbus and extends his hand to the first of them. His other arm is bent against his chest and originally held, between extended thumb and forefinger, a slender now unidentifiable object. The crowned woman on the left, next to him, looks in his direction and raises her arm to her chest; she too, once held an object. The scene takes place against a ground of overlapping scale-like patterns (see Fig. 10). Meanwhile, the foolish Virgins, one of whom carries a downward turning lamp that spills its contents, move along the broken left face toward the seated woman who pays them no heed. They are barred from approaching her by a carefully detailed, locked gate which the first figure seems to be trying to open while the second one clutches, with tensely extended fingers, at her own arm. All four of the surviving Virgins are nimbed. The carving telescopes several independent events into a single scene.

On the more beautiful, unbroken, but purportedly unfinished double capital, the seated woman is veiled, not crowned, and Christ is bearded but still long-haired and cross-nimbed (see Fig. 11). He carries a crown as a prize, to be offered rather than worn, in the hand he holds in front of his chest; a second crown was very likely offered by the hand he extends to the approaching Virgin who arrives on his left side. Christ turns more pronouncedly towards the wise Virgins in this sculpture; they carry flowering sceptres rather than lanterns. An ornamental tree, silhouetted against bare ground, marks the beginning and end of action on the short rear face. Immediately to the right of it begins the unfinished carving that blocks out four foolish Virgins. They are crammed onto the space of the remaining double side and lack the luxury of spilling over onto the far face as their wiser sisters do. They appear to be barred from making contact with the seated female by a tall, slender, rectangular form which, because work on this side was never finished, is not clearly defined. Nor can the foolish Virgins be understood beyond the obvious expressive bunching of their forms, the internal antagonism of their poses and the suggestion of tipped lanterns. There is no hint of and no room for halos around their drooping heads. A fine ornamental band, which runs along the background at the level of the wise Virgins' halos, unites those figures with the seated couple.

The double capital appears to represent the culminating part of the parable, perhaps as Emile Mâle said, "for itself," although he did not tell readers of his book on twelfth-century religious art what he meant by that.[30] The sculpture is not narrative; it does not present the parable in vignette form by showing the sleeping Virgins, their negotiations with the oil merchants or their exclusion from the heavenly feast, scenes which are independently visualized elsewhere. These same scenes also form the text of the contemporary *Sponsus* play with which Mâle associated the Toulouse carvings.[31] Neither is the subject of the capital marked by associations with punishment as it was to be, just a short time later, at St-Denis in an arrangement which impressed Mâle so much that he claimed it to be one of the major inventions of its time. By identifying the paired Virgins there as some sort of symbols of the Last Judgment (the theme of the adjacent tympanum), he provided the story with an "iconographic" interpretation that is based on the context within which it appears at that particular church.[32]

The double capital, by substituting sceptres for lanterns and depicting Christ with a crown in his hand, indicates that the version of the parable it presents goes beyond the text by showing the rewards for watchfulness, the impressive virtue that the wise Virgins display. These figures approach the bridal couple, whom the seated pair must be understood to represent,[33] to receive a prize for their vigilance. The alternation of their body movements conveys the restless rhythm of a slow procession, in itself a ritual occasion. The center and framing figures pivot on crossed legs; the two remaining Virgins are caught up in internal movements. One holds fast to her cape so that her leg is exposed as though she too will soon twist; the other rests her hand on her forward neighbor's shoulder in a gesture that frees her body from its own weight.

The wise Virgins, justly celebrated for the refinement of their postures, the elegance of their poses, and the delicacy of their draperies make fine figures in more than one sense of the word. Their apparently diaphanous garments fall gently over their limbs, clinging to their lithe forms, outlining their thighs and puddling at their ankles. Capes, veils and richly ornamented neckbands add to the dense layering of material on these figures; the pronounced hand gestures they make of caressing, holding and signaling with thumb, forefinger and palm extended, all stimulate association with the senses of seeing and touching. Indeed, in terms of proportion, the body parts that are most exaggerated on these maidens are the heads, with their large globular eyes, and the hands. The sculpture, in emphasizing these physiognomic aspects along with the elegance of their robes, brings to mind the words of Hugh of St. Victor when he describes the senses as a garment resplendent with jewels for display.[34]

The female figure who sits on Christ's left extends her palm in front of her chest in order to hold off those who approach her from the side; she looks in the other direction (see Figs. 11, 14). These figures, as Meyer Schapiro noted, have been "blocked out and partially modelled . . . the cutting is sufficiently advanced to enable us to judge the composition of the figures, their relative mass, the directions of the main lines and the gestures. But no features are visible. The heads are simple eggs, the hair, broad, unstriated surfaces in high relief. It is remarkable that the shoes have been carried further than other parts of the figures, perhaps because of their simple shape."[35] It has often been argued, by myself among others, that the capital is unfinished; that because of a change of plan after work had begun, reassignment of it to an engaged rather than free-standing position resulted in the abandonment of attention to one of its faces.[36] Such a claim seems logical and is easy to assert since there is neither archeological nor documentary evidence to the contrary. But the evidence of the capital should not be ignored. The selected stages of finish that are apparent on the foolish Virgins, as well as the posture of the seated female whose gesture responds to those maidens while she turns away from them, suggest deliberate execution with a sense of the whole, not an early rejection of one side. The seated woman, after all, takes note of the unfinished ones, something that could have been corrected if these figures, from an early moment on, were not intended to exist. Since another capital, the now fragmentary one, had already presented in a literal fashion the high point in the story when the foolish Virgins, with overturned lamps, knock at the door and find it barred, it was not necessary for this carving to repeat that scene.

Following Augustinian precepts, the capital may have presented the canons with examples of two kinds of behavior. On one face is shown an image of the wise Virgins in their allegorical condition as vigilant victors, sensually alive, physically alert and poised for action. The "unfinished" side may display an allegory of the foolish Virgins, the victims of failed watchfulness, as eternally condemned to the entrapment of insufficiency. Hugh's remarks in a treatise for the canons at Hamersleben near Halberstadt provide a relevant verbal analogue for what is seen here, without precisely describing it. Evil lives, he says, are constant warnings and examples for the welfare of the good; their iniquities cause the good to seek virtue more resolutely. Elsewhere he notes that evil is the defective, deficient state of man's nature.[37]

The exceptional finish given to the carved shoes on the foolish Virgins calls to mind a remark by Ambrose who singled out footwear, in a treatise on Virginity, and likened it to bodies; each, he observed, provides a means by which the soul can move toward a loftier goal. This comment, which took as its source Canticles 7:1 ("How graceful are your feet in sandals"), seizes on a particular word in that passage and develops the word's meaning metaphorically; the concrete sandal generates an image on which Ambrose's lesson turns. While it is possible that Ambrose's text may have been known in the twelfth-century circles of Toulouse's Augustinians, and thus could have stimulated the focus on shoes that we see in the sculpture, such, equally, may not have been the case.[38] Since Ambrose's method of commenting on Scripture was appreciated and practiced widely in diverse communities throughout the Middle Ages, his procedure rather than his precise prose should be emphasized in this regard. But while this kind of textual commentary is well attested by students of literature, its utilization in the construction of material images has

been little explored even though the same exegetical principles certainly underlie medieval visualization of Scripture. Painted and sculpted works, which are frequently regarded as illustrations of textual commentary, should be understood instead as independent formulations that employ the same interpretive strategies as do texts. The art may often parallel written commentary because it proceeds in similar fashion from the same source in Scripture, and not because it uses the written commentary for its program.

It is nonetheless difficult to imagine a twelfth-century sculptor employing a technical strategy of this sort—incompleteness—to evoke such a meaning—insufficiency, even though insufficiency of oil and its implications are the issues at the heart of the parable. It is difficult for us to view the image in that way because we are not accustomed to thinking about the range of possibilities that are open to an artist to allegorize in visual language. A life-like representation, we too often assume, is natural, that is it imitates the world as it really is. In fact, it should be understood as a construction of what its author wishes us to experience, as well as a projection of our own conventions concerning what we are prepared to accept.[39] At La Daurade, the detailed simulation of settings and spaces and the clarity of action create a sense of immediacy which authenticates for the viewer the reality of Christ's Passion. At St-Etienne, the avoidance of details of place and the complexity of gesture contribute to our perception of ambiguity in the activities of those depicted, as well as our acceptance of multiple meanings for their behavior. One kind of image is perceived to be factual because of its manner of presentation; another, for the same reason, is viewed as figural. If, at times, we are unable to tell the two apart, as has long been the case in regard to the Toulouse carvings, it may be because of our pre-disposition to accept images primarily as matter-of-fact records of reality. In these circumstances, the "illustration," or physical realization of metaphor burdens the image with literalism; the viewer loses his or her capacity to see any allusion beyond the thing depicted.[40]

The problems we have with images, and I believe that this is one of them, may not have troubled the twelfth-century viewer. At that time, the figural potential of description was readily perceived, as any encounter with the evidence of contemporary literature indicates. Bernard of Clairvaux, for example, used aggressively figural language in his sermons in order to stimulate in his audiences a visual record of what they heard.[41] The strategy could be reversed as well, with images evoking figures of speech.[42] When considered in the contemporary context of intense word/image interaction, the interpretation I have here suggested for the incomplete Virgins does not seem so implausible: their unfinished condition offers the viewer an outward manifestation of their inner imperfection.[43]

Sculptures, I argued in the case of La Daurade, must be understood in the context of their location, for they both impose on and receive from their environment particular associations. The carving of the Wise and Foolish Virgins assumes further meaning when experienced, imaginatively, in the vicinity of the Salome capital at St-Etienne.[44] In such a setting, the wise Virgins would stand as models of vigilance and watchfulness, on the lookout for those dangerous vices that can be around at any time. They are alert, as well, to the menacing sprout of apathy or weariness which is not an evil in itself but which hampers the exercise of virtue. Indeed vegetation "replaces" one of the five foolish Virgins on the capital, signalling their insufficiency as a group while marking the source of the companions' strength (see Fig. 13).[45] When read in this way, three of the surviving capitals made for the Augustinians at St-Etienne become a mini-program about the rewards of virtuous living in which there is an invitation to conversion instead of the threat of condemnation.[46] There is, as well, an unjudgmental acknowledgment of imperfection and of the susceptibility to temptation. Like Herod, the Virgins have not done anything wrong; they have failed to do something. Herod gives in to Salome's appeal; the Virgins are unprepared when the Bridegroom calls. That unreadiness is shown as their condition and the cause of their despair.

The double capital presents the story as an allegorical image, one which invites meditation on both the demands of self-discipline and the bondage of inactivity. It does not present itself as a mirror of reality for imitation. Like a parable, the image is open-ended; it requires of its viewers interpretation for completion and rewards with ever increasing understanding those who confront the image knowledgeably.[47]

The mature regular canons at the Cathedral of Toulouse would have constituted an audience of informed "insiders," to borrow the words of Frank Kermode. In the privacy of their communal cloister space, possibly in their chapter house where they were admonished to confess their transgressions and where they would have been chastized for them, the canons would have reflected upon the capitals.[48] The carvings would certainly have provided the canons with guides for the performance of their duties; but they may have assisted individuals in their ongoing struggles with self-discipline as well. For them the sculptures may have served as outlets for the expression of issues that either needed monitoring or demanded control. In particular, the use of sensual imagery to erotize a story, which we see in the St-Etienne capitals, may have functioned in this manner. Such a practice finds its analogue in the language of love that is employed by mystic writers of the time to vivify their ideas for their readers. The structure of Hugh's *De arrhâ animae*, for example, with its movement toward an intense climax, followed by what one critic has identified as "calm and satisfaction," conveys to the reader "the notion of the feeling which the soul now bears for the lover."[49] In a similar way, Bernard's sermon language is often developed around an impulse or element from his monks' past experience, such as aggressiveness—which in Leclercq's words needed an "outlet in action."[50]

The canons would have identified in varied ways with these carvings, taking in with their outer eyes what Bernard presented in his sermons to his brothers for the ear (and the inner eye). Indeed the power of carved images to address and engage an audience rivals the capacity of texts to do the same. It may be that the proliferation of Romanesque sculptures' new forms, such as figured capitals and tympana, was, in the late eleventh and early twelfth centuries, in part, an effort to press an alternative claim to authority. Tangible carvings, such as the capitals I have discussed here, appropriate the sense of sight for visual versions of texts; in doing so they re-create the phenomenon of personal witnessing which is an essential element of oral and prophetic experience. The struggle between seeing and hearing, which had engaged Augustine centuries earlier, is renewed as a rivalry between image and text.[51]

Perhaps Bernard's hostility to depictions in a cloister, among the brethren who knew how to read, can best be understood in the context of this challenge. For the Cistercian, the sounds of sermons were intended to unlock the operations of the listeners' inner eye; hearing came, for them before seeing.[52] In contrast, the testimony of the Benedictine and Augustinian images which I have examined suggests that considerable trust was placed in those quarters—however distinct the goals—in the silent discrimination of the eye. In our time, any attempt to come to terms with the medieval monastery must accord an important place to *both* categories of information.[53]

Notes

1 Bernards oft cited comments appear, in their entirety, in J.P. Migne, ed., *Patrologia Latina*, CLXXXII, cols. 914-916. For the English text as well as Jean Leclercq's valuable commentary, see *The Works of Bernard of Clairvaux. Treatises I. Cistercian Fathers Series I* (1970), pp. 3-69.

2 Meyer Schapiro has examined several twelfth-century texts on art, including Bernard's, in "On the Aesthetic Attitude in Romanesque Art," *Romanesque Art* (New York, 1977), pp. 1-27.

3 The reader unfamiliar with the way in which I define my task might wish to consult Michael Baxandall, *Painting and Experience in Fifteenth-Century Italy* (Oxford, 1972), for a clear demonstration of a similar, although not identical enterprise. In regard to literature, see the remarks of Franz H. Bäuml, "The Unmaking of the Hero: Some Critical Implications of the Transition from Oral to Written Epic," in *The Epic in Medieval Society: Aesthetic and Moral Values*, ed. Harald Scholler (Tübingen, 1977), pp. 86-99. Janet Wolff has summarized many of the theoretical arguments supporting such an approach in *The Social Production of Art* (New York, c1981) as Laura Spitzer has so kindly reminded me. On the suitability, for a study of medieval art, of a dynamic, interactive notion of vision and meaning, see Margaret Miles, *Image as Insight. Visual Understanding in Western Christianity and Secular Culture* (Boston, 1985), wherein the eye is said to catch the object rather than the object catch the eye (p. 45).

4 The documentation on the cloister of La Daurade has been studied by Kathryn Horste, "The Passion Series from La Daurade and Problems of Narrative Composition in the Cloister Capital," *Gesta* 21 (1982), pp. 34-37. My own study of St-Etienne originally raised questions about the reliability of the late eighteenth and early nineteenth-century plans and descriptions of that cloister ("A Romantic Forgery: The Romanesque 'Portal' from Saint-Etienne in Toulouse," *Art Bulletin* 50 [1968], pp. 33-42). Horste has recently reviewed this scholarship and provided additional documentary evidence ("A New Plan of the Cloister and Rampart of Saint-Etienne, Toulouse," *Journal of the Society of Architectural Historians* 45 [1986], pp. 5-19). See also my remarks in n. 7, below.

5 The basic study on the original work at La Daurade is by M. Lafargue, "Les sculptures du premier atelier de La Daurade et les chapiteaux du cloître de Moissac," *Bulletin monumental* XCIII (1938), pp. 195-216 and the same author's monograph, *Les chapiteaux du cloître de Notre Dame la Daurade* (Paris, 1940). The date of the first campaign has been placed in the early 1100s by Marcel Durliat, "La date des plus anciens chapiteaux de la Daurade à Toulouse," *Estudios dedicados a Duran y Sanpere: Cuadernos de arqueologia e historia de la ciudad de Barcelona* (Barcelona, 1967), pp. 195-202.

6 Arthur Kingsley Porter, *Romanesque Sculpture of the Pilgrimage Roads* (Boston, 1923), I, 242. Horste's interest in the lively narrative is discussed in her article, "The Passion Series." My own exploration of the subject, on which much of what follows is based, can be found in the paper "Installation as Inspiration: The Passion Cycle from La Daurade," *Gesta* 25 (1986), pp. 83-92.

7 My analysis of the La Daurade capitals may be read either as contrast or as complement to Horste's (above n. 4). I have attempted to provide an intellectual rather than archeological reconstruction of the capitals, utilizing for this enterprise information from the twelfth-century sculptures rather than evidence from eighteenth and nineteenth century plans. The latter are either opaque or inconsistent on most matters concerning the specific disposition of sculptures in the cloister and are unreliable because of their date and the circumstances of their production for determining the original characteristics of the architecture. The material is not without import but efforts to utilize it should evaluate its selectivity in light of what is known about pre- and post-Revolutionary attitudes towards the Middle Ages. See, on this matter, Claude Laroche's review of the recent exhibition in Toulouse ("Toulouse et l'art médiéval de 1830 à 1870," *Bulletin monumental*, 144 [1986], pp. 367-70). Although the sculptures are lonely survivors of much larger wholes, it is inappropriate to treat them as independent entities; attempts to insert them piecemeal into an overall plan of the cloister sacrifice aspects of subject matter to an architectural paradigm of uncertain reliability. The effort undertaken here and in the work to which this study is related focuses on prevailing thematic characteristics as clues to meaningful arrangement.

8 On the Washing of the Feet as a theme in cloister decoration of the time see Léon Pressouyre, "St. Bernard to St. Francis: Monastic Ideals and Iconographic Programs in the Cloister," *Gesta* 12 (1973), pp. 71-92. In regard to the meal, see, most recently, Peter Fergusson's study of refectory architecture and decoration which he so generously brought to my attention ("The Twelfth-Century Refectories at Rievaulx and Byland Abbeys," in C. Norton and D. Park, eds., *Cistercian Art and Architecture in the British Isles* [Cambridge, 1986], pp. 160-80). Horste emphasized the frieze-like nature of the two capitals in question in her study, "The Passion Series,"

pp. 46-7.

9   E.C. Parker, *The Descent from the Cross: Its Relation to the Extra-Liturgical "Depositio" Drama* (New York, 1978), pp. 8-10 and 202-3. I have made additional comments on this in "Installation as Inspiration," n. 30.

10 Migne, P.L., CLXXXVIII, 59 and the recent edition and translation by Marjorie Chibnall, *Orderic Vitalis: The Ecclesiastical History.* 6 vols. (Oxford, 1969-78).

11 Three of the double capitals, none of which I treat here, present paired scenes under hanging arcades: Christ's appearance to Mary in the garden and the visit of the apostles to the tomb; the journey to and meal at Emmaus; the Doubting Thomas and a scene which I identify as Jesus' appearance to his apostles just before his meeting with Thomas. The fourth one, which would have followed the triple capital of the Ascension both chronologically and, I believe, sequentially, displays the Pentecost in a unified manner around both drums. For photos, see my "Installation as Inspiration," as well as Horste's "The Passion Series." These capitals, I believe, would have been installed, in sequence, after the first seven, possibly in an adjacent walk.

12 Paul Meyvaert, "The Medieval Monastic Claustrum," *Gesta* 12 (1973), p. 54.

13 The use of seven narrative capitals centered on a strong axis—the triple column—may have been intended to evoke both the fraction of the host during the Mass and its disposition on the paten in the shape of the Cross, an evocation, possibly, of the "missing" Crucifixion. On the relation between septiform and cruciform see Steven G. Nichols, Jr., *Romanesque Signs* (New Haven, 1983), p. 107.

14 On monastic self-discipline, see Jean Leclercq, "The Imitation of Christ and the Sacraments in the Teaching of St. Bernard," *Cistercian Studies* 9 (1974), pp. 36-54, and, on the monk as a figure of the resurrected Christ, see George Klawitter, "Dramatic Elements in Early Monastic Induction Ceremonies," *Comparative Drama* 15 (1981-2), pp. 219-23.

15 On this issue see Jean Leclercq, "Monachisme et pérégrination du IXe au XIIe siècle," *Studia monastica* 3 (1961), pp. 33-52; Giles Constable, "Opposition to the Pilgrimage in the Middle Ages," *Studia Gratiana* 19 (1976), pp. 123-46; and Ilene Forsyth, "The *Vita Apostolica* and Romanesque Sculpture: Some Preliminary Observations," *Gesta* 25 (1986), pp. 75-82. Bede Lackner also talked of the monks' need to see the heavenly not the earthly Jerusalem in "The Monastic Life According to St. Bernard," in *Studies in Medieval Cistercian History.* II. Cistercial Studies Series 24 (1976), p. 59, n. 33. For an account of what monks might have seen in the Holy Land had they gone there, see Bernard Hamilton, "Rebuilding Zion: The Holy Places of Jerusalem in the Twelfth Century," *Renaissance and Renewal in Christian History.* Studies in Church History 14 (1977), pp. 105-16.

16 I treated issues of style and the relation between the La Daurade and St-Etienne sculptures in *Romanesque Sculpture from the Cathedral of St-Etienne, Toulouse* (New York, 1977), pp. 105-33. A proposal that extends the work of the atelier responsible for both projects over some four decades has been made by Denis Milhau, *Les grandes étapes de la sculpture romane toulousaine: des monuments aux collections* (Toulouse, 1971), pp. 11-60, esp. 15-44.

17 What is implied here is that artists made profound adjustments in their art when they were employed by patrons with particular desires. This challenges customary claims about medieval craftsmen's working methods and suggests that carvers had a sophisticated appreciation of the meaning of the forms they carved. Style is viewed here less as a diagnostic marker of authorship and more as an agent of communication. Willibald Sauerlaender has argued that the useful concept of style has blinded art historians "to the sheer information . . . objects offer to an observer who . . . is not mentally prestylized." "From Stilus to Style: reflections on the fate of a notion," *Art History* 6 (1983), pp. 253-70, esp. p. 267.

18 Hugh of St. Victor recommended that the student first learn history, "reviewing from beginning to end what has been done, when it has been done, where it has been done, and by whom it has been done." *Didascalicon of Hugh of St. Victor; A Medieval Guide to the Arts,* trans. Jerome Taylor (New York, 1961), p. 136. Jean Leclercq has discussed the study of Scripture in the monastery in *The Love of Learning and the Desire for God,* trans. Catharine Misrahi (New York, 1974; 2nd ed.), pp. 16-22.

19 Horste treats the history of the monastery in "The Passion Series," pp. 33-34.

20 *The Didascalicon,* pp. 145 and 136, for the quotes.

21 I have treated the John the Baptist capital in some detail in my paper "Salome and the Canons," *Women's Studies* 11 (1984), pp. 29-66. What follows draws on portions of that study. The texts describing John's martyrdom are in Matthew 14:1-12 and Mark 6:14-29. The Parable text is in Matthew 25:1-13. Only one other capital that survives from St-Etienne can be closely associated with this group. It presents the story of St. Mary of Egypt in a style that relates closely to that of the carvings discussed here. See n. 45, below.

22 See Margaret Miles, "Vision: The Eye of the Body and the Eye of the Mind in Saint-Augustine's *De Trinitate* and Confessions," *The Journal of Religion* 63, no. 2 (1982), pp. 125-42.

23 For *De Sacramentis* see Migne P.L., CLXXVI, 329 and the comments by Kevin Herbert in *Hugh of St. Victor: Soliloquy on the Earnest Money of the Soul* (Milwaukee, 1956), pp. 8-9. On imagination, see *The Didascalicon,* p. 66.

24 Caroline Walker Bynum, "Docere verbo exemplo. An Aspect of Twelfth-Century Spirituality." Harvard

Theological Studies 31 (1979), p. 86 for the quote and pp. 41-50 more generally.

25 G.R. Evans, "Sententiola ad aedificationem. The Dicta of St. Anselm and St. Bernard," *Revue Bénédictine* 92 (1982), pp. 159-71.

26 For this see "Salome and the Canons," esp. pp. 40-1.

27 Charles-Joseph Hefèle, *Histoire des Conciles*, trans. J. Leclercq (Paris, 1912), V, pt. 1, 631-39 and 725-33.

28 The Salome-John Baptist capital carved for the Benedictines at La Daurade in the first series of sculptures done for the cloister there does not offer such intimate imagery as can be found on the St-Etienne capital. Herod, on that sculpture, is seated at table while Salome is shown dancing off to one side. The presentation of the head is made to Herodias alone who is seated on a throne on the opposite side of the capital from the feast. For illustrations, see "Salome and the Canons," figs. 1-4.

29 Parts of what follows formed part of a presentation at the Robert Branner Forum for Medieval Art in the spring of 1985. My thinking on this theme in particular was greatly enhanced by the work of colleagues whose papers were presented at the conference of which the present volume constitutes the proceedings.

30 Emile Mâle, *Religious Art in France. The Twelfth Century: A Study of the Origins of Medieval Iconography.* Bollingen Series XC.1, trans. M. Mathews (Princeton, 1978), p. 182. The implication of his comment is that the representation of the parable at Toulouse does not have the same significance that he attributes to it elsewhere.

31 Ibid., pp. 151-53, where the play is discussed in terms of the influence of liturgical drama on art. Clifford Davidson has criticized Mâle and offered additional observations on the play ("On the Uses of Iconographic Study: The Example of the *Sponsus* from St. Martial of Limoges," *Comparative Drama* 13 [1979-80], pp. 300-19). For the bilingual text of the play, see W. Cloetta, "Le Mystère de l'Epoux," *Romania* 22 (1893), pp. 223-29, and, more recently, with a modern French translation and much commentary, the work of Lucien-Paul Thomas, *Le Sponsus.* Université libre de Bruxelles, Travaux de la Faculté de philosophie et lettres (Paris, 1951), pp. 174ff. The broken capital from St-Etienne appears to follow the story line of the parable more closely than does the unfinished one. This difference may help to explain why there are two visual versions.

32 "At St-Denis (the parable) suddenly takes on a profound meaning: united with the Last Judgment which they prefigure, the ten Virgins become the image of the two halves of mankind to be separated by God on the final day." *The Twelfth Century*, p. 182. While there is nothing wrong with the logic of Mâle's approach to this sculpture, his conclusions should

be applied on a case by case basis and not extended automatically to all carvings of the parable. In other words, because the parable relates to the Last Judgment at one church does not mean that it does so somewhere else, especially if it is accompanied by other sorts of images and is located in another type of architectural space.

33 The bride and bridegroom are the central figure of the Songs of Songs and the 44th Psalm; their appearance in the midst of the parable on the two St-Etienne capitals (when the bridegroom alone is required by the text) indicates an infiltration of the imagery of one text by another. Since feasts, Virgins and betrothals are featured in each, this interchange of images is not surprising. Leclercq has identified the Songs of Songs as the most read and commented upon book in the medieval cloister in *The Love of Learning*, p. 106. For the most celebrated commentary on the poem, see Bernard's sermons (*The Works of Bernard of Clairvaux*, vols. 2 and 3, trans. by Kilian Walsh OCSO, in Cistercian Fathers Series, nos. 4 and 7 [Kalamazoo, 1977 and 1976]); three recent additions to the literature have been particularly helpful to me: Joseph R. Jones, "The *Song of Songs* as a Drama in the Commentators from Origin to the Twelfth Century," *Comparative Drama* 17 (1983-84), pp. 17-39; Marie-Louise Thérel, *A l'origine du décor du portail occidental de Notre-Dame de Senlis: Le Triomphe de la Vierge-Eglise. Sources historiques, littéraires et iconographiques* (Paris, 1984), esp. pp. 136-45 and 186-93; Brian Stock, *The Implications of Literacy. Written Language and Models of Interpretation in the Eleventh and Twelfth Centuries* (Princeton, 1983), pp. 410-51. Thérel sees the two enthroned women on the Toulouse capitals as representing crowned Ecclesia and the Virgin Mary; according to her, the processions symbolize in the first instance vigilance and, in the second, virginity (*Le Triomphe de la Vierge-Eglise*, pp. 178-79). My own reading emphasizes the theme of vigilance in regard to both renderings of the parable but especially in regard to the unbroken capital. In this sculpture I see the veiled seated woman as the soul, an interpretation that follows Bernard (see below, n. 45).

34 See *De arrha animae*, Migne, P.L., CLXXVI, 951-70. The betrothal metaphor plays a central role in this effort of Hugh to lift the soul from a lust for temporal things to the love of eternal ones. The text appears in English editions by F. Sherwood Taylor, as *The Soul's Betrothal-Gift* (Glasgow, 1945), and Kevin Herbert, *Soliloquy on the Earnest Money of the Soul* (Milwaukee, 1956).

35 Meyer Schapiro, "The Romanesque Sculpture of Moissac- I," *Romanesque Art* (New York, 1977), p. 198 and fig. 128.

36 Seidel, *Romanesque Sculpture from St-Etienne*, pp. 145-46 and p. 160, n. 28, with reference to earlier material.

37 I refer here first to the English of Kevin Herbert's translation, *Soliloquy on the Earnest Money of the Soul*, pp. 20-21 and, in the second instance, to *The Didascalicon*, p. 52. Siegfried Wenzel stresses the explicit association of *acedia* and monasticism throughout the early middle ages. He notes that twelfth-century writers began to emphasize the "inner phenomenon" of mental slackness and lack of fervor in spiritual pursuits with its resultant exposure of the monk to other temptations. These were not necessarily sinful, but the best protection against them was constant watchfulness. *The Sin of Sloth: Acedia in Medieval Thought and Literature* (Chapel Hill: University of North Carolina Press, 1960, 67), pp. 30-34.

38 I found the reference in Thérel, *Le triomphe de la Vierge-Eglise*, pp. 137-38. Ambrose's treatise, *De Institutione virginis*, is in Migne, P.L., XVI, col. 326-27. On the link between *acedia* and the feet, see Wenzel who cites twelfth-century writings by Richard of St-Victor, Bernard of Clairvaux and Aelred of Rievaulx in this connection. *The Sin of Sloth*, p. 108.

39 See the important reflections on this matter by Murray Krieger in "The Ambiguities of Representation and Illusion: An E.H. Gombrich Retrospective," *Critical Inquiry* 11-2 (1984), pp. 181-84 with Gombrich's rejoinder, pp. 195-201.

40 I have reflected recently on metaphors in medieval art. See my paper "Images of the Crusades in Western Art: Models as Metaphors," in *The Meeting of Two Worlds; Cultural Exchange between East and West during the Period of the Crusades*. Edited by Vladimir P. Goss and Christine Verzár Bornstein. Studies in Medieval Culture 21 (Kalamazoo, 1986), pp. 377-91.

41 See Stock's comments, *The Implications of Literacy*, pp. 408-9 and 441. Leclercq stressed the contemplative character of the Song of Songs and emphasized the different qualities that distinguish scholastic from monastic commentaries on the poem (*The Love of Learning*, pp. 106-9). The latter remarks parallel the enterprise I have attempted here in differentiating among kinds of images.

42 The sounds of words and phrases could function in this way too. See the iconographic study based on sound association between Romanesque images and Biblical texts: William R. Cook, "A New Approach to the Tympanum of Neuilly-en-Donjon," *Journal of Medieval History* 4 (1978), pp. 333-45.

43 For commentary on the issue of man's image-likeness to God in early twelfth-century theology as well as the craftsman's work as a kind of *meditatio*, see John Van Engen, "Theophilus Presbyter and Rupert of Deutz: the Manual Arts and Benedictine Theology in the Early Twelfth Century," *Viator* 11 (1980), pp. 147-63. Wenzel considers no visual renderings of sloth in his chapter on iconography yet his references to verbal images of the transplanted tree and to

Biblical individuals whose failures or defeats resulted from a lack of vigilance draws his analysis close to that which is offered here (*The Sin of Sloth*, pp. 97-126). The Foolish Virgins are not included among his examples although other parables from Matthew, such as the withered fig tree and the guest without garment (Matthew 21 and 22) are cited as instances of religious slackness (*The Sin of Sloth*, pp. 101-102).

44 The original location of the capitals is not known although a location in a chamber off of the cloister was originally suggested and has long been assumed. Neither is it established beyond all doubt that the carvings in fact came from the Cathedral precinct. But available evidence does suggest that the sculptures originally belonged to that vast complex which contained a great deal of sculpture that is now lost. I suggest here that similarities among carvings within a circumscribed area would provoke in viewers reminiscences and reflections on the relationships that they observed among them; precise location is not in question. Through these associations, additional meanings would be generated. The role of cloister sculptures as facilitators of memory is being explored by Leah Rutchick in the context of the Moissac cloister. Such thinking may also prove helpful in reconsidering the significance of capital arrangement, including the role of alternative supports in a cloister; cf. n. 7 above. For further discussion of the role of recollection, see Grover Zinn, "Hugh of St-Victor and the Art of Memory," *Viator* 5 (1974), pp. 211-34, esp. p. 226.

45 The exhortation to the Virgins to be vigilant, which occurs in the opening lines of the *Sponsus* play, expresses the importance of this theme to the twelfth-century audience. See the references in n. 31, above. The theme appears again in Bernard's sermons on Canticles, when the soul is promised the embrace of the Bridegroom if it is vigilant in the pursuit of virtue. For tree imagery and virtue in his sermons, see the discussion by Luc Brésard in "Bernard et Origène commentent le *Cantique*," *Collectanea Cisterciensia* 44 (1982), pp. 183-209.

46 The fourth capital from St-Etienne with figurative imagery that relates to the three discussed here presents the story of the harlot Mary Egyptian who repents during a visit to the Holy Land and lives out the remainder of her life as a hermit. There is an obvious relationship between this unusual saint's story and the material of the other carvings. For photos and discussion, see Mâle, *The Twelfth Century*, pp. 241-44 and figs. 188-91. Wenzel notes that among the Old Testament examples of those who failed through lack of vigilance, which were offered by medieval writers, were several examples of men who trusted women, e.g., David, Samson, Sisaran, Isboseth, Holofernes. *The Sin of Sloth*, p. 101.

47 I borrow here and below the characterization of parable that is offered by Frank Kermode, *The*

Genesis of Secrecy; On the Interpretation of Narrative (Cambridge, Mass., 1979), pp. 24-5 and thank Steve Nichols for suggesting that I might find the book helpful.

48 Chapter meeting was the place at which the *circator*, the watchman whose role it was to search out negligence on the part of the canons, made his report. See the paper in this collection by Hugh Feiss, OSB, "*Circatores* in the *Ordo* of St. Victor," pp. 53-58.

49 Kevin Herbert, *Soliloquy on the Earnest Money of the Soul*, p. 12.

50 Jean Leclercq, "Aggressiveness or Repression in St. Bernard and his Monks," *Monks and Love in Twelfth-Century France* (Oxford, 1979), pp. 86-108. The connection between Bernard's and Hugh's ideas were long ago pointed out by Etienne Gilson, *History of Christian Philosophy in the Middle Ages* (New York, 1954), pp. 164-71.

51 On the aural/oral aspects of monastic reading see Leclercq, *The Love of Learning*, pp. 18-22 and, more generally, Walter J. Ong, *Orality and Literacy* (London, 1982), pp. 31-6 and 117-23. On Augustine, see Miles, "Vision," as in n. 22 above.

52 Stock's treatment of the medieval material is fundamental to my point here and has influenced my thinking greatly. *The Implications of Literacy*, pp. 407-09.

53 On the political nature of the struggle between pictorial and linguistic signs, see the critical comments of W.J.T. Mitchell, *Iconology. Image, Text, Ideology* (Chicago, 1986).

Photo notes: The capitals that illustrate this article are all in the collection of the Musée des Augustins, Toulouse. I have been assisted in my most recent efforts to study them through the good offices of the conservateur, M. Denis Milhau, to whom I am most grateful. The sources of the photographs are as follows: Figs. 1-9, 11-14: James Austin; Fig. 10: Bildarchiv Foto Marburg.

Analogues of the Cistercian Abbey Church

Emero Stiegman

Scholarship on the broad religious reform movement of the eleventh and twelfth centuries has made possible the discovery of a handicap under which Cistercian history has long been laboring: the foil against which we have studied Cîteaux has been Cluny, to such an extent that the rest of the historical landscape has functioned as a complex of accessories. Naturally, we have perceived the issue in black and white. What is now made possible, however, is not automatically assured: the study of twelfth century Cistercian art has not yet greatly benefited from a wealth of new data in the history of religious ideas, data that could provide the art history of the period with a more adequate theological setting.[1] It is still common to interpret the twelfth-century abbey church of the white monks simply as a reaction to the third basilica at Cluny and the opulence of Romanesque sculpture in the pilgrimage shrines, and to find in St. Bernard's *Apologia* on the subject, not a tract relating regular observance to interiority—a document that spoke for the entire reform movement—but a grandiloquent denunciation of Cluny.[2]

It is clear that the *Apologia* was critical of Cluniac churches and that the Cistercian manner of building developed in contrast to what was criticized; nevertheless, an understanding of this manner requires complementary perspectives. We must place St. Bernard's abbey church among those of twelfth-century reform groups, monks and canons. Comparing the Cistercian idea of the perfect Christian life to corresponding ideas held by earlier reform groups, historians have found telling similarities. Would some knowledge of the architecture of these earlier groups reveal ways of embodying their religious ideals similar, likewise, to Cistercian solutions? The possibility is too compelling to be left unexplored. Only the limited vista of our customary Cluny-Cîteaux dichotomy can explain that this possibility has been little studied. If examples were available to us for making a comparison between the Cistercian church and its antecedents among reform groups, we would be spared that feeble but frequent interpretative exercise in which one attempts to identify *what* the religious values of Cistercian architecture are while failing to explain, with any historical credibility, *how* these values take architectural form.

All too regularly the effort to discern the nature of Cistercian creativity—to determine, for example, whether there is a "Cistercian style" of architecture—has suffered from a debilitating distinction between content and form—or, better, from a willingness to allow the distinction to mark off separate disciplines. Under such rubrics, Cîteaux is found to be either a revolutionary reform, in contradiction to scholarly findings on the eleventh- and twelfth-century reform movement, or simply the largest institutional example of contemporary religious renewal, in denial of any claim to originality. Consistent with this atomizing analysis, the study of form is reduced to the tracing of a lineage in the history of stylistic elements: the Cistercian church is stripped-down *Romanesque* or transitional *Gothic*. Its aesthetic essence is rendered opaque by an evasive formalism. It is doubtful that we can improve upon this unpromising approach without a broader view of the stylistic *terminus a quo* in the development of the Cistercian abbey church. That we need an improved approach is clear from the fact that, in our century, the specifically architectural explanation we have so far given of Cistercian buildings fails to account for what both experts and the general viewer deeply admire. Art studied as reaction is art deprived of serious consideration. It seems desirable that a formal description not be aesthetically irrelevant.

Art history has done us the service of identifying the Cistercian church as a special case in the development of styles: while basically Romanesque, it abstains, for example, from architectural sculpture and other forms of ornamentation which typified this idiom; or, it is early Gothic in its emphatically selective use of such features as the broken arch, a more studied harmony of proportions, and eventually the rib vault.[3] Specialists have advanced the case by striving to relate these omissions and inclusions to the religious mind (the "spirituality," we say) of the Order.[4] It is specifically the functionality of these churches which is most praised: they are the prayerhalls of monks who designed an environment to foster their special approach to contemplation.[5] Seeing austerity here as an ascetical ideology or as an early version of the puritanical spirit is a reductionist and unhistorical perception. To the white monks, the abbey church was the *oratorium* prescribed in St. Benedict's rule, the oratory or praying-place, and every element of the building was to meet this purpose. To the twentieth-century observer, such disciplined functionality is singularly admirable. Was it, indeed, the Big Bang of functional church architecture?

Our current consensus seems to assume it was just that, largely because the question is hardly allowed to emerge. Even so erudite a specialist as the Cistercian Anselme Dimier found the Cistercian oratory to be "une nouvelle conception de l'architecture monastique."[6] Dimier's generic acknowledgment that the oratory was neither the first nor the only instance of the era's quest for a new architectural simplicity was something of a dismissal of earlier attempts on the grounds that their relative significance was all too slight. While this could prove to be true in relation to the historical impact of a fully achieved Cistercian architecture, it is an approach which discourages the perception of an architectural movement and delays questions leading to instructive comparisons between the developmental stages of such a movement and its eventual maturity.

To broaden our artistic perspective and include the architecture of earlier reform groups, it would be necessary in the end to possess precise art history on the monuments to be included. But, rather than wait until such definitive scholarship is available, we must consider where our present information leads us and, perhaps more significantly, the direction in which it points us. Rigorous students of architectural history, meanwhile, have not hesitated to suggest specific analogues to the twelfth-century Cistercian oratory.[7] Not the least benefit of some attention to these suggestions may be the stimulation of archeological research on the churches under consideration. Since in every department of monastic life it has been enlightening to set Cîteaux alongside its predecessors and contemporaries in the renewal, we must insist on asking what light this comparison may shed in the area of architecture.[8]

Development of the Cistercian Oratory

The one reform architecture we have studied with some diligence is, of course, that of the Cistercians. Their order was founded when a group of monks under Robert of Molesme, in pursuit of a cenobitism in closer accord with the desert spirituality of the era, left the monastery of Molesme in 1098 to establish another at Cîteaux. At the heart of desert spirituality was a drive toward ever greater religious interiority and contemplative prayer. The conditions most promoted by new communities, because altogether indespensible to this objective, were poverty and solitude. The church building of the "New Monastery," as Cîteaux was called, would reflect this ethos, and reflect as well some arrangements deemed necessary to it: the liturgy was greatly reduced, lay brothers or *conversi* (who, for the most part, tended the fields) were seated separately, and no laity were admitted. In the early legislative documents of the order, the *Summa cartae*

Fig. 1. Cistercian abbey church of Fontenay (Cote d'Or), the nave facing west (courtesy P. Lefevre).

caritatis and the *Exordium parvum,* and in successive General Chapters after 1134, strict prohibitions were launched against "superfluities" in the abbey church. From Cîteaux in Burgundy, "le pays des beaux clochers," came the order forbidding tall bell towers.[9] There was to be no narrative sculpture, no stained glass, no paintings, no tapestry. Saint Bernard had called into question the monastic appropriateness of Cluny's most ambitious efforts.[10] Now, after the first Cistercian generation, when new monastic buildings had to be erected to provide for enlarged communities, the white monks' thinking on church architecture had to move to a positive statement, in stone. In 1135 St. Bernard's abbey of Clairvaux took the initiative. Clairvaux II was completed in 1145.

The architecture of Bernard's oratory is known to us only through buildings which reproduced its solutions.[11] Among those erected under the abbot's immediate influence and still standing, Fontenay

(Côte d'Or), the earliest, is the model inevitably referred to in studies of Cistercian architecture (Figs. 1-4); but over one hundred and fifty oratories which adopted a reduction of the basic plan and elevation of Clairvaux II are either extant or known in historical records.[12] Abbeys founded from the other Cistercian motherhouses (Cîteaux, La Ferté, Morimond, and Pontigny) are not significantly different. They run so true to type that in the thirteenth century the architect Villard de Honnecourt was able to enter into his sketchbook an ideal plan for a Cistercian abbey church: its dominant characteristic was a modular construction which, in Villard's drawing, used the width of the square crossing as module (Fig. 5).[13] Cistercian churches remain distinctive also in their restrained use of the structural detailing which became a mark of the early Gothic, in their preference for the mural continuity which defined their space as enclosed (Fig. 7), and in their commitment to the formal simplification of a declared architectonic geometry. This easily recognizable conception is expressed in a variety of regional idioms—e.g., in Provence, in Lombardy, in

Fig. 2. Fontenay, detail looking north into aisle (photo: Stiegman).

Fig. 3. Fontenay, the west portal (photo: Stiegman).

England, and in Germany.[14] At Sénanque (Vaucluse) and Le Thoronet (Var), as instances, the square apse of the sanctuary, so favored by the Cistercians, becomes hemicyclic (Fig. 6); and the series of transverse vaults over the aisles, observed at Fontenay (Fig. 2), gives way to the continuous rampant vault (a half-arch vault) buttressing the nave (fig. 8). But, in all its variety of regional versions and its differences in scale, the Cistercian oratory of St. Bernard's generation makes a strong claim upon the modern imagination as a building that moves with chaste directness towards its objective; it is an uncompromising environment of prayer.

The Monastic Reform Movement

Heightened sensitivity to the built environment was a characteristic of desert spirituality. By the middle of the eleventh century, Peter Damian, from his hermitage at Fonte Avellana, had made it known that he held no admiration for the renowned building abbots, who enlarged their churches and ornamented their abbeys.[15] All the founders of the monastic reform wished their church building in one way or another to promote interiorization. And there was no vagueness about how this should come about; all insisted upon poverty and upon a curbing of visual curiosity, of concupiscientia oculorum.

Perhaps there is no objective way of narrowing the compass of what we are calling the reform movement any tighter than the very ecclesia semper reformanda. Cluny, the great Benedictine establishment which many reformers found uncongenial, had itself begun (in 909) as a strategy for monastic reform. But as Europe moved into the higher Middle Ages, several factors such as increased population, improved technology, and better education produced a social evolution calling for institutional response. Religious stirrings were first observed in monasticism: earlier forms exercised a widespread attraction. There seems to have been a spiritual invasion from the East—or, more precisely, the second wave of that invasion which had begun in the generation of John Cassian and had issued in the rule of St. Benedict.[16] Once again our fathers in the faith were the desert fathers.

We have read of the principal new foundations, of Camaldoli, Fonte Avellana, Vallombrosa, Grandmont, and the Grande Chartreuse. We are aware of how closely shared were their conceptions of the perfectly Christian life—all emphasizing solitude and an asceticism grounded in poverty and oriented to contemplative prayer. What interests me here is the fact that all shared as well a determination to make their church building a radically functional housing of this prayer activity, and that all assumed that the building, just as the rest of that milieu which their daily regimen was to create, would promote contemplation; it would foster, in some undetermined way, that solitude for which the paradigmatic desert was only an unnecessary condition. The necessary condition was a suppression of sensory or imaginative excitement—a premise with strong architectural consequences.[17]

This understanding of the church building emerges in the scholarship studying reform communities. We know extremely little of the oratories constructed by hermits.[18] More information becomes available as groups of hermits begin to build more permanent structures. Jean-René Gaborit observes Vallombrosa with its oratio continua ambition: here the liturgy of the Divine Office reflected the splendor of Cluny; and yet, because of St. John Gaulbert's desire for the circumstances of a solitude free of distractions, the Office took place in an unornamented wooden oratory (consecrated in 1038) in the wilderness.[19] Gaborit's archeological survey concludes that the congregation of Vallombrosa remained faithful to their own type of construction, a composite model of their churches, datable to the half-century following the death of the founder in 1073. In churches such as St. Paul of Razzuolo, St. Reparata of Marradi, St. Mary of Montepiano, and St. Cassiano of Montescalari (all near Florence), vestiges of the late eleventh-century buildings reveal a mentality quite in accord with St. Bernard's later censure of Cluny. One detects a choice limiting both size and such ornamentation as architectural sculpture (Fig. 9).[20] In a later generation Cistercian efforts in exactly these directions reached a masterful consummation.

Of the Carthusians, we read that they centered their cells around a common oratory in which they gathered, at the beginning, only for Matins and Vespers. Their liturgy was simpler than the Roman rite, and in their chapel the altar was of wood and the chalice of silver.[21]

In René Crozet's review of the churches of Grandmont (founded in 1073), again a distinct type of monastic construction is discovered. Although none of the monuments examined can be dated before the middle of the twelfth century, Crozet implies that they are in continuity with a Grandmontine building tradition going back to the early years of the order. The community rule demanded, "That the church and every other edifice of our order be nude and free from all useless luxury."[22] Characteristic features can be listed. The church had a long, low nave (six or seven meters of average height) with broken barrel vaulting and no transverse arches, no aisles, no transepts, and no lateral lighting. Would this design not dramatize the shafts of white light penetrating the nave east and west? Would it not etch the structural members in sharply contrasting tones? Would it not, above all, emphasize the sense of enclosure? The closest approximation to this Grandmontine experience today would be a visit to a Cistercian oratory of the period. As in Cistercian practice, vertical wall mouldings were characteristically arrested by corbels.[23] There was no west portal or façade; instead, two doors without tympana pierced the sides of the nave.

We might easily insert some of Crozet's most significant observations on Grandmont into an essay on the Bernardine oratory. He writes: "One sees great unity and great uniformity in the constructions of the order. Though their buildings were of extreme simplicity, the Grandmontines neglected nothing that might give them *harmonious proportions* (emphasis mine), something particularly noticeable in their churches and chapter houses." This is "an elegant and sober architecture," he concludes, one "impregnated in the character of Limoges."[24] The Cistercian Anselme Dimier, recognizing the family resemblance, balks nevertheless at the extent of Grandmont's abnegation: it was, he says, an architecture "which reached the extremity of rigor and renunciation."[25]

These, then were the artistic models available to the third abbot of Cîteaux, St. Stephen Harding, as he moved through Italy and France.[26] These were

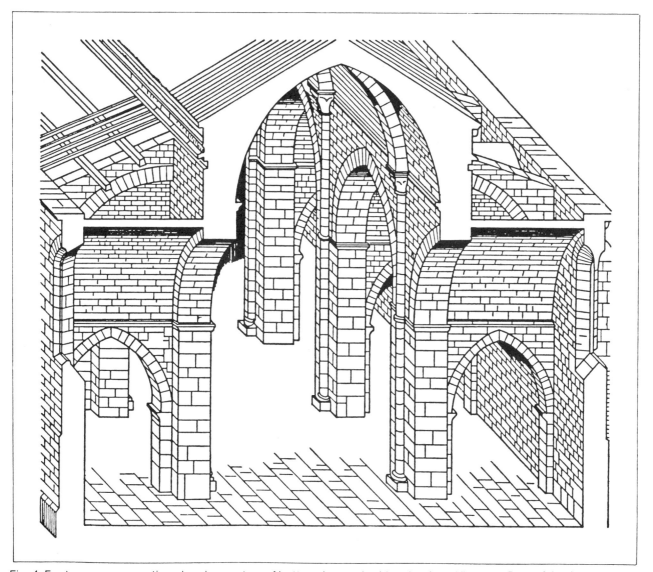

Fig. 4. Fontenay, cross section showing system of buttressing vaults (drawing from Viollet-le-Duc, 19th c.).

some of the oratories in which St. Bernard prayed.

It has been suggested that the economical plan of a rectangular chevet, found in all the abbey churches of a Clairvaux filiation during Bernard's lifetime, could have been observed by the saint at Hirsau.[27] In about 1082 Abbot William of Hirsau built the church of Saints Peter and Paul, borrowing from Cluny II, but simplifying the plan (Fig. 10).[28] The Hirsau reform, which during William's lifetime attracted one hundred and thirty monasteries, stressed building practices and, in fact, gave rise to a school of monastic architecture.[29] The legislation which informed this school insisted upon an austere simplicity. Unnecessary towers, for example, were not allowed.[30] Retention of the basilica style of elevation, with timber ceiling, was seen as a contact with Roman origins. The barrel vault of Romainmotier (ca. 1000 to 1030) and the groined vaults of Sangerhausen (the Ulrichkirche, ca. 1100)— both buildings employed extensive corbeling—gave way to the restored model of nave covering at Alpirsbach (1095 to 1125) and Schaffhausen (ca. 1104).[31] The practice of decorating walls with sacred paintings, as at Reichnau and Hildesheim, was discontinued. Building plans were oriented more strictly

to housing the monastic liturgy; so that, while the sanctuary was enlarged, crypts, which had always been popular as the sites of saints' relics, were eliminated.[32] The "Hirsau churches," as they were called, were an architectural reform reflecting much of that interiorizing spirituality which, in the experience of some monastic groups, demanded an accen-

Fig. 6. Cistercian abbey of Sénanque (Vaucluse), facing the rounded sanctuary apse (photo: Stiegman).

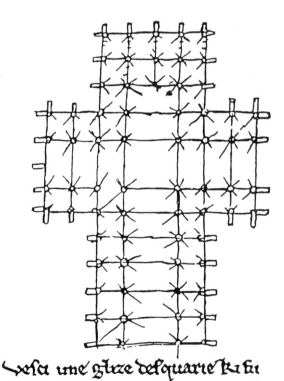

Fig. 5. Plan for a Cistercian church (from the sketchbook of Villard de Honnecourt 13th c.).

Fig. 7. Sénanque, the nave facing south (photo: Stiegman).

Fig. 8. Cistercian abbey of Le Thoronet (Var), looking from north aisle across the nave into south aisle (photo: Stiegman).

tuation of the difference between monastic churches and those built for the laity. St. Bernard's language and the Cistercian oratory became the classic statements of the difference.[33]

Reform of the Canons Regular

For those ecclesiastics whose days were absorbed in prayer but who accepted a certain active involvement with the laity, this difference in church architecture did not on that account disappear. The reform spirit of the era, remember, saw the life of prayer as demanding both solitude and community, and the precondition to both was religious poverty. It should not be surprising, therefore, if we find in the churches of the canons regular, as indeed we do, the manifestation of a complex of needs not always distinguishable from those of monks. The *regularization* of the canons in the eleventh century was a movement of reform; the *regula* adopted, even when it was not that of St. Benedict, was perceived to be in that spirit of desert spirituality which the Cistercians would later claim to find in the Benedictine rule. It was a canon regular, Hugh de Fouilloy, who in matter, manner, and motive, anticipated St. Bernard's censure of ornate monastic churches. In his *De claustro animae* Hugh railed satirically against sculpting the stone of monastic churches, against the decorating of walls, and against the menacing possibility that the written text of the Bible might be supplanted by narrative murals: "One should read Genesis," he said, "in the book and not on the walls."[34] Bernard of Clairvaux was the

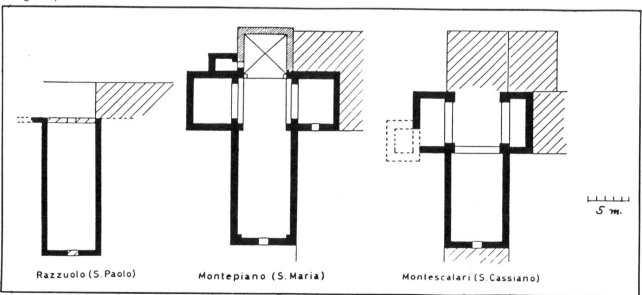

Fig. 9. Plans of churches in the Order of Vallombrosa (drawn by Stiegman after Gaborit).

superior writer and the more influential spokesman, but there is some significance in the fact that his architectural views were demonstrably not those of a solitary aesthetic prophet, nor indeed original to the early Cistercians. The canons regular had spoken out before him.

Evidently, some knowledge of the nature and direction of the canonical movement and of its size and strength is necessary in any attempt to re-create the religious and architectural setting of the Cistercian oratory.

We speak of the *canons regular* today most ordinarily in ignorance of how synthetic and unhistorical a category this is, failing to acknowledge that what evolved through at least two centuries is projected as a definition onto specific communities, though few of them may conform to this prescriptive notion. Confusion was planted early when the chroniclers of the twelfth and thirteenth centuries lumped the era's rich complexity of forms into an entity they mistakenly called the Order of St. Augustine. What is identified in the concrete by canon regular, common life, and the rule of St. Augustine is, as Charles Dereine has demonstrated, impossible to tell.[35] One reads through 60 of 144 canonial documents assembled by Dereine, or through a period of 92 years, before coming upon any mention of a Rule of St. Augustine. A study of Curial documents reveals that there are no terms which define the canonial form of life nor the function that "canons" filled in the Church.[36]

Unlike monks, whose communities were more closely organized, therefore more powerful, the canons did not write history nor leave much documentation, and the little they did provide has been poorly used. This situation has made the canons, in the words of Jacques Dubois, "les grands méconnus de l'histoire ecclésiastique médiévale."[37] It suggests why the problem has been, as Giles Constable says, "rather badly studied."[38] Some figures of the era even seemed to relish as wholesome the institutional disorientation they occasioned, such as the founder of Grandmont, Stephen of Thiers, who refused to be called either monk, hermit, or canon.[39] Attempting to identify the wellsprings of change, we might say that a certain maturing of secular society in the high middle ages spawned new insights into the relationships between Church and world, and into the possibilities and needs of the laity. Institutional identities were questioned. St. Bernard, confessing his failure to understand his own irrepressible involvement as a monk in ecclesiastical matters regarding the laity, is the very paradigm of a confused and vibrant age.[40]

In the twelfth century the major canonial *institutiones*, as they are called in the documents, were the Canons Regular of Prémontré, of Arrouaise, of Saint Victor, and of Saint Rufus. But there were a great number of small congregations. Our attempt to discover what the ecclesiastical world and its churches were like when the Cistercians arrived on the scene requires some awareness of these lesser communities.

Jean Richard calls one of these to our attention.

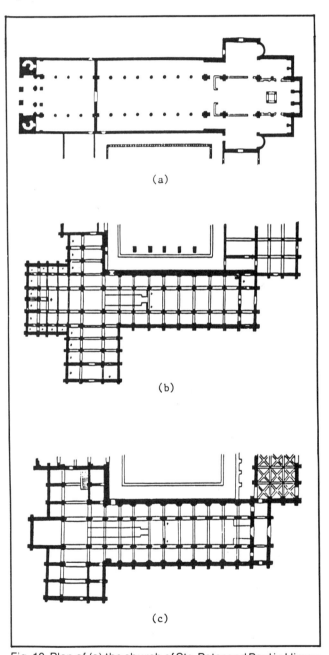

(a)

(b)

(c)

Fig. 10. Plan of (a) the church of Sts. Peter and Paul in Hirsau (drawn by Stiegman after Badstübner); (b) Clairvaux II, and (c) Cîteaux III (both after Dimier).

Fig. 11. Church of St.-Jean-L'Evangeliste at Bar-le-Regulier (Cote d'Or), the nave looking east (photo: Stiegman).

the common life. Early in the twelfth century we read that they follow the rule of St. Augustine.[43]

The bishop of Autun did not limit his commitment to the well-being of his people to providing them with a local congregation of canons. He soon became involved in the foundation of a Benedictine monastery at Saint-Rigaud. Here the monk Eustorge, who had become a hermit, helped to settle other monks who wished to incorporate some eremitic elements in the new community. Eustorge is a presage of Robert of Molesme, who will found Cîteaux. A similar history unfolded at the monastery of La Chaise-Dieu.[44] Saint-Rigaud became an abbey and established several priories in the region. We hear little about it except that its practices were so austere that in 1251 Pope Innocent IV mitigated them.

Richard situates on a map the several houses of the

We might begin in the small unprepossessing Burgundian parish church of St. Jean-l'Evangéliste at Bar-le-Régulier (Côte d'Or).[41] In its plan (rectangular chevet and transept chapels), two-story elevation, pointed barrel-vaulted nave, omission of clerestory windows, very plain corbels, unadorned colonnade wall, unenriched surfaces, and a certain harmony of proportions, it seems very Cistercian (Figs. 11-12). The congregation of Canons Regular of Saint-Germain-en-Brionnais, founded in about 1070 by Aganon de Mont-Saint-Jean, bishop of Autun, established a priory here sometime before 1085. Richard makes a strong case for these dates—about fifteen years earlier than those found in standard references—although dating is not as important in his argument as it is in mine.[42] After a brief while the priory at Bar-le-Régulier instituted daughter houses of its own in the area. Within the pontificate of Gregory VII, Aganon decreed that the several houses of the congregation could serve parishioners as long as the canons observed poverty and

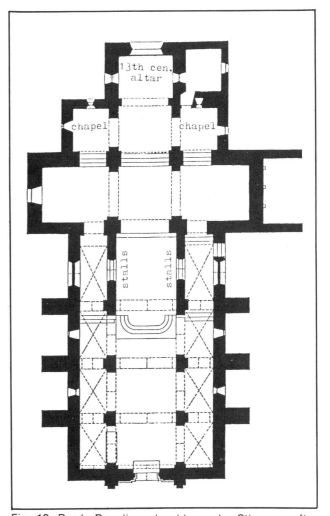

Fig. 12. Bar-le-Regulier, plan (drawn by Stiegman after Bernard Richi in *Pays de Bourgogne* 33 [1961]).

Fig. 13. Cistercian abbeys surrounding the diocese of Autun, mid-twelfth century (drawing by Stiegman after Richard).

Canons Regular of Saint-Germain-en-Brionnais, together with the foundations from Saint-Rigaud, located in the diocese of Autun (Fig. 13). On the perimeter of this area are the Cistercian monasteries of La Ferté-sur-Grosne, Reigny, Fontenay, La Bussière, Septfons, and La-Benisson-Dieu. No Cistercian house penetrates the circle. Checking against van der Meer's *Atlas*, one notices that this empty space, in the heartland of Cîteaux, is about the largest on the map of Cistercian France.[45] What fills the territory are not the Cluniac communities but those of the canons (and the monks of Saint-Rigaud) founded by Aganon, the local apostle of poverty and solitude. Richard acknowledges that the untypical absence of Cistercians in the Autun area may betray the resistance of Cluny to Cîteaux. "But," he asks, "is it not also because the recruits whom the Cistercian abbeys would have attracted had found in these modest foundations the response to their aspirations toward a life of poverty and eremitism?"[46]

Encountering a community of canons regular whose spirituality was so Cistercian before the Cistercians, we might suspect their church architecture would bear some resemblance to the Cistercian oratory. But, we settled that, before learning of Aganon and his canons regular, when we discovered the austerely simple and effectively prayerful parish church at Bar-le-Régulier.

It is important to realize that such buildings, products of the reform mentality, could not have come about in total independence of the building tradition of Cluny. Raymond Oursel believes the motherhouse of Bishop Aganon's canons, Saint-Germain-en-Brionnais, marks the moment when Cluniac building modes penetrated the Brionnais territory. The church of Saint-Germain exercised a strong architectural influence in the area.[47] Clearly, this observation brings little solace to those who insist upon keeping the genealogical lines of architectural history well separated.

Regarding other canonial churches of Burgundy to which historians of Cistercian architecture direct our attention, my remarks can be only selective. The four-bay nave of Saint-Ferréol de Curgy (Saône-et-Loire), with simple barrel vault, transverse arches, no direct lighting, and rampant buttressing vaults over the aisles, represented a complex of solutions which later Cistercian builders were certainly aware of. The surfaces of this eleventh-century church, inside and out, are unenriched (Fig. 14).[48]

One sees the same avoidance of "superfluities" at Saint-Savinien-de-Sens (Yonne), one of the most venerable churches in France, rebuilt in the eleventh century (Figs. 15, 16).[49] The nave communicates with its aisles through arcades almost totally bereft of any structural articulation—that is, through an "arcade wall," similar to the solution later employed at such twelfth-century Cistercian oratories as Bonmont (near Geneva), Sénanque (Vaucluse) (Fig. 7), and, to a lesser extent, Aiguebelle (Drome). But it is to the mathematical ratios of this eleventh-century

Fig. 14. Church of Saint-Ferréol de Curgy, west front (photo: Stiegman).

building that I would call the special attention of those historians bent on linking Cistercian geometrism to later influences from the school of Chartres:[50] the height-width ratio of the nave appears to be a graceful two-to-one. Perhaps one should not discount this altogether after learning that the original unvaulted ceiling was modified; for, the distance from the floor to the second-story windows—a dimension well marked by a stringcourse on the west wall, even as at Fontenay—seems equal to the width of the nave. This square of the lower west wall is then duplicated to the top of the present timber vault. The original spacial feeling is, with this modification, explicitly completed rather than violated.

I cannot support this perception with precise archeological data; but I must say that to experience the proportions of Saint-Savien-de-Sens is to be left

Fig. 15. Church of Saint-Savinien de Sens, west front (photo: Stiegman).

with some disquietude about current theories which explain the prominence of harmonious Cistercian ratios as a twelfth-century innovation prompted mainly by literary sources. Measurements would be important to a conclusive argument; but no amassing of ratio tabulations, of itself, constitutes an argument. Are the "perfect ratios" of the Cistercian oratory a rediscovery from late antiquity, or are they "a revival of the Carolingian feeling for space" already observable in churches of the reform?[51] One

might look for this revival where ancient churches like Saint-Savinien have been rebuilt on the site of earlier buildings. Then again, it is inherently probable that attention to areas and volumes was the gradual outgrowth of the renunciation of attention to surfaces—a renunciation that monks and canons regular of the reform movement accepted. With the Cistercians the experimental process succeeds.

That the Cistercian oratory was recognized as an architectural success is most conclusively demonstrated in the response of many groups of regular canons: they offered the compliment of imitation. In England (where the canons well outnumbered the Cistercians) the Premonstratensians, Augustinians, and Gilbertines became the first propagators of Cistercian building practices.[52] The extent of Cistercian influence in France may be observed in the mother church of the Premonstratensians, Saint-Martin de Laon (Aisne), in a Bernardine plan and in an elevation suggesting the august sobriety of the rib-vaulted Romanesque treatment at Pontigny (Yonne).[53] Dimier finds Cistercian characteristics also in the churches of Beauport in Brittany, Lucerne in Normandy, Dommartin in Artois—all twelfth-century foundations from Prémontré.[54] The close sharing of spiritual ideals between Cîteaux and Prémontré (a later foundation), even as the friendship between St. Bernard and St. Norbert, was well known. In 1142 an act of confraternity strengthened the bond.[55] From what we have seen, however, of the character of reform in the earlier canons, we must conclude that Prémontré, and the canons generally, could sometimes imitate the architecture of Cîteaux only because the Cistercian oratory effectively embodied what had always moved the canons regular and what, in some measure, had been evident in canonical churches before the founding of Cîteaux.

The Cistercian Synthesis

In some measure, I say. Can we be more specific and determine the measure? The genius of Cîteaux, the reason that history discovers to explain the blanketing of the map of Europe with Cistercian abbeys in the twelfth century, has to do with systematization. All the elements of spirituality, of governance, and of economy which comprise the Cistercian order were taken from the broad eleventh- and twelfth-century movement of reform. Cîteaux's originality was to synthesize them.[56] We must say the same for Cistercian architecture. All the expressions of religious values in the Cistercian oratory were found in various ways in the churches of the reformed monks and the canons whom we have considered. As one kneels in the church of Bar-le-Régulier or Saint Ferréol de Curgy or Saint-Savinien-de-Sens, one is made forcibly aware of a mentality that may be precisely formulated in consultation with texts on the religious aspirations of the eleventh- and twelfth-century reform. Yet, various qualities emerge in varying degrees of success. One is not likely to pronounce any of these buildings a complete embodiment of that prayer to which the reformers aspired. In the end one feels a tension between the demands of humility (poverty) and of majesty. What is ostentatious and distracting has been eliminated; compatible efforts to suggest grandeur have been made. But, this is not enough to leave us with the sense that we are witnessing, in the words of St. Bernard, a "controlled interplay of lowliness and exaltation," that we are in a building where everything is "absolutely congruent" with that perfect combination of "earthly tent and heavenly palace."[57] Striving for the same objectives and employing similar solutions, a Cistercian oratory like Bonmont or Le Thoronet, of small scale and meagre resources, will be judged to have reached a superior integration and balance. Here Bernard's words, spoken of the soul as the Bridegroom's earthly dwelling, may be enthusiastically excerpted as apt description.

Art historians who have responded to this majesty and exaltation have traced the Cistercians' borrowings of stylistic elements, praising the accomplishment for high discipline, simplicity, and the use of advanced techniques. They tend to suggest that a new religious vision assembling these elements constitutes Cistercian originality. The nature of this elusive aesthetic excellence is surely more human—that is, more accessible to cultural analysis—than that. Unless we are prepared to work from idyllic assumptions about the art of artlessness, we must ask how the Cistercian builder transposed his religious experience into an effectively religious building. Had he had occasion to judge the effect of the means he planned to employ? Or, was he innocent of all architectural effects? The view that the Cistercians, all unsuspecting, backed their way into artistic success is, strangely, rather common. Although the debt of students to Anselme Didier is immense, one should not avoid noticing that this author marveled at what he considered a paradox in his order's history: "Chose curieuse: . . . de cette résolution de ne pas faire œuvre artistique, devait sortir cet art nouveau, cette architecture nouvelle, qu'on peut appeler l'architecture cistercienne."[58] Frederic van der Meer is equally insistent: "Le point

de vue des premiers Cisterciens était au-dessus de toute considération esthétique; . . . la majesté qu'ils cherchaient . . . est née malgré eux."[59] Such a conviction seems to derive from the lingering romantic notion that true art surges irrepressibly out of the truth of human experience. Is it not this view, however questionable, which explains some part of our

Fig. 16. Saint-Savinien de Sens, the nave facing west (photo: Stiegman).

willingness to account for what is characteristic and wonderful in Cistercian architecture by direct appeal to Cistercian spirituality, bypassing the mediation of the architect as artist? This manner of thinking would then legitimate the historian's neglect of architectural antecedents.

At this point, to contrast medieval concepts of art with those of later times would make no critical contribution to our question. We are not concerned here with knowing how people of the twelfth century identified and organized their intellectual categories; we want to know concretely whether Cistercian builders cared enough about the aesthetic end-product of their planning to ask carefully what this would be. An historicism content to lock the twelfth century into its own vocabulary—to the point where we can no longer recognize our own questions in the era—simply evades this issue. It sanctions the highly suspect proposition that obviously careful builders, producing powerfully effective work, did not know what they were doing.

The buildings that come before St. Bernard's oratory in the age of monastic reform do not betray so integral a conception of an aesthetic end-product as does the Cistercian oratory. They seem to be only partly successful in their transposition of desert spirituality. Yet, they point the way. We are familiar with the synthesizing of ideas and attitudes; but how do qualities ascertained in a variety of buildings—a good solution in one, another in another—become a system? The student of religion and of aesthetics here relies upon the architectural engineer. In an elegant effort to analyze the effect of the Cistercian oratory, the art historian François Bucher explains how the parts relate to one another.[60] Take Fontenay, all too briefly (Figs. 1-4): the nave is covered by a broken barrel vault with transverse arches; it is of moderate height, producing good acoustics for the chant. The flat chevet is not only economical; it allows much window space which, together with windows from the west wall, provides indirect white light for the vault of the nave. Since the Office to be sung is known by heart, clerestory windows which could provide reading light are omitted, producing a strongly unified one-story elevation. The aisles are covered by transverse broken barrel vaults which act, economically, as buttresses to the nave vault. From small windows under these vaults come channels of light which outline the bays of the nave. The proportions of the church are based on a modular construction, using the width of the crossing (one side of a square) as a unit.[61] The height of the nave in relation to its width is two to one. The cross-section of the building is a perfect square.

I do not think we have come very far in analyzing the contribution of these and other solutions to the housing of that function for which the oratory was built, and in clarifying, therefore, how the architecture is "functional"; nevertheless, Bucher makes an installment on the project. Such studied proportions, he says, produce a calming effect, the positive counterpart to the elimination of narrative sculpture, colored glass, and various types of ornamentation: "The clearly interbalanced simplicity of all

the elements throws us back on ourselves."[62] To that widespread constituency in twelfth-century Christendom which sought a place of solitude to pray together, in contemplative longing for the Bridegroom, this was a good place. It was the perfectly functional church.

The inventiveness of St. Bernard's oratory lay, not in austere renunciation, nor even in more genuinely theological objectives. The originality of Cistercian architecture was specifically architectural. That it came about suddenly sometime before 1135, when a group of talented builders directed by St. Bernard laid the plans for Clairvaux II—that it was the issue of a first effort, a kind of spontaneous generation in architecture—strains credibility.[63] That such a view is contradicted by the evidence I have tried to assemble should be clear.

If, by some timid diminution of architectural scope, we set Cistercian oratories in art history merely as an exhibit in the transition from Romanesque to Gothic, one may tend, however incorrectly, to see them as an ascetical reaction against beautiful things. If, instead, we set them in the milieu from which they truly arose, the reform movement of monks and canons regular, who cherished their own tradition of church building, they will be discovered as the mature realization of long established building aims. St. Bernard's abbey church was the gathering place of those who longed for the beauty of that kingdom which is within. Its distinction lay not as much in a characteristic spirituality as in a synthesis of architectural solutions governed by that spirituality. In strictly artistic terms, where one speaks not about experiments (the partial and the instrumental) but about performance (the totality and the final effect), there are *no* analogues of the twelfth-century Cistercian abbey church; but, perhaps it is unhelpful to conceive of analogues that narrowly. The reformers who, in successive efforts through many decades, strove to build an environment inducing a prayerful state of soul, must be associated with the achievement of St. Bernard's builders. The shared accomplishment of these pioneers becomes fully visible finally in the Cistercian oratory, a building type that, in its power to communicate, can lay claim to the first completely realized single-minded architectural functionality in the Western tradition. Like the Cistercians themselves, St. Bernard's oratory is the consummation of a movement.

Notes

1 Research for this study was made possible by a leave-fellowship grant from the Social Sciences and Humanities Research Council of Canada, and by the generous welcome of Cistercian abbeys in France, Belgium, and Switzerland.

2 *Apologia ad Guillelmum abbatem* in Jean Leclercq and H. M. Rochais, ed. *S. Bernardi opera*, 8 vols. (Rome: Editiones cistercienses, 1963), III, 5-108. Michael Casey, trans. "An Apologia to Abbot William," *The Works of Bernard of Clairvaux: Volume One, Treatises I*, CF 1 (Shannon: Cistercian Publications, 1970), pp. 33-69. Jean Leclercq's Introduction to this translation, pp. 3-30, is uncommonly helpful on the character of the tract. In "Saint Bernard: The Aesthetics of Authenticity," *Studies in Cistercian Art and Architecture*, ed. Meredith Parsons Lillich, CS 66 and 69 (Kalamazoo: Cistercian Publications, 1982, 84), II, 1-13, I have discussed misuses of the *Apologia* by historians.

3 See, e.g., Joan Evans, *Art in Mediaeval France, 987-1498* (Oxford: Clarendon, 1948), pp. 62-73; Henry Focillon, *The Art of the West in the Middle Ages*, 2 vols. (London: Phaidon, 1963), II, 20-25; Robert Branner, *Burgundian Gothic Architecture* (London: Zwemmer, 1960) ch. 2. The pioneering survey is Marcel Aubert and the Marquise de Maillé, *L'architecture cistercienne en France*, 2 vols. 2nd ed. (1943; Paris: Editions d'art et d'histoire, 1947); see esp. II, 207-213.

4 See, e.g., Anselme Dimier, "Architecture et spiritualité cistercienne," *Revue du moyen âge latin*, 3 (1947), 255-74. For this author's most comprehensive statement, see Joseph (Anselme) Dimier, Introduction to *Recueil de plans d'églises cisterciennes* (Grignan, Drome: Abbaye ND d'Aiguebelle, 1949), I, 2-45.

5 François Bucher, "Cistercian Architectural Purism," *Comparative Studies in Society and History* 3 (1960-61), 89-105, stresses functionality. See esp. pp. 98-103.

6 "Sur l'architecture monastique au XIIe siècle," *Centre international d'études romanes* 3 (1969), 20-48, at p. 28.

7 R. De Lasteyrie, *L'architecture religieuse en France à l'époque gothique*, 2 vols. (Paris: Picard, 1926-27), II, 98-99, mentions St.-Lazare d'Avallon, Montréal, and Pont Aubert; Marcel Aubert, I, 165nl, speaks of St.-Ferréol de Curgy, St.-Savinien de Sens, Appoigny, St.-Martin du Bourg at Avallon, Crain, St.-Martin de Langres, Michery, Montréal, Nuits-sous-Beaune, St.-Martin de Challon, and St.-Seine. François Bucher, *Notre-Dame de Bonmont und die ersten Zisterzienserabteien der Schweiz* (Bern: Benteli

1957), p. 280, calls attention to St.-Vorles in Challon, Farges, Uchizy, Sts. Peter and Paul at Hirsau, and other churches, incl. English examples of the flat chevet. Robert Branner, p. 19, links Cistercian churches to the "Romanesque Avallonais" type, listing St.-Martin du Bourg at Avallon, St.-Savinien de Sens, St.-Verain, Sermaize, and Goaille in the Franche Comté. Ernst Badstübner, *Kirchen der Mönche: Die Baukunst der Reformorden im Mittelalter* (Vienna: Rusch, 1980), pp. 140-217, views the Cistercian oratory in the context of the eleventh- and twelfth-century reform, with special emphasis on the Hirsau churches.

8 The most comprehensive treatment of Cîteaux's debt to the reform movement is Bede K. Lackner, *The Eleventh-Century Background of Cîteaux*, CF 8 (Kalamazoo: Cistercian Publications, 1972), with excellent bibliography at pp. 277-96. See p. 276.

9 René Crozet, *L'art roman*, 2nd ed. (1962; Paris: Quadrige, 1981), p. 121.

10 *Apologia*, pp. 28-29; in Casey, pp. 63-66.

11 Anselme Dimier, "L'église de l'abbaye de Foigny," *Bulletin monumental*, 118 (1960), 191-205; and "En marge du centenaire bernardin; l'église de Clairvaux," *Studi su S. Bernardo di Chiaravalle nell' ottavo centenario della canonizzazione*, Bibliotheca Cisterciensis 6 (Rome: Editiones cistercienses), 317-25.

12 Bucher, "Cistercian," p. 92.

13 H.R. Hahnloser, *Villard de Honnecourt: Kritische Gesamtausgabe des Bauhüttenbücher ms. fr. 19093 der Pariser Bibliotek* (Vienna: Schroll, 1935). An excellent demonstration of the unity of Cistercian architecture in the twelfth century is C. Bruzelius, "The Twelfth-Century Church at Ourscamp," *Speculum* 56 (1980): 28-40.

14 For England, e.g., see Peter Fergusson, *Architecture of Solitude: Cistercian Abbeys in Twelfth-Century England* (Princeton: Princeton UP), pp. 101-110: the Cistercian oratory in England had a greater stylistic unity with the French examples (i.e., it was less "Anglo-Norman") than has been acknowledged.

15 Jean Leclercq, "La crise du monachisme aux XIe et XIIe siècles," *Bolletino dell' Instituto Storico Italiano per il Medio Evo* 70 (1958), 19-41, at p. 23.

16 Louis J. Lekai, "Motives and Ideals of the Eleventh-Century Monastic Renewal," *The Cistercian Spirit: A Symposium in Memory of Thomas Merton*, ed. M. Basil Pennington, CS 3 (Shannon: Cistercian Publications, 1970), 27-47, at pp. 37-38, argues plausibly that the eleventh century's fascination with earlier models of monasticism was a response to changed local conditions rather than the direct influence of hermits newly arrived from the East.

17 For the Cistercians, see Dimier, *Recueil de plans* I, 18-19.

18 Jean Hubert, "L'érémitisme et l'archéologie," *L'eremitismo in occidente nei secoli XI e XII* (Milan: Università

cattolica del sacro Cuore, 1965) 462-87. Jean Owen Schaefer, "The Earliest Churches of the Cistercian Order," *Studies in Cistercian Art and Architecture,* I, 1-12, at p. 12n32, calls attention to the powerfully suggestive fact that, before there were "Cistercian" oratories, some of the earliest Cistercian communities (e.g., Pontigny, Morimond, Fontenay, Hautecombe, Les Dunes, Aulps) took the hermits' structure for their own.

19 Jean-René Gaborit, "Les plus anciens monastères de l'ordre de Vallombreuse (1037-1115): étude archéologique," *Ecole française de Rome: mélanges d'archéologie et d'histoire* 76 (1964), 451-90, and 77 (1965), 179-208. See 76 (1964), 474-76, for the author's insistence that Vallombrosa was a cenobitic community, not a group of hermits as is frequently claimed. For the splendor of their liturgy and the construction of their church, see Lackner, p. 191, with further documentation.

20 Gaborit in *Ecole française* 76 (1964), 479-80 for Razzuolo; pp. 488-89 for Marradi; pp. 480-82 for Montescolari; and *Ecole française* 77 (1965), 190-92 for Montepiano, and p. 207 regarding the choice of these elements. The author does not speak of spatial experiments; these are inferred from the plans he has collected. My examples are at fig. 9.

21 Lackner, p. 209 and n145. For details of spatial organization in the Carthusian monastery, see Dimier, "Sur l'architecture monastique," pp. 44-46.

22 René Crozet, "L'architecture de l'ordre de Grandmont en Poitou, Saintonge, et Angoumois," *Bulletins et mémoires de la société archéologique et historique de la Charente* 11 (1944), 221-41, at p. 224.

23 Crozet, "L'architecture," pp. 232, 241. The author offers illustrations at pp. 230, 233, and 236.

24 Crozet, "L'architecture," pp. 98 and 241.

25 Anselme Dimier, *Les moines bâtisseurs* (Paris: Fayard, 1964), p. 97, commenting upon the priory of Saint-Jean-des Bonshommes near Avallon in Burgundy. Dimier describes the austerity of Grandmontine architecture more extensively in "Sur l'architecture monastique" 42-44. Some of the Grandmontine houses spoken of by Crozet are La Carte (Deux Sèvres), Sermaize (Charente-Maritime), Barbe-Torte (Vendée), Bonneray (Vendée), Chassay (Vendée), Notre-Dame de la Garde (Charente-Maritime), and Puy-Chevrier (Vallée de la Dive).

26 R. Duvernay, "Cîteaux, Vallombreuse, et Etienne Harding," *Analecta sacrae ordinis cisterciensis* 8 (1952), 379 ff., at 423. Duvernay believes the Cistercian *Carta caritatis* contains direct borrowings from Vallombrosa, where Stephen Harding had spent some time. See also Maur Cocheril, "Les Cisterciens," *Les ordres religieux: la vie et l'art,* ed. Gabriel Le Bras, 2 vols. (Paris: Flammerion, 1979-80), I, 338-561, at p. 344.

27 Karl Heinz Esser, "Les Fouilles à Himmerod et le plan bernardin," *Mélanges Saint Bernard: XXIVe*

Congrès de l'association bourguignonne des sociétès savantes, 8e Centenaire de la mort de Saint Bernard (Dijon: Marilier, 1953), pp. 311-15, at p. 315. Esser calls attention both to formal resemblances and to the probability that St. Bernard visited Hirsau before work began on Clairvaux II.

28 Badstübner, pp. 67-68.

29 Werner Weisbach, *Religiöse Reform und mittelalterliche Kunst* (Einsiedeln-Zürich: 1945), p. 51. Badstübner, pp. 67-68.

30 Badstübner, pp. 127-28.

31 See Badstübner for illustrations of Sangerhausen, pp. 88-89; of Alpirsbach, p. 94; of Schaffhausen, pp. 92-93.

32 Weisbach, p. 50.

33 A divide between monks and the laity is built into the very texture of Bernard's language; but the pertinent statements concerning churches are in the *Apologia,* 28, *Opera* 3:104-06: *Illud autem interrogo monachus monachos. . . . Et quidem alia causa est episcoporum, alia monachorum. . . . Denique quid haec ad pauperes, ad monachos, ad spirituales viros?* My translation: "I ask you about this as a monk addressing other monks. . . . Bishops and monks deal with different affairs. . . . What, finally, do these things [church ornaments] hold for poor men, for monks, for spiritual men?"

34 Victor Mortet, "Huges de Fouilloy, Pierre le Chantre, Alexandre Neckham et les critiques dirigées au XIIe siècle contre le luxe des constructions," *Mélanges d'histoire offerts à M. Charles Bémont* (Paris: Picard, 1913) 105-35, qtd. in M.-M. Davy, *Initiation à la symbolique romane (XIIe siècle)* (1955; Paris: Flammarion, 1977), p. 206.

35 "Vie commune, règle de Saint-Augustine, et chanoines réguliers au XIe siècle," *Revue d'histoire ecclésiastique* 41 (1946), 365-406. Reference to Rule of St. Augustine, at p. 375.

36 Jacques Dubois, "Les ordres religieux au XIIe siècle selon la Curie romaine," *Revue Bénédictine* 78 (1968), 283-309, at p. 309. Dubois concludes that from Curial terminology one can infer only that the regular canons were Religious with the traditional vows.

37 "Les moines dans la société du moyen âge," *Revue d'histoires de l'église de France* 60 (1974), 5-37, at p. 16.

38 "Cluny-Cîteaux-La Chartreuse: San Bernardo e la diversità delle forme di vita religiosa nel XII secolo," *Studi su San Bernardo,* pp. 93-114: "Questo problema è stato piuttosto mal studiato" (p. 105).

39 Lackner, p. 198.

40 Constable 114, referring to Bernard's famous uncomfortable remark that he was the chimera of his century.

41 Jean Richard, "La congrégation de Saint-Germain-en-Brionnais: L'evêque Aganon d'Autun et le renouveau de la vie commune au XIe siècle," *Mémoires de la Société pour l'Histoire du Droit et des Institutions des anciens pays bourguignons, comtois, et romands*

24 (1963), 289-98. I am indebted to the author for a generous interview.

42 Albert Colombet (membre de la Société Française d'Archéologie), *L'église de Bar-le-Régulier et ses magnifiques stalles* (Dijon: L'Arche d'Or, 1961), p. 3, sets 1100 as the foundation of the priory, and the twelfth century as the date of the church. The *Dictionnaire des églises de France 2*, A24 dates the church thirteenth century, possibly with an eye to such additions as the lantern tower.

43 The *Necrologium* of the diocese of Mâcon, qtd. in Richard 293n3, speaks of the knight Renier, who became a religious in the congregation, *"sub norma sanctissimi Augustini."*

44 Richard, p. 295n4.

45 Frederic van der Meer, *Atlas de l'ordre cistercien* (Paris and Brussels: 1965), map II.

46 Richard, p. 298.

47 Raymond Oursel and A.-M. Oursel, *Les églises romanes de l'Autunois et du Brionnais (Ancien Grand Archidiaconé d'Autun): Cluny et sa Région* (Mâcon: Protat, 1956), pp. 268-71.

48 The date is from *Dictionnaire 2*, A58-59.

49 *Dictionnaire 2*, A147-148.

50 E.g., Otto von Simson, *The Gothic Cathedral: Origins of Gothic Architecture and the Medieval Concept of Order* (1956; New York: Pantheon, 1962), pp. 21-58.

51 Phillippe Verdier, "St. Denis and Chartres," rev. of *The Gothic Cathedral* by Otto von Simson, *The Yale Review* 46 (1956-57), 145-49, at p. 148, prefers to explain early Gothic ratios as "a revival of the Carolingian feeling for space" rather than as the influence of a Cistercian rediscovery of Augustine, as von Simson would have it. Re Carolingian influences, see Walter Horn, "On the Author of the Plan of St. Gall and the Relation of the Plan to the Monastic Reform Movement," *Studien zum St.-Galler Klosterplan* (St. Gallen: 1962), pp. 103-27; also subsequent works of Walter Horn, such as "On the Selective Use of Sacred Numbers and the Creation in Carolingian Architecture of a New Aesthetic Based on Modular Concepts," *Viator* 6 (1975), 351-90.

52 Fergusson, pp. 108-10.

53 Dimier, *Les moines bâtisseurs*, pp. 111-14, speaks of Cistercian influence upon Premonstratensian architecture. Fergusson, pp. 109-10, affirms the influence but notes that it was not always in one direction. William W. Clark, "Cistercian Influences on Premonstratensian Church Planning: Saint-Martin at Laon," *Studies in Cistercian Art and Architecture*, II, 161-88 at pp. 179-80, would restrict Cîteaux's architectural influence upon Prémontré to the plan of the transept chapels.

54 "Sur l'architecture monastique," p. 47.

55 J.B. Valvekens, "Actus confraternitatis inter Ordinem Praemonstratentium et Ordinem Cisterciensem," *Analecta Praemonstratensia* 42 (1966), 326-30.

56 Lackner, p. 276.

57 *Sermones super cantica canticorum* 27.14, *opera* 1:191, lines 23-24: . . . *deiectio ista, et ista celsitudo . . . ea moderatione sibi pariter contemperantur;* well rendered by Kilian Walsh, trans. *On the Song of Songs II*, SF 7 (Kalamazoo and London: Cistercian Publications, 1976), 86, as "controlled interplay of lowliness and exaltation." From the same paragraph, I translate *"plenum . . . congruentiae* as "absolutely congruent"; and *"terrenum habitaculum, et caeleste palatium"* is translated by Walsh as "earthly tent and heavenly palace," p. 86.

58 "Architecture," p. 268.

59 *Atlas*, p. 39.

60 "Cistercian," esp. pp. 100-03.

61 The best discussion of Cistercian proportions is an excursus in Hanno Hahn, *Die frühe Kirchenbaukunst der Zisterzienser* (Berlin: Mann, 1957), pp. 314-39.

62 "Cistercian," p. 103.

63 C. Edson Armi, *Masons and Sculptors in Romanesque Burgundy: The New Aesthetic of Cluny III*, 2 vols. (University Park, PA and London: Pennsylvania State UP, 1983), I, 8-10, gives an excellent presentation of the weaknesses in a theory that explains a great building achievement by the genius of one person and all similar buildings as imitations of his work.

The Way of Mary or That of Martha: Conceptions of Monastic Life at Savigny, 1112-1180

Kathryn L. Reyerson

The monastery of Savigny, dedicated to the Trinity, was one of several monasteries founded in Normandy in response to the spirit of ascetic monasticism which spread throughout Europe in the last decades of the eleventh and the early twelfth centuries. Previous scholarly research on Savigny has been concentrated in institutional and economic history.[1] Given the continuing interest of monastic history in the conceptions of twelfth-century religious life, I have focused instead on the interpretations of monastic life at Savigny from its foundation in 1112 until about the year 1180.[2] The lives of two abbots and two monks of Savigny provide the major source material for my study.[3] From an analysis of these works, I will describe the early conception of monastic life under the founder Vitalis and then examine elements of continuity and change with the second abbot Geoffrey and two monks, Hamo and Peter, who lived after the merger of Savigny with the order of Cîteaux in 1147.

The founder of Savigny, Vitalis of Mortain, selected as a site for his monastery a valley where there were ruins of an old château.[4] The *Vita B. Vitalis* describes the site as "a land which thorn bushes, thorny plants, and unfruitful trees inhabited. . . ."[5] The choice of a barren and isolated spot for foundation was a common practice of most twelfth-century ascetic movements.[6] A local lord, Raoul of Fougères, donated the forest of Savigny along with one thousand pounds of annual revenue and high and low justice.[7] In spite of clearance, drainage efforts, and new cultivation, Vitalis needed additional resources. Through a recovery of alms which had earlier been surrendered to the church of St. Etienne of Caen and through other donations, Savigny became deeply involved in the feudal and economic system of the twelfth century.[8] In contrast to early Cistercian practice, Savigny received tithes and patronage of churches, mills and wine-presses

from the beginning of its history.[9] It also leased lands, carried primitive mortgages as a means of investing its capital and held vassals.[10] When merger with the Cistercian order came in 1147, numerous exceptions were made on behalf of Savigny permitting it to retain the monasteries and persons of its filiation under its control and to continue the empiricism of its existing economic policies and organization.[11] It is within this context of involvement that an inquiry into the spiritual life at Savigny must be set.

Scholars have related the ascetic spirit of monasticism of the late eleventh and early twelfth centuries to new interpretations of the *vita apostolica*.[12] On the one hand, the *vita apostolica* might suggest an imitation of the evangelical activity of the apostles; on the other, it could refer to the life style of the primitive church whose Christianity people of the medieval period much admired. In monastic movements, the impetus of the *vita apostolica* called forth a return to solitude and meditation from some individuals and evangelical preaching and service in the world from others. Institutionally, in fact, there were several types of response ranging from the severity of Carthusian practice to the evangelical involvement of the Premonstratensians.[13] Beginning with the life of abbot Vitalis by Stephen of Fougères, grandson of the first lay patron, I will follow the evolution in the conceptions of monastic life at Savigny through the later twelfth century.

In the study of saints' lives, the modern historian must read on several levels, keeping in mind that the purpose of hagiography was not so much an objective narrative of the facts as the creation of an edifying image of the saint, from legend as well as fact. In my analysis, I have read on the level of fact for information about the saint, that is, for descriptions of his actions, for the author's opinion of the saint, and for the points of spirituality which the author sought consciously to emphasize. On another level, and of equal interest for my topic, were the unconscious revelations of the author's preconceptions and attitudes. My conclusions in many instances must remain tentative, for the men whom I am studying did not leave theoretical discussions of their views of the *vita apostolica*.

The *Vita B. Vitalis* does not provide dates in the life of Vitalis, but scholars have established that he was born about 1050 in Tierceville in the Bessin of devout parents of humble background.[14] After an early education in letters and a later period of study away from home, Vitalis became chaplain of the count of Mortain, a position which he left about 1094 to pursue an eremitical life lasting seventeen years in Normandy and Brittany, punctuated by several trips to England.[15] Because of his success as a spiritual leader and preacher, Vitalis found the need to supervise more effectively the scattered hermits under his tutelage. He established a monastery for the men and one for the women who followed him.[16] Early in the *Vita*, Stephen established Vitalis' religious vocation as that of evangelical preacher.[17] As the author portrayed him, Vitalis sought at all times in his life to spread the seeds of God's word. He led men from evil to the way of eternal life.[18]

Claude Auvry, a seventeenth-century monk of Savigny and author of a history of the order, suggested that Vitalis interpreted his sphere of action as the total community, that is, as both the secular and religious worlds; he did not confine his preaching to the monastic community and to his hermits.[19] While Auvry cited the *Vita B. Vitalis* as the source for this contention, I have found no passage which corresponds to the citation. However, I believe that Auvry's statement can be corroborated by other information in the *Vita*.

The greatest stumbling block to the establishment of the fact that Vitalis preached in the lay community after the founding of Savigny is the confusion of chronology in the *Vita*. Stephen wrote the *Vita* as a series of episodes, a standard hagiographical procedure. Early in the *Vita* he made reference to the petition of Vitalis to Raoul of Fougères for the founding of the monastery of Savigny. There is no further mention of the monastery until very near the end of the *Vita*.[20] Stephen gave no dates for the episodes which he described. The fact that most of these are set in the world indicates that Stephen and the men from whom he drew his information conceived of Vitalis outside the monastic context. Stephen did not portray Vitalis in interaction with his monks; instead Vitalis' actions took place in the

secular community. Whether the incidents related occurred after the foundation of Savigny or before is impossible to determine with certainty, but the likelihood that they took place after the founding is strong.

The following offers an example: Vitalis became lost for three days in a wood without food. Finally stumbling into a town and finding people gathered, he began to preach. He ignored his lack of food until a monk who was with him reminded him of it.[21]

It is possible that the monk in question was a member of one of the Norman monasteries other than Savigny, although there is not much evidence that Vitalis, a cleric and chaplain by background, had extensive contact with any monastery before the founding of Savigny. More plausible is that the monk was a member of Savigny and that the episode displays Vitalis' preaching in the lay community after the founding of the monastery.[22] Stephen also described more traditional instances of Vitalis preaching at religious gatherings such as church councils before and after the founding of Savigny.[23]

In the *Vita B. Vitalis* there was no mention of the monks of Savigny engaging in the active life of regular canons which could have included preaching and parish service. However, here again Auvry made a tempting suggestion that the monks of Savigny, in imitation of Vitalis, performed pastoral duties.[24]

Vitalis' interpretation of the *vita apostolica* is quite clear from the actions which Stephen chronicled. During the seventeen years which Vitalis spent in eremitical life, he labored to restore peace among discordant factions, providing food and clothing for the poor and lepers, found legitimate marriage partners for prostitutes, offered hospitality to travelers, and obtained grace for prisoners.[25] In addition he performed several miracles such as the raising of a man from the dead.[26] Vitalis' actions resembled those of the apostles of the *New Testament*. Stephen conceded that some of Vitalis' actions might seem radical, but he saw Vitalis as one who did not fear to pluck out the poison tooth.[27] For Stephen, Vitalis' evangelical role was analogous to that of Christ and the apostles who were fishers of men: "just as fishermen drew fish out of the river, so he (Vitalis) will remove men from the world."[28]

Stephen reinforced Vitalis' evangelical role with references to the efficacy of his eloquence.[29] The twelfth-century Norman ecclesiastical historian, Ordericus Vitalis, corroborated this estimate of Vitalis' eloquence: "All the world trembled before his rebukes; and crowds of both sexes were filled with shame at the misdoings he revealed."[30]

Vitalis was a saintly man of action in the minds

of his contemporaries. Examples of Vitalis in retirement or meditation are lacking in the *Vita*. The nature of early Savigniac monasticism, influenced as it was by Vitalis, must have reflected the founder's preoccupation with service in the community . That Vitalis probably chose the Rule of St. Benedict for his monks, rather than, for example, the Augustinian Rule for regular canons, suggests that he thought monasticism could incorporate a commitment to service in the secular world.[31] How this interpretation evolved over time is the focus of the remainder of this study.

At Vitalis' death in 1122, Geoffrey of Bayeux became abbot of Savigny. By the time of his death in 1138, he had established some twenty-nine monasteries under the order of Savigny.[32] While Vitalis represented the active preacher and servant in the secular world, with Geoffrey we find the same talent of preaching employed to buttress the institutionalization of the Savigniac order. During Geoffrey's abbacy, Savigny began to assume a more traditional monastic organization.

The anonymous author of the *Vita B. Gaufridi*, perhaps a monk of Savigny, writing in all likelihood after the merger of Savigny and Cîteaux, projected an image of Geoffrey as that of an eloquent man who was in many ways similar to the evangelical preacher, Vitalis.[33] Through Geoffrey's mouth "divine wisdom appeared to speak."[34] Geoffrey appealed to the whole community with what was a genuine oratorical style.[35]

At one point, however, Geoffrey underwent a transformation.[36] His life opened on a new contemplative phase, recalling the contemplative life as it was described by St. Augustine, Pope Gregory I and St. Bernard.[37] Yet, instead of surrendering his vocation for preaching to one of contemplation and retreat, Geoffrey spent time in Paris, studying in order that he might bring to his commitment to preaching a greater spiritual depth.[38] Herein is a similarity with the regular canons of whom Jean Leclercq noted:

> They have to study, not at all like monks, in order to pray better, to know better the Lord whom they serve, but to preach. They must correct, console, nourish, take back; they are 'light,' they discharge the priestly function, they are judges, they 'bind and loose,' they announce the word of God.[39]

The function of regular canons was more expansive than that which the author of the *Vita* describes for Geoffrey, but some of the same tendencies were present in the latter.[40]

The tension between life in the world and life in the monastery was central to the evolution of monasticism in the twelfth century. Such a tension must have been a part of Savigniac monasticism, for by his actions Vitalis had demonstrated his belief in an apostolic life of service to the community outside the monastery.[41] It is not easy to deduce from the *Vita B. Gaufridi* what Geoffrey's ideas about religious life were. On the one hand, his establishment of the order of Savigny can be seen as a commentary on his view of the world as something to be escaped. Here he would fall directly in the monastic tradition. After his entry into a monastery, Geoffrey no longer preached to the secular world. On the other hand, within the monastic context, Geoffrey's actions speak to an unquestionably evangelical role of saving souls.[42] It is probable that Geoffrey saw the development of a strong monastic order as the most effective means of salvation for the greatest number of people. Ironically, Geoffrey himself was frequently absent from Savigny in visits to daughter abbeys during his later life.[43]

The remaining men in my discussion of Savigniac monasticism, the monks Peter of Avranches and Hamo of Landchop, present alternative approaches to monastic life. Peter sought a life of contemplative retirement from the world, and indeed, from direct participation in the monastic community. In him there was a strong eremitical strain. Hamo, by contrast, was a man who combined the active and contemplative lives. The author of the *Vita B. Petri* was much concerned with a theory of these two sorts of lives whose equality before God he emphasized in men such as Hamo and Peter.

The *Vita B. Petri Abricensis* was probably written before 1182 and after the death of Peter which is thought to have been about the year 1172 preceding that of Hamo who died in 1173.[44] Peter was born in Avranches and, attracted first to worldly delights and music, he studied the liberal arts in which he became quite a competent scholar.[45] He experienced a moment of conversion when, through God's mercy, he was shown the horrible penalty of hell, the fearful judgment, and, in contrast, the joy of a pure life in future beatitude. Peter then began to think of flight from the world in monastic retirement, the traditional means of minimizing the temptation of secular vices. He retired at Savigny because of its reputation for religious fervor.[46] In the anonymous author's description of Peter's life and spiritual development at Savigny, there are several crucial passages which bear particularly on the conception of monastic life and on the place of preaching at the monastery.

Peter turned inward in search of spiritual perfection rather than outward in service to the world.

Peter's withdrawal is epitomized in the passage entitled, "How much he desired silence and how he shunned, as he could, public speech."[47] Among the observances referred to at Savigny which Peter chose to avoid were the "colloquia publica tam religiosorum quam secularium."[48] It is not beyond the realm of possibility that what was understood was an audience assembled to hear someone preach. Jean Leclercq has said that in the canonical orders, especially that of Prémontré, there could be preaching and ministry of souls in the monastic routine but that this was not necessarily a predominant feature of any house.[49] If the terms, "colloquia publica," were to refer to some sort of public preaching, such an interpretation would support the involvement of monks of Savigny in preaching and contact with secular people. The author of the *Vita B. Petri* in an aside to his readers in the same passage included the statement: "Therefore, let us speak completely in an evangelical manner, we who are evangelical men. May our speech diffuse an odor of the law, the prophets and the apostles; from their words, let us draw our language."[50] The author was clearly interested in the relation of the monks to the apostles and made the connection through the word "sermo" meaning "talk," "speech," or possibly, "sermon." The author's concern with the quality of speech, with eloquence, and with its evangelical purpose is evident in the remainder of the passage.[51]

In another passage of the *Vita B. Petri* the author dealt with the question of active and contemplative lives. Here, he contrasted the monks Peter and Hamo, beginning with a statement that Peter, choosing always to remain in the house of God, sought to be abject and humble, and to avoid all worldly glory and vanity.[52] Then, turning to Hamo, he described him returning from the king's court. The contrast of Hamo, active in the world, as opposed to Peter, in retirement, is very sharp.[53] The author concluded that both men followed ways of life which were acceptable to God: "Thus it is agreeable that they, fervent fighters and untiring soldiers of Christ, hastened, moreover, to the one prize of the highest vocation by diverse means."[54]

Although in his examples and in his contrast between Hamo and Peter, the author's purpose seems to have been to demonstrate that the active and contemplative lives were of equal value before God, he did at one point early in the *Vita* cite the example of Mary and Martha as types of the contemplative and active lives, respectively. The author identified with the traditional view when he stated, "Because it is pleasing that Martha merit divine grace by ministering officially to the Lord Jesus Christ, Mary nevertheless chose the best and sufficiently sweeter part; she, sitting at the feet of the Lord, was nourished by him at celestial feasts."[55] This statement and his development of the Mary/Martha images must become a qualification of the author's endorsement of the equality of the active and passive lives.

However, the remaining evidence of the *Vita* reinforces the author's inclination towards equality of interpretation. In order to illustrate his point that there was no real priority of one way of life over another in the search for God, he related the example of the abbots Arsenius and Moses.[56] A monk prayed to God to show him which of the two men was more pleasing to him: "One, on account of Your name, flees from seeing and controlling men; the other, on account of Your name, is sociable with men."[57] This brother then saw two boats in a vision. "In one he saw the abbot Arsenius sailing silently in peace; in the other, truly, the abbot Moses and saintly angels placing honey in his mouth and teeth."[58] The author of the *Vita B. Petri* sought to show by the strongest argument available to the Middle Ages— fate in the afterlife—the equality of the active and contemplative lives.[59]

Peter's own experience demonstrated the possibility of almost complete retreat within the monastic community. A life of isolation and retreat was probably an option from the beginning years of Savigny because of Vitalis' many years of contact with hermits before the founding of Savigny. Clearly, this conception of monastic life was still much alive through the third quarter of the twelfth century.

In turning to the *Vita B. Hamonis*, it is interesting to remark that, while for the author of the *Vita B. Petri*, Hamo filled the role of a man of the active life, the author of the *Vita B. Hamonis*, less concerned with the theory of the active versus the contemplative life, showed Hamo as a monk who combined elements of both lives. Hamo's sphere of activity seems to have been the whole community— secular and ecclesiastical—much as Vitalis' was. While there is no evidence that he was specifically involved in preaching or in celebrating mass for men other than the monks of his congregation, he interacted with the whole community in his acts of charity, in the building of churches, and as a spiritual leader.

The *Vita B. Hamonis* is by an anonymous monk of Savigny.[60] It is possible to date the work with some certainty from internal evidence to the period between Hamo's death in 1173 and 1178.[61] The author wrote as a contemporary of Hamo. Scholars have conjectured that Hamo was born about 1100 in

Landchop in Brittany.[62] He studied the liberal arts only to reject the vain glory of the world and take the religious habit.[63]

The author of the *Vita B. Hamonis* depicted Hamo in an evangelical relationship with the monastic and secular communities, as a leader.[64] Hamo's many miracles with relics speak to the apostolic nature of his life.[65] He was frequently absent from Savigny in his ministry of souls, spending time at the side of Henry II of England, before Louis of France, with the count of Mortain or in the presence of Mathilda of England.[66] He came in the capacity of confessor, urging more saintly behavior or with a petition in matters concerning Savigny. He was the spiritual leader of congregations other than that of Savigny.[67]

Much of Hamo's contemplative life was taken up with visions in which Hamo gave himself wholly to God. The author compared him to the apostles as being worthy of receiving communication from God, "to whom God, just as to the apostles, deemed it worthy to impart the holy spirit in kindling tongues."[68] Hamo also sought time for meditation and study of divine literature, participating in a contemplative tradition which was that of St. Augustine, Pope Gregory I and St. Bernard.[69]

Hamo seemed to feel a tension between service in the world and the traditional retirement in search of spiritual perfection, doubting his worldly deeds and needing confirmation of God's approval. His actions, those of confessor, spiritual guide, and almsgiver, were apostolic in nature. Hamo was a savior of souls, and he related his communication with God, for the most part, to this vocation, as a means of inspiration and guidance. Here, too he joined Bernard and Gregory who believed that a combination of the two lives, active and contemplative, was desirable.[70]

In the twelfth century the regular canons had begun to elevate the active life to equality with the contemplative. An exponent of this trend was Anselm, Bishop of Havelberg, a disciple of St. Norbert of Xanten, founder of the Premonstratensians.[71] Anselm, reinterpreting the example of Mary and Martha, considered the two lives as equal in importance when exemplified in the person of Jesus who combined both.[72] He was clearly trying to shift the emphasis of discussion from a dichotomy of lives in which Mary was superior to their fusion in the figure of Christ. The author of the *Vita B. Petri* was making an even more radical argument when he affirmed that the two lives were equal.[73] The idea of a mixed life and the elevation of a life of action to spiritual equality with a life of con-

templation were new conceptions in the twelfth century. They would be embraced wholeheartedly by the friars such as St. Thomas Aquinas in the thirteenth century.[74]

In its interpretations of the *vita apostolica*, Savigny made a place in its monastic system for contemplative retirement and for evangelical service in the world. Vitalis set the tone of Savigniac monasticism in its early years through his evangelical preaching and his service in the lay community. Under Geoffrey, Savigny became an institutionalized order, assuming more of the characteristics of traditional monasticism. Geoffrey viewed the monastery as a refuge from the contamination of the lay world, though he, himself, continued to spend much of his time as abbot in the lay community.

After its merger in 1147 with Cîteaux, Savigny had more direct contact with the Cistercian order and its ideals, which, by 1147, were well developed.[75] Abbot Serlo's admiration for St. Bernard of Clairvaux undoubtedly had some influence on the nature of Savigniac conceptions of monastic life.[76] Bernard felt that "It is often needful to leave the sweets of contemplation for the sake of labours which give nourishment (*lactantia ubera*) and that no one must live for himself alone, but for the good of all. . . ."[77] After the merger, the *vitae* of Peter and Hamo provide evidence of contemplative retirement and of the fusion of the active and contemplative lives. Savigny interpreted the ideal of the *vita apostolica* with a flexibility resembling that of contemporaneous regular canons. Hamo's fusion of the two lives, similar in conception to that of some regular canons such as Anselm of Havelberg, reflected a new trend in spirituality in the twelfth century.

Notes

1   I first studied the topic of Savigniac spirituality in my senior honors thesis of 1967 at Harvard entitled, "The Conceptions of Monastic Life at Savigny: 1112-1180." The history of the order of Savigny has been the subject of some reinterpretation in recent years. See Bennett D. Hill, "The Beginnings of the First French Foundations of the Norman Abbey of Savigny," *The American Benedictine Review* 31:1 (March 1980), 130-152 and *English Cistercian Monasteries and Their Patrons in the Twelfth Century* (Urbana, IL: University of Illinois Press, 1968), and Mary Suydam, "Origins of the Savignac Order. Savigny's

Role within Twelfth-Century Monastic Reform," *Revue Bénédictine* LXXXVI (1976), 94-108. Earlier institutional and administrative studies include Jacqueline Buhot, "L'Abbaye normande de Savigny, chef d'ordre et fille de Cîteaux," *Le Moyen Age* XLVI (1936), 1-19, 104-121, 178-190, 249-272; Anselme Dimier, "Savigny et son affiliation à l'ordre de Cîteaux," *Collectanea Ordinis Cisterciensium Reformatorum* (1947) IX, 351-358. The most elaborate study of Savigny was written by a monk of Savigny, Claude Auvry, in the seventeenth century. It was edited with an introduction by Auguste Laveille as *Histoire de la Congrégation de Savigny*, 3 v. (Rouen: A. Lestringant, 1896-1898).

2 Background on twelfth-century monastic spirituality can be found in Marie-Dominique Chenu, "Moines, clercs, laïcs au carrefour de la vie évangélique," *Revue d'histoire ecclésiastique* XLIX (1954), 59-89, translated and reprinted in M.-D. Chenu, *Nature, Man, and Society in the Twelfth Century*, ed. and trans. by Jerome Taylor and Lester K. Little (Chicago: University of Chicago Press, 1968), 202-238.

3 These four saints' lives were edited and published by E.P. Sauvage in the *Analecta Bollandiana*. See Stephen of Fougères, *Vita B. Vitalis, A. B.* 1:358-390 (Brussels, 1882); *Vita B. Gaufridi, A. B.* 1:390-409 (Brussels, 1882); *Vita B. Petri Abrincensis, A. B.* 2: 479-500 (Brussels, 1883); *Vita B. Hamonis, A. B.* 2:500-560 (Brussels, 1883).

4 Claude Auvry, *Histoire de La Congrégation de Savigny* 1:166. The date of foundation given by the *Chronicon Savigniacense*, ed. by Etienne Baluze, *Miscellaneorum* 2 (Paris: F. Muguet, 1678), 310-323 is 1112. On the foundation date, see Buhot, "L'Abbaye normande," p. 6; Hill, "The Beginnings," pp. 130-132 and "The Counts of Mortain and the Origins of the Congregation of Savigny," *Order and Innovation in the Middle Ages: Essays in Honor of Joseph R. Strayer*, eds. William C. Jordan, et al. (Princeton: Princeton University Press, 1976), pp. 237-253.

5 *Vita B. Vitalis*, p. 359: "terram quam vepres et tribuli arboresque infructuosae occupabant, . . ." Buhot, "L'Abbaye normande," p. 5 stated that the rich soil of Savigny was a guarantee of prosperity for the monk-farmers. In spite of the seeming contradiction between this statement and that of the *Vita*, it is possible that the site of foundation was wild and barren, but that with cultivation, as in Buhot's statement, the land proved fertile.

6 The Cistercians provide the best example of this practice. On the Cistercians, see briefly Richard W. Southern, *Western Society and the Church in the Middle Ages* (1970; rpt. New York: Penguin Books, 1977), pp. 250-261.

7 Jeanjacques Desroches, "Analyse des titres et chartes inédits," *Mémoires de la société des antiquaires de Normandie* XX, 2nd series X (Paris, 1853), 258.

8 Ibid., p. 256.

9 Buhot, "L'Abbaye normande," pp. 117ff.

10 Norman monasteries frequently acted as sources of credit. See Robert Génestal, *Rôle des monastères comme instruments de crédit étudié en Normandie du Xe à la fin du XIIIe siècle* (Paris: Arthur Rousseau, 1901).

11 Buhot, "L'Abbaye normande," pp. 188-189, 250, 260, 271-272. See also D. Guilloreau, "Le démêlé entre Serlon, abbé de Savigny et Pierre d'York, abbé de Furness, 1147-1150," *Revue catholique de Normandie* XXV (1916), 132.

12 The literature on this topic, some of it written long ago, is vast. See note 2 above and as examples, Ursmer Berlière, *L'Ordre monastique des origines au XIIe siècle*, 3rd ed. (Lille: Desclée, De Brouwer & Cie, 1924); G. Morin *L'Idéal monastique et la vie chrétienne des premiers jours*, 5th ed. (Paris: Desclée, De Brouwer & Cie, 1931); Edward Cuthbert Butler, *Benedictine Monachism*, 2nd ed. (1924; rpt. Cambridge: Speculum historiale, 1961); David Knowles, *The Monastic Order in England*, 2nd ed. (Cambridge: Cambridge University Press, 1963); Jean Leclercq, *La spiritualité au moyen âge* (Paris: Aubier, 1960) and "La spiritualité des chanoines réguliers," *La vita comune del clero nei seculo XIe e XII. Miscellanea del centro di studia medioevali* (Milan, 1962), I: 117-136; Ernest W. McDonnell, "The *Vita Apostolica*: Diversity or Dissent?" *Church History* XXIV (1955), 15-31; Philibert Schmitz, *Histoire de l'ordre de saint Benoît*, 2nd ed. III (Namur: Editions de Maredsous, 1948), IV (Namur: Editions de Maredsous, 1949).

13 See, for example, François Petit, "L'Ordre de Prémontré de saint Norbert à Anselme de Havelberg," *La vita comune del clero nei seculo XI e XII* (Milan, 1962), I:465-481. See also the comments of J. Leclercq, "La spiritualité," *Vita comune* I:190-197, on the monastery of La Grande Chartreuse under Bruno.

14 Buhot, "L'Abbaye normande," p. 2. Vitalis' father Rainford and his mother Rohais were devout and simple people.

15 *Vita B. Vitalis*, 360, 362 n. 1, 373 n. 1, 380. See also Buhot, "L'Abbaye normande," p. 3 and Auvry, *Histoire* I:125.

16 Auvry, *Histoire* I:140 and Buhot, "L'Abbaye normande," pp. 6, 14.

17 *Vita B. Vitalis*, p. 359: "Merito, inquam, tali nomine meruit insigniri qui et vitam caducam posthabuit, et ad coelestem pia animi aviditate anhelavit, et ad hanc multos verbis et exemplis animare sategit."

18 *Vita B. Vitalis*, p. 374. *Vita B. Vitalis*, p. 359: "Jure siquidem tali refulsit vocabulo, qui et diaboli versutias prudenti argumentatione patefecit, multosque ab ejus ore pestifero salubri consilio retraxit, vitaeque coelesti pristinae sanitati reintegratos restituere curavit."

19 Auvry, *Histoire* I:251-252. The passage of the *Vita B. Vitalis* to which Auvry referred in his footnote

to substantiate the above statement does not do so in the *Analecta Bollandiana* edition. Indeed, no similar passage seems to exist. Auvry cites "Vit. S. Vitalis, ibid., 1, II, art. 3." The *Analecta Bollandiana* edition divides the *Vita* into two parts, with articles numbered, but there is no three-part system of numbering such as that of Auvry's citation. Léopold Delisle, ed. *Chronique de Robert de Torigni* II (Rouen: A. Le Brument, 1873), 74, mentioned in a footnote that there was a copy of the *Vita B. Vitalis*, then unpublished, at the end of the manuscript history of the congregation of Savigny. This manuscript history is probably that of Auvry which was published in 1896. Since Auvry was a monk of Savigny, he would logically have had access to this *Vita* which might have had a different numbering system from that of the *Analecta* edition.

20 *Vita B. Vitalis*, pp. 382-383.

21 *Vita B. Vitalis*, p. 370: "Quarto tandem die egressus, quamdam villam ingreditur, fameque posthabita, praedicationi occupatur, sermoque ab eo fere ad mediam diem protrahitur, donec, monacho qui cum eo erat submurmurante, quod tamdiu jejunus erat a populo cognoscitur."

22 Given the monastic vow of stability, it would have been unlikely for a monk from other than Vitalis' monastery to travel about with him. For an example of St. Bernard of Clairvaux's opinion on the principle of stability, see *The Letters of St. Bernard of Clairvaux*, ed. Bruno S. James (London: Burns, Oates, 1953), Letter 8, pp. 26-38. There remains the distant possibility that author Stephen called Vitalis' companion a monk in retrospect, reflecting a later vocation.

23 *Vita B. Vitalis*, pp. 376-379.

24 Auvry, *Histoire* I:208. Auvry gave as his source for this contention "Lib. ms. de transl. S.S. Savign." I have not been able to locate this source; however, the first source which suggests itself as a possible interpretation of the Auvry reference is the *Liber de miraculis sanctorum Savigniacensium*, excerpts of which I have read in the edition of the same title by Léopold Delisle, published in *Recueil des historiens des Gaules et de la France* XXIII (Paris, 1876), 587-605. It does not seem inconsistent with Vitalis' example that his monks might also preach and work in the community and accompany him in his travels.

25 *Vita B. Vitalis*, p. 382.

26 *Vita B. Vitalis*, pp. 375 and 382. There were, in fact, many other episodes in the *Vita* which portrayed Vitalis in roles outside the monastery. In several he was seen in the fields, preventing robbers from stealing sheep or under attack himself from enemies (pp. 372 and 377). In these incidents he prevailed with the help of God. In one incident the wife of a soldier dreamed that she should prepare food for the coming of Vitalis (p. 377). His presence among these people indicates that he was away from his monastery, probably on a journey or engaged in pastoral work.

27 *Vita B. Vitalis*, p. 371. Throughout the *Vita*, Stephen spoke of Vitalis in terms which suggest an intimacy with God, terms such as "vir sanctus," "Vir Dei," "testor Deum," "Pater sanctus," "famulus Dei." In spite of the chronological problems in the work, we can safely assume that at least some of the episodes described would have taken place after the foundation of Savigny, and, indeed, since the petition for the foundation of Savigny occurred in an early chapter of the *Vita*, perhaps many of them were after the foundation. See pp. 264-365.

28 *Vita B. Vitalis*, p. 361: "sicut piscatores pisces extrahunt ex fluvio, ita hic erupturus erat homines de mundo."

29 *Vita B. Vitalis*, p. 374.

30 Ordericus Vitalis, *The Ecclesiastical History of England and Normandy*, trans. with notes and introduction of Guizot by Thomas Forester, III (London: G. Bohn, 1855), 52.

31 See below for arguments about the similarity of the Savigniacs and regular canons. There is considerable controversy concerning the early customs of Savigny. The *Chronicon*, p. 310, stated in connection with Vitalis: "Hic beatus vir modernas institutiones in aliquibus Cisterciensibus similes monachis suis imposuit, virtutibus & miraculis claruit." Most contemporary twelfth-century opinion indicated that Vitalis gave Savigny customs similar to the Cistercian customs. Knowles, *The Monastic Order*, p. 202, n. 3, quoted a statement of Robert of Torigni which makes a point similar to that of the *Chronicon*. (See L. Delisle, *Chronique* II:189.) Auvry, *Histoire* I:169-172, demonstrated the inconsistency in attribution; he cited a charter of Henry I of 1118 stating that Savigny was under the Benedictine Rule and later (p. 172), Auvry mentioned that Odericus Vitalis stated that Vitalis did not give his monks Cluniac customs but rather new customs, presumably along the Cistercian line. Buhot, "L'Abbaye normande," p. 7, referred to the statement by Ordericus. Auvry, 1:172, and Buhot, p. 105, argued that the reference to gray robes of the Savigniac monks in *Vita B. Gaufridi*, p. 401, probably indicated the same untreated, natural-colored wool of which Cistercian garments were made. In recent years, Bennett Hill and Mary Suydam have reconsidered the matter of Savigny's first customs. See note 1 above. Hill, *English Cistercian Monasteries*, pp. 92-100, argued for a Cluniac model at Savigny.

32 *Vita B. Gaufridi*, p. 408. In the *Chronicon Savigniacense*, p. 310, Geoffrey's term of abbacy was stated as 1122-1138; presumably 1138 was then the year of his death. However, at the end of the *Vita B. Gaufridi*, p. 408, the year of his death was given as 1139. Buhot, "L'Abbaye normande," p. 9, gave his tenure of office as 1122-1139, citing no reference for her dates.

The anonymous author of the *Vita B. Gaufridi* was identified by Sauvage as a monk of Savigny because of his one use of the expression "patrem nostrem," when speaking of Geoffrey. See the introduction by Sauvage, p. 356. The *Vita* was written after the death of Geoffrey in 1138 or 1139, and Sauvage suggested that it dated from after the merger of Savigny and Cîteaux in 1147 because of a mention of Savigny under "disciplina Ordinibus Cisterciensis."

33   *Vita B. Gaufridi*, pp. 390-396.

34   *Vita B. Gaufridi*, p. 396: "Per os illius divina sapientia loqui videretur."

35   *Vita B. Gaufridi*, p. 396.

36   *Vita B. Gaufridi*, p. 396: "Nam in seipso cor mundum sevare desiderans, collegit pro posse totum se intra se, publicum fugitans et amans habitare secum, lectioni, meditationi et orationi, in quantum permittebat humana fragilitas, diligenter inserviens."

    Geoffrey also chanted the whole psalter, an act of devotion which the author praised in *Vita B. Gaufridi*, p. 397: "Psalmi daemones fugant, tenebras illuminant, virtutes accumulant."

37   Edward Cuthbert Butler, *Western Mysticism* (London: Constable & Co. Ltd., 1922), part II, treated the idea of these men on the active and contemplative lives.

38   *Vita B. Gaufridi*, p. 398.

39   Leclercq, "La spiritualité," *Vita comune* I:121: Ils doivent étudier, non point, commes les moines, afin de mieux prier, de mieux connaître le Seigneur qu'ils servent, mais afin de prêcher. . . . Ils doivent corriger, consoler, nourrir, reprendre; ils sont 'lumière,' ils 's'acquittent du sacerdoce,' ils sont juges, ils 'lient et délient,' ils 'annoncent la parole de Dieu.'"

40   *Vita B. Gaufridi*, p. 391. Before the twelfth century the possibility of a pure life in the world was not acknowledged, but with the regular canons of the twelfth century, apostolic action in the world was first valued in western Christian medieval spirituality. Charles Dereine commented on this point in the *Discussione* at the end of Leclercq's article, "La spiritualité," in *Vita comune* I: 136, with reference to the regular canons.

41   See notes 22-24 above.

42   *Vita B. Gaufridi*, p. 403.

43   *Vita B. Gaufridi*, pp. 403-404.

44   The *Vita B. Petri Abricensis* was attributed by Sauvage to an anonymous monk of Savigny, p. 479, n. 1. For the probable dates of death of Peter and Hamo, see pp. 492-499 and 560.

45   *Vita B. Petri Abricensis*, p. 479.

46   *Vita B. Petri Abricensis*, p. 480.

47   *Vita B. Petri Abricensis*, p. 481: "Quantum silentio studuit, et qualiter colloquia publica pro posse declinavit."

48   *Vita B. Petri Abricensis*, p. 481. The passage is as follows: "colloquia publica tam religiosorum quam secularium necnon et consortia declinare studuit, quantum permiserunt Ordinis observantiae, fraternae pacis honestas et obedientia magistrorum."

49   J. Leclercq, *La spiritualité au moyen âge*, pp. 175ff.

50   *Vita B. Petri Abricensis*, p. 481: "Evangelice igitur ex toto loquamur, qui viri evangelici sumus. Sermo noster legem redoleat, prophetas et apostolos; ex eorum verbis linguam nostram exacuamus."

51   *Vita B. Petri Abricensis*, pp. 481-482.

52   *Vita B. Petri Abricensis*, p. 484.

53   *Vita B. Petri Abricensis*, p. 484: "Beatus siquidem Hamo eminenter praeditus erat sapidae charitatis affluenti benignitate, beatus vero Petrus vividae charitatis et veritatis districta severitate."

54   *Vita B. Petri Abricensis*, p. 484: "Unde, licet diverso itinere gratiarum, ad unum tamen supernae vocationis bravium currebant, tanquam ferventes Christi pugiles et milites indefessi." A literal translation would state "by varied way of gifts."

55   *Vita B. Petri Abricensis*, p. 486: "Quia, licet Martha divinae gratiae mereretur Domino Jesu Christo officiosissime minitrando, Maria tamen optimam partem elegit et satis dulciorem, quae sedens ad pedes Domini dapibus coelestibus ab ipso pascebatur."

56   *Vita B. Petri Abricensis*, p. 485.

57   *Vita B. Petri Abricensis*, p. 485: "Unus, propter nomen tuum, homines videre et compellare fugit; alter vero, propter nomen tuum, hominibus comunis est."

58   *Vita B. Petri Abricensis*, p. 485: "In una vidit abbatem Arsenium cum silentio in requie navigantem, in altera vero abbatem Moysen et angelos sanctos favum mellis ori ejus et dentibus inferentes."

59   *Vita B. Petri Abricensis*, p. 485: "Qua quidem revelatione Dominus ostendit quod utrumque sanctum gratanter approbavit, utriusque modum, licit dissimilem in conspectu hominum, coram angelis tamen bonitate non disparem dignanter acceptavit." Peter's own experience demonstrated the possibility of almost complete retreat within the monastic community. To portray the saintly qualities of Peter's life and his love of solitude and secret, the author described a vision of heaven and hell which a soldier experienced while he was ill. In heaven he saw one monk placed near the throne of God, and he was told upon inquiry that the monk was one of the community of Savigny. The soldier, recovering from his illness, went to Savigny to seek the monk whose glory he had foreseen in heaven. At first the soldier saw no one in the gathering of monks who resembled the blessed monk. Finally, the prior recalled that Peter was not present, as it was his custom to shun such gatherings. Peter was summoned, and the soldier recognized him as the chosen monk. Peter was pained by such a demonstration, but he suffered it. The fulfillment of Peter's life of retirement is clear from such an example. As the fruit of his retirement, Peter was praised for his gift of prayer and the grace of tears. See pp. 490-497.

60 The version of the *Vita B. Hamonis* which is found in the *Analecta Bollandiana* is a compilation of some seven codices, consulted by the editor, Sauvage. See pp. 475-78.

61 *Vita B. Hamonis*, pp. 526-527, n. 1 and n. 2; Auvry, *Histoire* II:79. A reference to the conversion and subsequent saintly life of William of Caen, who is sometimes called William of Tholosa, permits the dating. The author described William as a simple monk. We know from the *Chronicon* of Savigny (Baluze, *Miscellaneorum*, p. 312) that William of Tholosa became abbot of Savigny in 1178 and abbot of Cîteaux in 1179. It is unlikely that the author of the *Vita B. Hamonis* would have omitted the above details about William if he had been aware of them, that is, if he had written after 1178. As a monk of Savigny, the author would have known of his own abbot. Because of a mention of the date of the death of Hamo in 1173 in the *Vita* (p. 560), we can be certain that it was written after 1173. Such a dating—shortly after Hamo's death—is consistent with the author's depiction of himself as a contemporary of Hamo.

62 Auvry, *Histoire* II:52.

63 *Vita B. Hamonis*, pp. 502-504. Hamo entered the novitiate at Savigny but was suspected of having leprosy and was not at first allowed to take the monastic habit. He proved himself to be in good health by serving the lepers of the monastery without acquiring the disease, and the monks relented, permitting him to receive the monk's habit.

64 *Vita B. Hamonis*, pp. 504-505: "Unde et multos a nefariis sceleribus ereptos ad tramitem confessionis reduxit, cophinumque stercoris (id est humilitatem poenitentiae) ad cordis radicem ponens, Deo fructificare perdocuit." See also p. 541 for the author's summary of Hamo's evangelical stance.

65 *Vita B. Hamonis*, p. 517.

66 *Vita B. Hamonis*, pp. 523, 531, 534ff for Henry; p. 524 for Louis; p. 529 for the count of Mortain; p. 546 for Mathilda.

67 *Vita B. Hamonis*, p. 550. See also Auvry's comments on Hamo's evangelism (*Histoire* II:59). The role of confessor was a common one for Hamo; the *Vita B. Petri*, p. 483, related that he was confessor of the community of Savigny.

68 *Vita B. Hamonis*, pp. 509-510: "cui Deus, sicut et apostolis, in linguis igneis Spiritum sanctum dignatus est impertire."

69 See Butler, *Western Mysticism*, pp. 195-222. The author of the *Vita B. Hamonis* described Hamo's position, p. 542: "Itaque, vitae contemplativae sectator indefessus existens, ad conditoris sui faciem contuendam jugiter anhelabat, prae amore ejus cuncta quibus inde averti poterat refugiens, omnesque cogitationes suas ac totam spem ex illius delectatione suspendens."

70 Butler, *Western Mysticism*, pp. 253-254. On similar twelfth-century responses, see the example of Adam Scot, mentioned by Leclercq, *La spiritualité*, pp. 198-199.

71 F. Petit, "L'Ordre de Prémontré," *Vita comune* I:477.

72 Ibid.

73 See notes 55-62 above.

74 Petit, "L'Ordre de Prémontré," *Vita comune* I:478.

75 See note 1 above.

76 Abbot Serlo retired at Clairvaux in 1153. See *Auctarium Savigneiense*, ed. Léopold Delisle in *Chronique de Robert de Torigni* (Rouen: A. Le Brument, 1873) II:156-164 and A. Wilmart, "Le recueil des discours de Serlon, abbé de Savigny," *Revue Mabillon* XII (Paris, 1922), 26-38. See also note 11 above.

77 Butler, *Western Mysticism*, p. 253.

Men's Houses, Women's Houses: The Relationship Between the Sexes in Twelfth-Century Monasticism

Constance H. Berman

It goes without saying that there was a relationship between the sexes in most parts of twelfth-century life, but it is generally assumed that the Church, and in particular the monastery, were exceptional places— that therein existed a world of sex-segregation. Traditionally, it has been thought that in this period after the Gregorian reform, the new purity that monks and other religious men sought for their lives allowed them little contact with women. It has generally been held that because only a few preachers and reformers responded to, or at least wrote about, the desire among women for a purified religious life, that their interest was less intense than that of men.[1] Scholars looking at its surviving literature have tended to see the period as one in which female participation in monasticism lessened, citing the misogynist tone in the letters and legislation of members of the new religious groups such as the Cistercians or the Praemonstratensians.[2] However, the most recent assessments suggest that the number of new religious houses for women in this period was significant and that women were not the negligible factor in the eleventh- and twelfth-century reform movement that they have sometimes been thought.[3]

It is the contention of this paper that the participation of women and their ties to men's houses within the religious reform dating to the late eleventh and twelfth centuries have been understated by historians, partially because of our traditional tendency to study the history of religious men or women within the context of particular congregations and orders—a bias which is built into the ways in which major archival collections are organized and in which studies of monasticism are published. If one is willing to look beyond the documents for a single religious order, however, and if one considers location and early patrons of male and female communities within a region, hitherto unnoticed relationships between male and female religious and

their communities sometimes emerge. Indeed, a careful scrutiny of such evidence suggests that women's houses in this period were even sometimes predecessors of those for men. Perhaps the typical methodologies of looking at communities of only one order, or looking at male communities first and then regarding female communities as satellites around them, or of looking at houses of one or the other sex exclusively, all tend to distort the reality of eleventh- and twelfth-century religious reform which turns out to have been less sex-segregated than is often thought. Indeed, if one considers findings for history of early Christianity and the barbarian period, there is considerable reason for thinking that lay women, women religious, and women's religious communities were equally or more important in the spread of Christianity than were their male counterparts.[4] One might hypothesize that women in the post-Gregorian reform period, as they were pushed out of the secular church, had an increasing impact on the monastic church. Thus, an effective approach to studying women's part in the monastic fervor of the high middle ages might be to look first at how females—as patrons and founders of male and female houses and as members of female communities needing to have priests or canons around them to care for their souls—influenced the foundation of monastic houses for both sexes, and only then to look at how those women eventually fit into the institutional framework of orders and congregations.[5]

In attempting to show how such a starting point might affect our assessment of women's participation in twelfth-century monasticism, this paper will examine relationships between three religious communities for women founded in southern France in the twelfth century, and three communities of Cistercian men with which they had ties. From these examples one can contend that there were much more complex relationships between monks and female patronesses, between monks and nuns, between the houses of monks and those of nuns, than the official picture of the early Cistercian order presents. Undoubtedly the examples which are discussed here: the women's communities of Nonenque, Lespinasse, and Le Vignogoul, with their counterparts: the Cistercian men's houses of Silvanès, Grandselve, and Valmagne respectively, reflect ties which existed between other male and female communities which have thus far gone unremarked and in many cases are probably undocumented.[6]

Any effort to discuss relationships between men's and women's monastic communities, when it relates to Cistercians of the twelfth century, encounters problems specific to the early history of that order. This is a period for which contact between women religious and the Cistercians has often been denied. Until recently, historians contended that the Cistercian order did not accept women until the last decade of the twelfth century. Moreover, it was generally believed that most entrances of women into the Cistercian practice were a result of the admissions *en masse* of transformed Praemonstratensian canonesses—the canons of Prémontré having allowed women into their congregation initially, but then ousting them in the late twelfth century because of the burden of providing them priests and administrators, as well as to avoid scandal.[7] This model has allowed historians of the Cistercian order to deny the presence of women within Cistercian practice during the early "Golden Age" of Cistercian monasticism, and to admit their presence in the order only in a period for which those historians are forced to admit that decadence had already begun to set in; there is consequently a self-reinforcing tendency to see women as symptomatic of decadence.[8]

This picture of the Cistercian early order and its "Golden Age" (without women) is based on faulty considerations of the order's early legislative documents and is belied by much of the surviving local archival evidence. Although it is true that some of the most famous foundations for Cistercian women were made during the thirteenth century, often with direct intervention by papal and secular authority, the entrance of women into Cistercian practice occurred much earlier.[9] The twelfth century, although not nearly as well documented, can now be shown to have been as important as the thirteenth for the participation of women in the fervor of the reform movement and for the influx of female communities into some sort of relationship with communities of Cistercian men. Indeed, the Cistercian reality of the twelfth century was probably similar to that of the Praemonstratensians; early Cistercian monks and abbots, like the regular canons, probably did encourage women to practice their observances and participate in the benefits of the order (such as tithe exemption), although the General Chapter and chroniclers of the order, as they projected the organization of the second half of the twelfth century back onto its earlier events, seem to have officially ignored that participation.[10] Unfortunately, particularly for the first half of the twelfth century, the local evidence is limited and open to a number of interpretations. Crucial information is not necessarily found among files of Cistercian documents. Moreover, because it comes from local archives rather than from the official Burgundian records of the order, it has often been dismissed as aberrant.[11]

Whatever the order's official position on women at the time, the existence in twelfth-century southern France of communities of women which had some tie to Cistercian houses for men is clear and is documented by local archival evidence. In addition to the three houses of Nonenque, Lespinasse, and Le Vignogoul discussed below in detail, there were, for instance, several other communities of women tied to Cistercian monasteries in the region near Narbonne and Montpellier. These included the house of Rieunette, founded in 1162, whose first abbess had earlier been a donor to the nearby Cistercian monks of Villelongue, or that of Netlieu founded in 1195, or that of St. Felix of Montseau also founded in the twelfth century, although generally listed as being Benedictine until the thirteenth, as well as the slightly later foundation at Les Olieux.[12] In the marquisate of Provence there was a female community at Bonlieu and another at La Vernaison. The first was described in 1291 as the daughter-house of the abbey of Cistercian men at Aiguebelle; it continued until the fourteenth century when it was taken over by a male community.[13] Were these and the many other twelfth-century houses for Cistercian women throughout France[14] simply aberrations?

It is not only that local evidence shows the contrary, but the denial by historians that there were twelfth-century Cistercian houses for women is based on weak arguments from the Burgundian legislative documents, on faulty dating or interpretation of the early Cistercian legislation, and on mistaken assumptions about the character of the early order. For instance, historians have denied that women were part of the twelfth-century order because "early" (and unreliably dated) statutes forbade the blessing of nuns,[15] or because women were not mentioned in the order's legislation until the 1190s and then in a "negative" way; in the latter case, historians have tended to assume that the refusal by the General Chapter to compel women on a specific issue constituted a denial that women were part of the order.[16] In general, these arguments assume that the twelfth-century legislative records of the order are complete and accurately dated, when they are neither.[17]

Moreover, despite assumptions to the contrary, the early order was not made up of identical units all in strict conformity to the edicts of the General Chapter. The legislation of that Chapter must be considered a set of guidelines towards which individual houses aimed, not binding or wholly-enforceable law, and while consistency of organization may have been the ideal, it was rarely the reality.[18] The monolithic view of the early Cistercians which we tend to take, particularly for the twelfth century, cannot be verified in local records. The conformity on any issue which we have tended to project back onto those early monks in their "Golden Age," did not exist.[19] Thus, particularly for the early period, that for which the order's surviving legislative documents are faulty and sparse and its organization weakest, local archival records may be more accurate than the order's legislation regarding almost any aspect of monastic practice. It must be accepted that there were discrepancies between ideal and reality in Cistercian practice for houses of men. If this is so, discrepancies are even more likely between theory and practice for women's houses or with regard to ties between houses of the two sexes. This was demonstrated by Catherine Boyd some years ago with regard to the Cistercian nuns of Rifreddo in northern Italy and the ownership of tithes, where the evidence from local archives was much more reliable than recourse to the order's idealizing "statutes."[20] Such relationships between early houses for women (whether Cistercian or not) and houses for men which eventually became Cistercian seem most likely to have occurred for southern French communities having roots in the eremitical tradition of reform coming from western and central France, rather than among houses founded *de novo* by the Cistercians. That western French reform, which is associated with Robert of Arbrissel, Gerald of Salles, and Bernard of Tiron, was extremely important in the spread of what would eventually be the Cistercian order in southern France.[21] That reform movement much more than the parallel movement of monastic reform in Burgundy (from which the Cistercian order originated) encompassed the religious desires and interests of women as well as of men. There were a number of houses of nuns

associated with western French reformers; not just Robert of Arbrissel, but Gerald of Salles, Bernard of Tiron, Vidal of Savigny, and Stephen of Obazine all seem to have founded communities for women.[22] As a result, it is not surprising that communities for men founded in southern France which were inspired by such western French reformers also took an interest in women's religious aspirations or were tied to similar communities for women.

The most famous of such reform houses for women in western France was Fontevrault, founded by the wandering-preacher, reformer, hermit, Robert of Arbrissel. Fontevrault, was not simply a great aristocratic house for contemplative women; it was the inspiration for an entire order of houses of "Fontevristes" including a number of such houses in southern France; such "daughters" of Fontevrault have, unfortunately, been much less studied than the famous "mother-abbey."[23] In addition, the "Fontevriste" pattern—houses founded by the dominant ladies of the region for female contemplatives with secondary communities of priests and lay-brothers attached—describes many other new communities of religious women having no specific tie to Fontevrault, but like Bellecombe and Nonenque discussed below, simply called Benedictine.[24] Some of the latter, as described above, seem to have been transformed in the thirteenth century into abbeys and priories of Cistercian nuns, while houses which had clear ties to Fontevrault were more likely to avoid Cistercian affiliation (perhaps needing that order less in terms of protection and tithe exemption).

Turning to the specific houses in question here, the clearest example of a community of women having a close relationship to a Cistercian house for men from the time of foundation is a case from the southern Rouergue: the convent of Nonenque which became associated with the monks of Silvanès. In this instance the house of nuns at Nonenque was elevated in 1251 to the status of Cistercian abbey and may have been considered a Cistercian priory from some earlier date. Although the 1160s chronicle of Silvanès claims that the house of Nonenque had been founded by Silvanès, this is one of many instances of that chronicle's unreliability.[25] Both Nonenque and Silvanès had pre-Cistercian roots and, as explained below, the foundation of a community of nuns at Nonenque was at least contemporary with and may have preceded the foundation of a men's house at Silvanès; at the outset it may also have been the stronger community, in both economic and political terms. In the twelfth century Nonenque also had more important pastoral rights and granges on the Causse de Larzac than Silvanès:

that Nonenque gradually fell under the control of Silvanès may well have been a result of the monks' need for access to pasture and Nonenque's need for protection from increasing competition coming from military religious orders for access to pasture. Nonenque also had, much more than Silvanès, received very important gifts at the outset—for instance, the large grange of Lioujas on the Causse Comtal north of Rodez, which came from Ermengarde of Creyssels, Countess of Rodez, who entered the community in 1170.[26] Ermengarde's special interest in Nonenque probably derives from the fact that her family came from the immediate area of that convent: their castle of Creyssels was located in the southern Rouergue, not far from Millau.[27]

As is so often the case, there is considerably more surviving material concerning the early history of the men's community than for the women's. As far as both the chronicle of Silvanès and that monastery's cartulary tell us, Silvanès was founded c. 1132 by a group of hermits, probably inspired by western French reform movements. They were led by a former knight from the region of Lodeve named Pons de Leras who had abandoned his life of violence after undergoing a religious conversion at the urging of his wife; he sold his goods, did penance before the bishop, made material amends for past wrongdoing, and persuaded his wife and children to enter religious houses. Then he undertook a pilgrimage with his followers, and finally founded a hermitage at Silvanès. The Silvanès chronicle describes his settlement there, the decision with his followers to adopt a rule, and the group's rejection by the Carthusians, who sent them to the Cistercian house of Mazan in the Vivarais, where some of the group seem to have done a novitiate. By c. 1138 their community had been transformed into a Cistercian abbey. Out of humility, Pons de Leras remained a *conversus*, but he seems to have acted as cellarer of the community and was involved in at least several of its early land acquisitions.[28]

Much less information survives for the early history of Nonenque. The community there appears to have been founded by local patrons with the aid of "Benedictine" nuns from Bellecombe in the Velay.[29] Although eventually developing ties to Silvanès, it was recognized as an independent community of women and not as an appendage of Silvanès, for example, in a papal exemption from tithes granted by Alexander III c. 1162.[30] The earliest surviving dated document concerning Nonenque is found in the Silvanès cartulary. It records that in 1139 the monks of Silvanès had been given land in the valley of Elnonenca.[31] The fact that this charter describes land conveyed as the valley of Elnonenca or Nun's valley, implies the presence of nuns there already at the time the charter was written—that is, prior to 1139. Thus, careful consideration of such local archives as survive suggests not only that the Silvanès chronicle that Nonenque was a foundation *de novo* as a dependency of Silvanès is simply untrue, but also that this "Benedictine" foundation for women had been made prior to the foundation of the nearby hermitage of Silvanès. Indeed, rather than seeing Nonenque as dependent on Silvanès from foundation, it is perhaps more appropriate to contend that it was the community of women at Nonenque who tolerated the foundation of a hermitage in their neighborhood. It is even possible that the story of Pons de Leras' conversion actually masks the transformation into a separate community of what had originally been a collage of canons or priests originally attached to Nonenque (like those of Fontevrault, or at houses like Ronceray in Anjou).[32] While Nonenque's mother-house of Bellecombe apparently remained Benedictine, Nonenque was brought under Silvanès' control, but despite claims of the Silvanès chronicle, only a considerable time after Silvanès' incorporation into the Cistercian order.

The transformation of such a community of priests attached to a house for women into a community of Cistercian men is even more likely to have occurred in the other cases discussed here, for instance, that of Lespinasse and Grandselve. In this second example, the community of women was one of Fontevristes at Lespinasse, located a few kilometers north of Toulouse on the right bank of the Garonne River; that of men was what would become the Cistercian house of monks at Grandselve, located not far to the west of Lespinasse on the opposite side of the Garonne from the women's community, but with many properties on either side of the Garonne.[33] Documents for Lespinasse tell us that a house of nuns in the order of Fontevrault was founded on March 12, 1114 by Philippa, Countess of Toulouse, wife of William VII count of Poitou and Ninth Duke of Aquitaine.[34] The foundation of Grandselve remains in obscurity, although Grandselve also claimed a foundation date of 1114, and its foundation is generally attributed to Gerald of Salles, an early associate and follower of Robert of Arbrissel. Unfortunately, the bulk of the recorded contracts for Grandselve are dated to the period after it was incorporated into the Cistercian order in the mid-1140s. The earliest surviving document concerning Grandselve is a letter concerning a group of hermits in the forest of Grandselve, who were commended to the king of England by a bishop of Toulouse; slightly later, possibly in 1117, there was a grant to those hermits by the bishop of that city of revenues from nearby churches for their support.[35]

The foundations at Lespinasse and Grandselve were thus both apparently made during the period when William of Aquitaine occupied Toulouse in the name of his wife Philippa and before their divorce of 1115, after which she seems to have retired to Lespinasse.[36] Late eleventh-century documents in the Trencavel cartulary record Robert of Arbrissel among witnesses to a feudal oath received by Philippa and thus confirm her relationship with the western French reformers; other accounts suggest that Robert enjoyed a stay at her "court."[37] Gifts originally made by Philippa to the community of Lespinasse were confirmed to it by a later count of Toulouse in 1150. Count Alphonse Jourdain similarly appears to have made or confirmed gifts to Grandselve.[38] This parallelism of confirmations by her successor suggests that Philippa was also involved in the foundation of Grandselve by Robert's follower and companion Gerald of Salles.[39] Indeed, it is possible, in keeping with the tradition of Fontevrault, to which Lespinasse was definitely affiliated, that the community of nuns there had originally been a "double house" with an associated community of priests and lay brothers which eventually developed into the community at Grandselve. It is at least suggestive that the two foundations were not only adjacent, but claim foundation dates of the same year, probably had many of the same patrons, and were both associated with western French reformers interested in such "double houses." Among Grandselve documents, Lespinasse is mentioned at least once and further prosopographical study of donors and witnesses in the acts for these houses might confirm or clarify an early relationship as well as providing information on its continuation.[40] Unlike Nonenque, Lespinasse never fell under Cistercian control, but remained tied to Fontevrault.[41]

A third pair of religious communities for men and women which eventually became very closely associated but which heretofore have not been linked in their origins, was the community of nuns at le Vignogoul in Languedoc and that of monks at Valmagne, located nearby. Despite opinion which calls Le Vignogoul a community of Benedictine nuns in the twelfth century and only ties it to Valmagne in the mid-thirteenth,[42] these two houses, like Nonenque and Silvanès and probably Lespinasse and Grandselve as well, had probably been closely associated since foundation. Although there are a number of unresolved questions regarding their early years, both Le Vignogoul and Valmagne probably had been founded by western French reformers or their followers in the south. Valmagne was a daughter of Ardorel in the Albigeois.[43] Le Vignogoul was apparently founded by 1130, was originally called Bonloc and was dedicated to St. Mary Magdalene; the date of the name change is not clear and surviving early charters are uncatalogued and inaccessible at present.[44] By mid-thirteenth century both houses were Cistercian, for the community of nuns at Bonloc or Le Vignogoul was elevated to the status of Cistercian abbey in 1246.[45]

It was the Countess Cecilia of Provence, wife of Bernard Aton IV of Carcassonne and Nîmes, who had made important gifts to the early hermit-monks of Ardorel in the early 1130s or before and although accounts often attribute its foundation to her son Raymond Trencavel, it was presumably also Cecilia who was most involved in the foundation of Valmagne by Ardorel. Early documents preserved in Valmagne's late twelfth-century cartulary record conveyances to the monks in the territory of Veyrac and near the port of Meze, where Cecilia is known to have held property.[46] Moreover, it was only after Cecilia's death in mid-twelfth century and only after a certain amount of hesitation that Valmagne was incorporated by the Cistercians, probably in 1155. The hesitation and difficulties over incorporation have been explained as a result of Cecilia's preference for the Fontevrault tradition over the Cistercians.[47] It is quite possible that Cecilia had met Robert of Arbrissel himself, for the Trencavel cartulary records Cecilia's husband Bernard Aton's presence in the court of Philippa of Toulouse in a charter to which that reformer was witness.[48] The fact that Bonloc was dedicated to St. Mary Magdalene is also suggestive of an interest in or relationship to Fontevrault, which was also dedicated to that saint. Thus, despite the availability of documentation, it seems likely that Cecilia was the founder of that house for women at Bonloc-Le Vignogoul along with Ardorel and Valmagne. At Le Vignogoul with Cecilia and perhaps with Guillelma of Montpellier, as was the case at Nonenque with Ermengarde of Creyssels and at Lespinasse with Philippa of Toulouse, there was thus a strong female patroness, one of the "viragos" described by Huyghebaert,[49] involved in the foundation of the female community, if not promoting what may have originally been a "double community." For Le Vignogoul, at least, the record is not closed, for further documents will eventually become available. Unlike at Lespinasse, however, the tie of the female community to Fontevrault was not retained, perhaps because of differing political conditions in Languedoc.[50]

Whereas the earliest relationship between Le Vignogoul and Valmagne remains obscure, it is clear that Valmagne did have ties by the late twelfth century to another religious house in the vicinity, a hospital for brothers and sisters under the direction of a female "procuratrix." This was the otherwise undocumented hospital of St. Martin which is mentioned in a contract in the Valmagne cartulary dated 1197.[51] That hospital was under the direction of a certain Guillelma, presumably Guillelma of Montpellier, Cecilia's daughter-in-law, wife of Bernard Aton V of Nîmes and daughter of William VI of Montpellier. Was this hospital perhaps the house of lay brothers and sisters associated with a double or triple house in the tradition of Fontevrault? Whatever the earliest relationships among these three communities of St. Martin, Valmagne, and Le Vignogoul, they seem to have grown out of the western French reform movement encompassing Fontevrault, which in southern France was gradually engulfed by the Cistercians.

In the three examples discussed in this paper, female communities having ties to or similarities to the "double community" of Fontevrault were made as early as, or even earlier than the nearby communities of men which eventually became Cistercian. Whatever the order or affiliation of those female communities in the twelfth century, it is clear that the three houses of Cistercian men discussed here had close ties to such women's houses even during the twelfth century. Moreover, the surviving evidence confirms that these women's houses were not simply satellites founded by houses of Cistercian men. Instead these foundations for women adhering to reform practices occurred very early. They were entities in themselves because they had the backing of those powerful local women in the twelfth-century Midi who were founders of communities of both sexes. The examples discussed here also show that reform houses for men and for women could survive side by side without scandal even in the "Golden Age" of Cistercian monasticism, when the white monks were purported not to have concerned themselves with women. Moreover, the association with women's houses did not bring about disrepute or decadence for the Cistercian men.

Whether one can say definitely that any or all the pairs of houses discussed here were originally "double communities" on the model of Fontevrault can probably never be resolved. The evidence, however suggestive, is too sparse. One interpretation of the little evidence available, however, is that these were female communities from which the male communities eventually sprang. It does seem probable that if such relationships were consistently searched for in surviving local documents for this and other regions, that more such pairs of houses, where women's needs for communities of priests may well have been the impetus for the later development of a community of men, would be uncovered, and that many such twelfth-century female communities can be found to have been at the origins of the so-called foundations of Cistercian women of the thirteenth century. The interpretation of evidence for the houses discussed here suggests a new direction for additional research.

Notes

1   Exceptions were Jacques de Vitry, Herman of Laon, and those interested in Hildegard of Bingen, see Herbert Grundmann, *Religiose Bewegungen im Mittelalter* (Berlin: Ebering, 1935), passim, or E.W. McDonnell, *The Beguines and Beghards in Medieval Culture, With special emphasis on the Belgian scene* (New Brunswick: Rutgers, 1954), or Simone Roisin, "L'efflorescence cistercienne, et le courant feminin de piété au XIIIe siècle," *Revue d'histoire ecclésiastique* 39 (1943): 342-78.

2   For example, R.W. Southern, *Western Society and the Church in the Middle Ages* (Harmondsworth, Eng.: Penguin, 1970), pp. 314-5.

3   See Janet Burton, *The Yorkshire Nunneries in the Twelfth and Thirteenth Centuries* (York: Borthwick Papers, no. 56, 1979), or the work of the Women's Religious Life and Communities: 500-1500 Project, under the direction of Suzanne Wemple, Barnard College, Columbia University.

4   For example, see Jo Ann McNamara, "Cornelia's daughters: Paula and Eustochium," *Women's Studies*, 11 (1984): 9-27, or Suzanne Wemple, *Women in Frankish Society. Marriage and the Cloister, 500-900* (Philadelphia: University of Pennsylvania Press, 1981), esp. pp. 127-87.

5   For example, Joseph Avril, "Les fondations, l'organisation et l'évolution des établissements de moniales dans le diocèse d'Angers (du XIe au XIIIe siècle)," *Les religieuses en France au XIIIe siècle*, ed. Michel Parisse (Nancy: Presses Universitaires, 1985), pp. 27-67, which includes a discussion of the organization of a community of canons to serve the needs of the religious women of Ronceray, or Nicolas Huyghe-

baert, "Les femmes laïques dans la vie religieuse des XIe et XIIe siècles dans la province ecclésiastique de Reims," *I Laici nella "societas christiana" dei secoli XI e XII*. Atti della terza Settimana internazionale di studio, Mendola, 21-27 agosto 1965. (Milan: Vita e pensiero, 1968), pp. 346-95, or Constance H. Berman, "Women as Donors and Patrons to Southern French Monasteries in the Twelfth and Thirteenth Centuries," *The Worlds of Medieval Women: Creativity, Influence, and Imagination*, ed. Constance H. Berman, Charles W. Connell, and Judith Rice Rothschild (Morgantown, West Virginia: University of West Virginia Press, 1985): 53-68.

6   This study grew out of research conducted for other purposes and unfortunately does not follow the research plan advocated here.

7   The official position is presented by Louis J. Lekai, *The Cistercians: Ideal and Reality* (Kent, Ohio: Kent State University Press, 1977), pp. 347-57, but see also Roisin, "L'efflorescence," esp. pp. 376-8, and Micheline de Fontette, *Les religieuses à l'âge classique du droit canon. Recherches sur les structures juridiques des branches féminines des ordres* (Paris: Vrin, 1967), pp. 13-63, or Ernst G. Krenig, "Mittelalterliche Frauenkloster nach den Konstitutionen von Cîteaux," *Analecta Sacri Ordinis Cisterciensis* 10 (1954): esp. 9-15, or Thompson article cited in note 11 below.

8   Bennett D. Hill, *Cistercian Monasteries and Their Patrons in Medieval England* (Urbana, IL: University of Illinois Press, 1968), pp. 92-115, or Southern, *Western Society*, pp. 312-18, or Lekai, *Cistercians*, pp. 347-57.

9   Often, houses which were founded in the twelfth century were only elevated to abbey status within the order in mid-thirteenth, as in the examples of Nonenque and Le Vignogoul discussed below. Others, like Marham in Norfolk were founded only in mid-thirteenth century; see, John A. Nichols, "The History and Cartulary of the Cistercian Nuns of Marham Abbey, 1249-1536," Kent State University Ph.D. dissertation, 1974.

10 That there was a certain amount of rewriting of their earlier history by Cistercians in the middle and second half of the twelfth century is now generally accepted, see Lekai, *Cistercians*, pp. 19-32.

11 This is the case with regard to the foundation of the house of Ardorel in the Albigeois, which has been described as practicing a mitigated form of the Cistercian rule, see L. de Lacger, "Ardorel," *Dictionnaire d'histoire et de géographie ecclésiastique*, 7 (1924): 1617-20. The tendency to give Burgundian documents or those of the General Chapter priority is also found in a recent article on the order's women; see Sally Thompson, "The Problem of Cistercian Nuns in the Twelfth and early Thirteenth Centuries," *Medieval Women*, ed. Derek Baker (Oxford: Blackwell for the Ecclesiastical History Society, 1978), pp. 227-52. Thompson begins with the assumption that the

Cistercian legislation and the minutes of the General Chapter are the most reliable source for the position of women within the Cistercian order. Although to some degree consulting the local evidence, she dismisses the claims by women's houses in England to Cistercian status, although that status is confirmed in local and papal documents, because she finds that such status is never mentioned in the early minutes of the Cistercian General Chapter meetings and is later denied at a particularly expedient moment, in 1270 by the abbot of Cîteaux. A good corrective to this view is that of Roger de Ganck, "The Integration of Nuns in the Cistercian Order, particularly in Belgium," *Cîteaux: comm. cist.*, 35 (1984): 235-47, although it would have been possible for the latter author to go further in the re-evaluation of the position of women within the order in the twelfth century; see note 16 below.

12 Vincent Ferras, *Documents bibliographiques concernant le rayonnement médiéval de l'ordre de Cîteaux en pays d'Aude* (En Calcat, France: 1971), p. 117 and passim, and Beaunier-Besse, *Archives Monastiques de la France* vol. 11 (Paris, 1911), pp. 125, 136, 141, 160, 173, 185, 201, 255.

13 Ibid., vol. 19, p. 120, or M. de Framond, "Historique de l'abbaye de la Vernaison," *Cîteaux dans la Drôme: Revue Drômoise* 83 (1980): 151-154, and other articles in that special issue.

14 See the article on early houses for women, including Tart by Jean de la Croix Bouton, "Saint Bernard et les moniales," *Mélanges Saint Bernard* (Dijon: Association bourguignonne des sociétés savantes, 1953), pp. 225-47. A survey of Beaunier-Besse, *Archives Monastiques*, shows several additional Cistercian houses dated to the thirteenth or later centuries, but which had an earlier history, for instance, St. Pierre du Puy in the diocese of Orange, which is listed as Benedictine until its incorporation by the Cistercians in 1200 (vol. 7, p. 114), or St. Véran in the diocese of Avignon, which was a Benedictine foundation from 1140 until it became Cistercian in 1436 (vol. 7, p. 139).

15 See Krenig, "Mittelalterliche Frauenkloster," loc. cit. which cites *Statuta capitulorum generalium ordinis Cisterciensis ab anno 1116 ad annum 1789* ed. J. -M. Canivez, "prima collectio" dated 1134, no. 29. "*Quod nullus nostri ordinis abbas monacham benedicat.* Prohibitum est ne quis abbatum vel monachorum nostrorum monacham benedicere, infantulum baptizare, vel etiam in baptismo tenere praesumat, nisi forte in articulo mortis fuerit, et presbiter defuerit."

16 Ibid., 1191, no. 27, "Domino regi Castellae, scribatur, quia non possumus cogere abbatissas ire ad Capitulum de quo scripsit, et si vellent ire, sicut eis iam consuluimus, multum nobis placeret," has been cited (along with the 1134 statute cited in previous note) by historians as evidence that until 1191 or later, the Cistercian order did not include women. See Lekai,

Cistercians, pp. 348-9 which relies on M. -A. Dimier, "Chapitres généraux d'abbesses cisterciennes," *Cîteaux: comm. cist.*, 11 (1960): 268-73; but why argue that this specific decision concerning a general chapter in Spain for women only excludes the possibility of any jurisdiction over women in other cases? Attempts are often made to explain Cistercian nuns as subsidiary groups or branches or not wholly part of the order, see Coburn V. Graves, "English Cistercian Nuns in Lincolnshire," *Speculum* 54 (1979), 492-99, Roisin, "L'efflorescence," 376-8, Fontette, *Les religieuses*, 27-63, or Thompson, "Problem of Cistercian Nuns," passim.

17 Cistercian legislative documents are sparse and unreliable for the order's earliest practice—for both men's or women's communities; it must be recalled that Canivez's edition is based on the collation of "available" surviving notes of General Chapter meetings which individual abbots took home or sent to daughter-houses; they are not official transcripts of proceedings. Moreover, for the order's earliest "statutes" such as the "prima collectio" of 1134, there is but a single manuscript source, whose dating may well be questioned. The statutes are interesting where they provide evidence of relationships and practices about which otherwise we know nothing; for example, records of a conflict between the monks of Bonneval in the Rouergue and the merchants of St. Gilles suggest a commercial contact otherwise undocumented (*Statuta*, ed. Canivez, 1200, no. 52). From such fragments we can know something of what early Cistercian abbots discussed, but there is absolutely no guarantee that they include the entire agenda. It is therefore inadmissible to assert that because the General Chapter *never* mentions nuns or the admission of a specific house of nuns into the order before the last decade of the twelfth century, that women in general or that specific house of nuns were not part of the order in earlier years.

18 See Louis J. Lekai, "Ideals and Reality in Early Cistercian Life and Legislation." *Cistercian Ideals and Reality*, ed. John R. Sommerfeldt (Kalamazoo, Michigan, 1978), pp. 4-29, on this new interpretation in general and Constance H. Berman, *Medieval Agriculture, the Southern French Countryside, and the Early Cistercians* (Philadelphia: American Philosophical Society, 1986), Chapter One with regard to early foundation history and economic practice, as well as idem, "The Growth of the Cistercian Order in Southern France," forthcoming, *Analecta Cisterciensia*.

19 For example in southern France there was often an ambiguous relationship among mother and daughter abbeys of male monasteries in the twelfth century. The daughter abbeys were treated as the actual property of the mother abbey, and the endowments of those houses used at the mother abbey's convenience, for example, see *Recueil des actes de l'abbaye de Bonnefont-en-Comminges*, ed. Ch. Samaran and Ch.

Higounet (Paris: Bibliothèque Nationale, 1970), no. 78 (1165); this is discussed with regard to pastoralism in Berman, *Medieval Agriculture*, chapter five.

20 See Catherine E. Boyd, *A Cistercian Nunnery in Medieval Italy: The Story of Rifreddo in Saluzzo, 1220-1300*. Cambridge, Mass. Harvard University Press, 1943.

21 Of forty-three Cistercian houses for men in that region, as many as twenty-one had roots linking them to that western French tradition or were founded by mother houses within southern France which had had such roots; see Berman, *Medieval Agriculture*, Table One, and idem, "Growth," passim.

22 Hill, *English Cistercian*, pp. 85ff., discusses Savigniac nunneries, Thompson, "Problem of Cistercian Nuns," pp. 230-232, and Jacqueline Smith, "Robert of Arbrissel's relations with women," *Medieval Women*, ed. Baker, p. 179, discusses other groups.

23 Fontevrault was a group of houses for contemplative nuns, for penitents (dedicated to St. Mary Magdalene), and communities of priests and lay-brothers to serve the material and spiritual needs of the nuns. Fontevrault has most recently been studied by Penny Schine Gold, *The Lady and the Virgin. Image, Attitude and Experience in Twelfth-Century France* (Chicago: University of Chicago Press, 1985), pp. 93-115, and idem, "Male/Female Cooperation: The Example of Fontevrault," *Distant Echoes: Medieval Religious Women*, vol. 1, ed. John A. Nichols and Lillian Thomas Shank (Kalamazoo, MI: Cistercian Publications, 1984), pp. 151-68. See also Jacques Delarun, "Robert d'Arbrissel et les femmes," *Annales, E.S.C.* 39 (1984): 1140-60, and Smith, cited in note 22. Whereas Fontevrault itself has attracted considerable attention, for a number of reasons, for instance with regard to the development of courtly literature by Reto R. Bezzola, *Les Origines et la formation de la littérature courtoise en Occident (500-1200)* (Paris: Champion, 1966), part 2, vol. 2, esp. pp. 275-92 (note that Bezzola can be unreliable on political details), other Fontevriste houses have received relatively little study thus far.

24 See the article by Avril, cited above note 5, and Mary Skinner, "The Benedictine Life for Women in Central France: 850-1100: A Feminist Revival," *Distant Echoes*, pp. 115-30.

25 *Statuta*, ed. Canivez, vol. II, 1251 no. 49, and 1255, no. 31, indicate a debate over control of Nonenque between Silvanès and its mother-abbey of Mazan. The introduction to *Cartulaire de l'abbaye de Nonenque*, ed. C. Couderc and J. -L. Rigal (Rodez: Carrère, 1955), p. xv, suggests that this debate occurred because the nuns at Nonenque had originally come from Mazan (which apparently founded a number of houses for women); this assertion, based on an assumption that Nonenque was a Cistercian foundation *de novo* is belied by the references to Bellecombe in other documents, cited below. Mazan and Silvanès were presumably fighting over control of Nonenque

in the thirteenth century because of its access to superior pasture rights on the Causse de Larzac, which control of that convent would have given either of them. (See next note.) Ibid., no. 72 (1254) is the first reference to an abbess as opposed to a prioress at Nonenque; that document does not refer to Cistercians and no earlier documents make reference directly to the Cistercians, so the contention that it was a Cistercian priory may be based simply on the notoriously unreliable Silvanès chronicle, discussed in note 28 below. All indications are that Nonenque was the stronger of the two communities—founding a daughter house in the region of Toulouse in the 1250s, ibid., intro. p. xvi; by the 1290s it was in considerable conflict with Silvanès and attempted unsuccessfully to remove itself from the Cistercian order; see ibid., intro. xvi-xix.

26 Specifics mentioned here are found in *Cartulaire de Nonenque*, nos. 17 (1170), 18 (1171), 32 (1189), and 53 (1206). On Nonenque's properties generally, see G. Bourgeois, "Les granges et l'économie de l'abbaye de Nonenque au Moyen Age," *Cîteaux: comm. cist.*, 24 (1973): 139-60. On the importance of pastoralism generally in the area, see Jacques Bousquet, "Les origines de la transhumance en Rouergue," *L'Aubrac: Etude éthnologique, linguistique, agronomique et économique d'un établissement humaine* (Paris: CNRS, 1971) vol. 2, pp. 217-55.

27 Raymond Noël, *Dictionnaire des châteaux de l'Aveyron*, I, pp. 337-8.

28 *Cart. de Silvanès*, pp. 370 ff. is the text of the chronicle; that chronicle, its general unreliability, and its relationship to the post-1160s Silvanès cartulary are discussed in detail in Constance H. Berman, "The Foundation and Early History of the Monastery of Silvanès: the Economic Reality," *Cistercian Ideals and Reality, Studies in Medieval Cistercian History* III, ed. J.R. Sommerfeldt (Kalamazoo, MI: Cistercian Publ., 1978):280-318.

29 *Cartulaire de Nonenque*, no. 3 (1152) indicates the relationship to Bellecombe in a conveyance of land to Silvanès; that early relationship is still referred to in the late thirteenth century when conflict arises between Nonenque and Silvanès, see, ibid., intro., pp. xix.

30 *Cartulaire de Nonenque*, no. 6 (1162) is the confirmation of a tithe exemption granted by Alexander III, which is made by Peter, bishop of Rodez.

31 *Cartulaire de Silvanès*, no. 47 (1139), *Cartulaire de Nonenque*, no. 1 (1139): "quicquid de nobis aliqua persona habet in valle Elnonenca."

32 See Avril reference in note 5 above, and references in note 23 above.

33 The presence of the Garonne between the two houses did not present an insurmountable barrier, since it is clear from Grandselve's documents that the monks of that abbey had granges and kept animals on both sides of the river. See Berman, *Medieval Agriculture,*

esp. Map 2, and Mireille Mousnier, "Les granges de l'abbaye cistercienne de Grandselve," *Annales du Midi* 95 (1983): 7-27.

34 On this house's association with Fontevrault, see John Hine Mundy, *Liberty and Political Power in Toulouse, 1050-1230* (New York: Columbia University Press, 1954), pp. 16-17, Bezzola, *Origines*, p. 290, and documents in Toulouse, A.D. Haute-Garonne, H 205 Lespinasse, liasse 1, a copy of a privilege of Alexander (III) granting exemption from both old and new tithes in the parishes pertaining to it. A short history of the abbey is found in ibid., liasse 12, in a sixteenth-century hand.

35 See Mundy, *Political Power*, p. 17; M. Jongler, "Monographie de l'abbaye de Grandselve." *Mémoires de la société archéologique du Midi* 7 (1853-1860): 179-234; Victor Fons, "Les monastères cisterciens de l'ancienne province ecclésiastique de Toulouse," *Revue de Toulouse et du Midi de la France* 25 (1867): 112-34; R. Rumeau, "Notes sur l'abbaye de Grandselve," *Bulletin de la Société de géographie de Toulouse* 19 (1900): 247-85; and Mireille Mousnier, "L'abbaye cistercienne de Grandselve du XIIe au début du XIVe siècle," *Cîteaux: comm. cist.*, 34 (1983): 53-76 and 221-44, which mentions the original double dedication to the Virgin and to Mary Magdalene.

36 Mousnier, p. 57, relying on Philippe Wolff, *Histoire de Toulouse*, (Toulouse: Privat, 1958), p. 95, says that she retired to Lespinasse and gives the date of Philippa's death as 1116; Mundy, *Political Power*, p. 17 also says that she retired to Lespinasse; Bezzola, *Origines*, p. 290, says that Philippa retired to Fontevrault itself and died there in 1117 or 1118; all interpretations are based on Alfred Richard, *Histoire des comtes de Poitou*, (Paris: Picard, 1903), vol. I, pp. 470-4, which cites an obituary notice from another Fontevriste house, that of Fontaines (Bas-Poitou) for Philippa. Bezzola's seems to be the inaccuracy; however, Delarun, "Robert d'Arbrissel," p. 1143, follows Bezzola without explanation. Given that William VII's first wife Ermengarde was living at Fontevrault at the time, it seems less likely that Philippa would also retire there; see next note.

37 Montpellier, Société archéologique, "Cartulaire dit de Trencavel," fols. 107-8, undated, published in Devic and Vaissete, *Histoire Générale de Languedoc*, (Toulouse: Privat, 1872-93), vol. 5, col. 845, in which Philippa receives a feudal oath from Bernard-Aton IV (Trencavel) (husband of the Cecilia of Provence discussed below) in the presence of Robert of Arbrissel. That Philippa is actively ruling in her own realm of Toulouse suggests that this would be the natural place for her to stay once abandoned by her husband William VII of Poitou, rather than to remove to Fontevrault.

38 Toulouse, A.D. Haute-Garonne, H 205 Lespinasse, liasse 12, no. 11, suggests that additional gifts were made by the count of Toulouse before 1150; Grand-

selve received gifts from the count Alphonse Jourdain before 1133, Paris, B.N. Latin MS 11011, fol. ir, (undated).

39 See Mundy, *Political Power*, p. 17 and 17, n. 22. Philippa's granddaughter, Eleanor of Aquitaine would also be interested in both Fontevrault and Cistercian foundations. See Gold, "Male/Female," her note 41, and M. Rossignol, "Une charte d'Aliénor, duchesse d'Aquitaine, de l'an 1172," *Revue d'Aquitaine et du Languedoc* 5-6 (1861):224-8, on efforts made by Eleanor to found a house in memory of one of her sons; the date, however, is probably not 1172, see Berman, "Women as Patrons," note 54.

40 Reference to Lespinasse's *nemora* as a boundary for property conveyed to Grandselve in 1163 is made in Paris B.N. Latin MS 11008, Grandselve, fols. 133v-134v.

41 Pressure was placed on Grandselve among other houses in that region to found a community for women; see Ibid., no. 65 (1164). Perhaps Lespinasse, despite remaining under the aegis of Fontevrault, did fulfill that function.

42 Beaunier-Besse, *Archives Monastiques* 12 (1911), p. 201, "Le Vignogoul, Sancta Magdalena de Bono Loco, d'abord prieuré avec la règle bénédictine, dont la fondation est antérieure à 1130, abbaye après 1245 avec les observances de Cîteaux, sous la dépendance des abbés de Valmagne . . ."

43 See Pierre de Gorsse, *L'abbaye cistercienne Sainte-Marie de Valmagne au diocèse d'Agde en Languedoc. Histoire de l'abbaye* (Toulouse: Lion, 1933), pp. 7 ff., and Berman, "Growth," forthcoming. Despite foundation by Ardorel it was incorporated into the Cistercian order in the filiation of Cîteaux, as a daughter of the Cistercian house of Bonnevaux in the 1150s.

44 Avril, "Fondations," note 13, mentions that a study of the religious houses for women in the "diocese of Maguelonne" is being conducted by Mme. Moreau, but whether this will include Vignogoul is unclear.

45 Beaunier-Besse, loc. cit. and *Statuta* ed. Canivez, vol. 2, 1246, no.

46 Albi, A.D. Tarn, H3 Ardorel (1138) refers to Cecilia's patronage of Ardorel, if not Valmagne, and Montpellier, Soc. archéologique, "Cartulaire dit de Trencavel," fols. 160v ff. (1157), shows her ownership of land near Mèze in the vicinity of Valmagne. Montpellier, A.D. Hérault, film (private deposit) "Cart. de Valmagne," I, 100r (1179), 100v (1180), 138v (1147), and 137v (1148) and 146 (1175), show the family's association with Valmagne. See also Devic, *Histoire de Languedoc*, vol. 3, p. 707, which attributes the foundation to Raymond Trencavel, her eldest son. Cecilia's daughter Trencavella was also among donors to Valmagne, see "Cart. de Valmagne," vol. 1, fol. 137v (1148).

47 See Gorsse, *Valmagne*, passim.

48 See note 37 above.

49 Huyghebaert, "Femmes laïques," pp. 373 ff.

50 A survey of Beaunier-Besse, *Archives monastiques*, passim, shows that most houses in the "order" of Fontevrault were located in western France.

51 "Cart. de Valmagne," vol. 2, fol. 86v (1196, n.s. 1197?).

Circatores in the *Ordo* of St. Victor

Hugh Feiss, OSB

The *Liber ordinis*, the customary of the monastery and congregation of the canons regular of St. Victor, seems to have been composed during the abbacy of Gilduin at St. Victor (1113-1155). Gilduin succeeded the founder, William of Champeaux, and under his regime the *ordo* of St. Victor was adopted by many other canonial communities. This diffusion of the *ordo* would have necessitated that the observances and customs of the Parisian abbey be put in written form. In the judgment of its recent editors, the *Liber ordinis* of St. Victor drew on traditional, monastic sources, rather than on the recently formulated customs of the Cistercians and canonical orders like Prémontré.[1]

Chapter 41 of the *Liber ordinis* is devoted to the office and tasks of the *circator*:

> Let a *circator* be chosen from among those of the community who are more conscientious and zealous for the *ordo*, one who will never spitefully report anyone out of personal animosity nor because of personal friendship pass over anyone's negligence in silence. It is the office of the *circator* to go around the workplaces of the monastery and take note of the negligences of the brethren and violations of the *ordo*. Whenever he makes his round, he should proceed conscientiously, in an orderly way, so that he may strike terror in those who see him and offer an example of conscientious religious observance. Moreover, he should also make his round quietly and seriously, so that he never speaks to anyone or gives anyone a sign. Let him simply scrutinize and investigate offences and negligences. He can make his round at any time, except at the time of the chapter or the *collatio*, when the doors of the cloister have already been shut, and during the night, after everyone, officials included, has retired.
>
> He should pay careful attention lest anyone ever miss the canonical hours without reason and lest anyone speak where or when he is not supposed to speak. After the prayer has been said in the dormitory following compline, let him take a dark lantern if it is needed and go and check out the entire cloister, the chapter room, the speaking rooms, the refectory, and the remaining workshops. He need not go out into the courtyard; he can look it over from the door of the speaking room and the other doors which adjoin the court. He must notice carefully whether anyone is in the cellar, in the refectory, or anywhere else, and why he is there. He should also check what is going on in the infirmary building: whether the sick have retired and how they are doing. It is not necessary for him to go to the bed of each; rather, he may stand in the middle of the infirmary and shine the light around in order to see everything. Then he returns and goes up to the dormitory, passes through the middle of it while shining the light of the lantern toward the beds of the brethren, looking on both sides, to make sure they are observing the rule in everything. When he has done this, let him extinguish his candle.
>
> While the brethren are eating he can leave the refectory without permission and make his round, provided he returns for the grace. When he finds some talking together, let him, insofar as he can in passing by, listen lest they speak without proper restraint. If they speak with permission let them say to him: "We speak with permission." If not, let them disperse and let him report them in chapter. However, if he finds someone speaking with an outsider, the speaker need not excuse himself then; but after the one with whom he was speaking has left, let him indicate to the *circator* whether he was speaking with permission.
>
> One who is in charge of the community, but not the abbot, can help the *circator* in making his rounds, whenever there is need and it is convenient for both of them. It is to be noted that if there are several *circatores*, they should not go around together, but in such a way that when one leaves a place, the other enters it not long afterwards.
>
> The *circator* ought to be carefully and respectfully heard in the chapter.
>
> The abbot should appoint one or two, or however many he wishes, of the brethren, so that the *circator* may entrust his office to one of them when he himself cannot fulfill it.

The *circator* can leave or enter at one of the canonical hours without permission; there is no need to change the seating arrangement just for him.[2]

There are two avenues toward understanding this office at St. Victor: (1) an historical study of the development of *circatores* in earlier Benedictine communities; (2) an appraisal of the function of the *circatores* at St. Victor itself.

Circatores in Earlier Benedictine Monasticism

In the *Rule of St. Benedict* the office of *circatores* is not mentioned explicitly. However, in chapter 48, lines 17-20, after discussing Lenten reading, the *Rule* prescribes:

> Above all, one or two of the seniors must surely be deputed to make the rounds (*circumeant*) of the monastery while the brothers are reading. Their duty is to see that no brother is so apathetic as to waste time or engage in idle talk to the neglect of his reading, and so not only harm himself but also distract others. If such a monk is found—God forbid—he should be reproved a first and second time. If he does not amend, he must be subjected to the punishment of the rule as a warning to others.[3]

The office of *circator* seems to have derived from this passage, just as the name derived from the verb it uses for making the rounds (*circumire*). In the Middle Ages this official and the round he made were both sometimes call a *circa* (a noun of the first declension). This noun is derived from the preposition *circa*, which St. Benedict uses five times: three times in reference to the abbot's care concerning (*circa*) brothers who are excommunicated, once regarding the concern a brother should have concerning (*circa*) sinful thoughts, and once with reference to the spiritual health which God will restore to (*circa*) a frequently reproved brother.[4] Hence, in the *Rule of St. Benedict* both *circumire* and *circa* have disciplinary connotations.

Non-Monastic Usages

There was some secular precedent for the emergence of the vocabulary and office of *circator* in medieval monasticism.

Frontinus mentions *circitores* as a class of inspectors for the waterworks of Rome.[5] Vegetius, in his *Epitome rei militaris*, writes of military *circitores* or *circuitores* who made the rounds at night and reported infractions during the night watch.[6] This secular use of the word-complex *circumire-circator-circa* was not unknown in medieval texts.[7]

One ecclesiastical use of these terms was in connection with episcopal visitations. Gregory the Great spoke of a bishop who customarily made the rounds of the churches under him (*ex more circuiret*).[8] Alcuin urged Eanbald, the archbishop of York: "Let not your tongue cease from preaching or your foot from going around (*circuiendo*) the flock committed to you."[9] Matthew Paris describes a very severe visitation which Robert Grosseteste, bishop of Lincoln, made of Ramsey Abbey in 1251, in which the bishop personally inspected the monks' beds and made the rounds of everything (*omnia circuit*).[10]

Early Benedictine Texts

Circatores have become distinct officials in the earliest Benedictine legislations, and they are already designated to make reports at the community meeting. The *Ordo Casinensis I* (after 750 AD) legislated:

> (7) We saw to it that great care was taken regarding youthful brethren. For this care are deputed two brothers of observant life in the monastery. The youths should not dare leave the sight of these two, day or night.
>
> (8) Also, two *circatores* made the rounds (*circuibant*) of the monastery at all hours when the brothers were awake, lest any brother be absent from his proper place. If one were absent, it was noted on tablets and presented in the gathering of the brethren in the presence of the abbot and corrected by the regular discipline, according to the degree of heedlessness involved . . .
>
> (11) If the aforementioned *circatores* noticed anyone laughing or whispering something, it was immediately noted on their tablets and kindly corrected at a suitable time.[11]

The *circatores* are mentioned a number of times in Carolingian legislation. One such text, the *Capitula notitiarum* (after 817 AD) specified that when the brethren went out to their assigned tasks, one *circator* accompanied them. The other *circator* stayed at home to watch the cloister.[12] The same document prescribed that when someone was admonished in the chapter, he was to ask pardon immediately. When ordered to, he arose and humbly rendered an account of himself. Those who refused to do this were to receive a double punishment.[13] The commentaries on the *Rule of St. Benedict* attributed to Paul the Deacon and Hildemar present the *circatores* as minor disciplinarians, who first admonished violators and then reported them to the abbot, who sometimes added excommunications to the public admonitions in order to correct the wayward. According to these commentators, another task of the *circatores*, who held office for a year, was to summon the brethren to choir.[14]

Two Literary Texts

Ekkehard of St. Gall (+ca. 1060 AD) tells of several striking events which show the *circatores* in good and bad light and serve to illustrate the damages of unofficial disciplinarians. The *circatores* were supervising the boys of the community at St. Gall. The boys had contrived to obtain a day or two of grace from punishment merited by their misdeeds on the feast of St. Mark in 937 AD. However, the *circatores* finally reported the boys' misdeeds to the master, who ordered one boy to go to get the switch. To try to free himself and his companions by diversionary tactics, the boy lit some sticks on fire and yelled that a building was burning. Tragically, the buildings actually did catch on fire.

Earlier in his narrative, Ekkehard tells of three friends at St. Gall: Notker, who was strict in matters of discipline (*acer exactor disciplinis*), Tutilo, and Ratpert, a kindly teacher but a rather stern disciplinarian (*disciplinis asperior*). Even though Ratpert thought impunity undercut claustral life, he only came to the chapter when summoned, since he had the very onerous duty of reproving (*capitulandi*) and punishing. The refectorian, Sindolf, disliked these three friends. While Ratpert was reluctant to do his official disciplinarian duties in chapter, Sindolf was a willing, volunteer informer and slanderer. Sindolf got the ear of the abbot, who listened to his slanders against the three friends, "even though the abbot knew that nothing was more harmful to prelates than to listen to whisperings of their subjects." One time Ratpert and Tutilo caught Sindolf eavesdropping in the dark. Pretending they thought he was a devil, they gave him a sound beating. The abbot compensated Sindolf by making him a dean, but eventually Sindolf's insolence earned him a taste of the regular discipline in chapter.

Ekkehard also reports about a time Tutilo was in Mayence on business. He was resting at the abbey of St. Alban's where he saw the *circator* getting ready to ride out and gather for vespers the brothers who were working on the harvest. Secretly the *circator* was looking to see if his "housekeeper" was at home. She came out to give him a drink. When he finished the drink, he began fondling her breast. When Tutilo saw this, he immediately jumped up and began horsewhipping the culprit. Later, Tutilo asked pardon for himself and this undisciplined *circator*.[15]

In the eleventh-century beast fable, the *Ecbasis cuiusdam captivi*, written by a German Benedictine, the "monastic fox" had been slandered to the lion (king). The fox approached the king warily, who brought up the accusations. To these the fox replied:

Let the inquisitor (*circator*) come, let him disclose
  my whole guilt that has been mentioned:
If it is deserving of death, let me be forced
  to succumb to the law;
If I am judged innocent, I shall rejoice in the
  palace of my master.[16]

French and English Legislation

The tenth-century customs of Fleury included the *circator* among the officials of the monastery. The *circator*, who was also called a sentinel (*excubitor*), was described as "a man who holds most firmly to monastic purpose; not flighty, but constant and a friend of regular discipline." The *circator* kept constant watch on the cloister and the workplaces. Like a spiritual trapper he took a dark lantern at night and looked for the negligences of the brethren. If he found things like books or clothes left lying around after compline, he collected them to return them at the chapter meeting. In the winter he checked the choir as well as the cloister to make sure no one was sleeping in the choir stalls or in bed. If someone was found sleeping in the choir, he took the lantern from the *circator* and in his turn went around the choir looking for monks who were sleeping.[17]

The *Regularis concordia* (ca. 972 AD) explains that the *circa* was so called because he made the round (*circuitus*). As at Fleury he used a lantern to see if brethren were sleeping during the night office. During the rest of the monastic day he was supposed to go frequently around the cloister (*circuire claustrum*) looking for brothers who had given in to sloth or other vanities. As at Fleury the *circa* also made the rounds after compline. He was to report misdeeds at the chapter next day, unless in the case of a slight fault a brother gave humble satisfaction immediately. At the chapter meeting, any brother conscious of having committed a fault might seek forgiveness. If a brother were accused by a senior official, he was not to say a word, but to bow down and give satisfaction.[18]

German Customaries

A tenth-century customary contained in a manuscript at Einsiedeln describes a gentler, less searching confession of faults at the daily chapter. All were asked to examine themselves to see if they had offended in speech, food and drink, or sleep. Then they declared their faults and received a penance of fasting or prayers. There is no mention of a *circator*.[19]

The customary of Fulda and Trier (11th century) legislates that at the end of the rest period after lauds on Sunday, the dean or the *circuitor* should wake

the brethren, when this seems fitting. This customary explains that the name "chapter meeting" (*capitulum*) was derived from the word for "head" or
"chapter" (*caput*), since "in a monastic community
if men are not checked by fear there is no religious
life." After the abbot's sermon at the chapter meeting, the monks accuse themselves. Some are accused
by the *circuitor*. No one is to excuse himself as blame-
less before receiving pardon.[20]

The customary of St. Vanne, Verdun, (11th or
12th century) devotes a separate chapter to the
circuitor. His job was to explore the monastery by
going around everywhere at unseasonable hours.
If he discovered an offense, it was his task to report
it in the morning chapter, but not to make rash
judgments. He also had an instrument to catch those
sleeping at vigils.[21]

Cluniac Usages

Circatores do not appear by name in the earliest
Cluniac customs, but thereafter they are a regular
feature of Cluniac customaries. The Cluniac *circatores* inherit much from their Benedictine predecessors.

The customary attributed to Bernard of Cluny
(ca. 1070 AD) discusses the *circatores* after the major prior and the claustral prior. To the latter was
assigned the round after compline; the morning
rounds were evidently made under his supervision
or by him personally. Regarding *circatores*, whose
institution he ascribed to St. Benedict, Bernard
noted that especially devout and fervent monks
were to be assigned for this office. Since their task
was to make the rounds of the monastery looking
for negligences of the brethren and violations of
the *ordo*, they were not to be the sort who accused
someone out of personal enmity or who concealed
faults out of friendship for an offender.

They were to make an inspection whenever they
thought something might be amiss, as well as at prescribed times. During these periods they were never
to talk; they were only to observe. As they walked
by, they were to try to catch the drift of the conver-
sation of lesser abbey officials, to make sure they
were not speaking frivolity. Brothers found talking
with each other were to indicate whether they had
permission to speak.

The *circatores* were to be heard attentively and
reverently in the chapter meeting. There, whenever
a brother confessed a fault or was accused of one,
he immediately prostrated and sought pardon. If he
answered anything before seeking pardon, he was
ordered to prostrate and receive a blow before being
assigned a penance.[22]

The tasks of the *circatores* are described in much
the same terms by other Cluniac and Cluny-inspired
customaries.[23]

Circatores at St. Victor

It is clear that the *circatores* at St. Victor had a
long ancestry stretching back through the centuries
to the *Rule of St. Benedict*. There is nothing astonish-
ingly new in the description of their offices in the
Liber ordinis of St. Victor. They were included in
the *ordo* of St. Victor because they were traditional;
presumably they were also included because traditionally they served some positive purposes.

The Chapter Meeting at St. Victor

At the daily chapter meeting, the superior began
the chapter of faults by saying: "Speak of your *ordo*."
First, those who by their own choice wished to confess
public faults did so in a specified order, in front of
the abbot, and loudly enough so that everyone could
hear clearly. Likewise, even if someone had permission to miss a liturgical hour or was allowed to
be absent from some other obligatory activity, he was
to declare it publicly. Next, at the abbot's bidding,
the *circator* made his accusations. Then other brothers
could make additional accusations. One who was
accused came before the abbot and listened patiently
to his brother's accusation, which was to be stated
simply and without exaggeration. If the accused saw
he was guilty, he was to confess his fault. If he was
not guilty, he was to say he did not remember doing
the alleged fault. The one who made an accusation
was not to accuse somone who had accused him.
Accusations were to be made only regarding what
one had seen and heard. If someone among the
accused was to be whipped in the chapter, he was
not to be whipped by one who accused him, nor by
one whom he had accused. No one was to speak to
anyone outside the chapter about faults dealt with
in the chapter.[24]

Interpretation

What, then, can one conclude about the role of
circatores at St. Victor specifically, and indirectly
about their role in earlier Benedictine monasticism?

Initially, one feels mystified, if not repulsed by the
office of *circatores* and the custom of accusations in
chapter. The fictional contemporary abbot of Pierre
de Calon's novel *Cosmas* probably gives the custom
a more benign interpretation than most twentieth-
century Christians would:

This custom, by which a monk denounced the faults of another, has now been suppressed. It used to come after the confession of one's own faults which took place two or three times a week in the chapter.... There was no question of commenting on personal failings, which belonged to the sphere of private confessions: the accusation was concerned with breaches of the Rule which could become obstacles to the progress of the community as a whole; ... when a monk seemed unaware of his faults or lacked the courage needed to confess them, fraternal charity performed this service on his behalf. It was a way of safeguarding the integrity of community life. But one also had to reckon with the effect on the monk who was accused. Personally I was not sorry to see the custom dropped; its effects could be very good or very bad, depending on the intentions of the "accuser" and the spiritual and mental state of the "accused."[25]

So much for the custom of accusation in recent monasticism. What about the *circatores* at twelfth-century St. Victor?

One obvious function of the *circator* was to act as an agent of social control, a watchdog of regular observance. The high value placed on the observances of the regular *ordo* is worthy of scrutiny, since it seems to be a significant clue to the mentality of medieval monasticism.

A second task of the *circator* was to contribute to the chapter meeting's function as an institutionalized and legitimate channel for "fraternal correction," which seems to have been an important element in Augustinian life. For example, the *Bridlington Dialogue* discussed fraternal correction at length as an evangelical and Augustinian value.[26]

Thirdly, closely if not overtly related to fraternal correction, is the function of defusing some of the annoyances of communal life. One reason to correct an erring brother is so he will stop doing things which bother the accuser. When the *circator* made his report, irritants were eliminated without the interjection of personal animosity. Even if one brother accused another in chapter, it was done in a form and setting which seems designed to provide checks on personal antagonisms.

Fourthly, the Victorine *circatores*, who at first glance seemed like unpalatable spies, were as much at the service of human community living as they were the guardians of discipline. Their role was so designed that others (especially those with proclivities to do so) would not feel obligated to scrutinize their brothers' behavior; and when correction and accusation occurred it took place in a public forum. Although the *circatores* and the chapter accusations could cause considerable anxiety,[27]

they assured that a brother had a chance to face his accusers. They served as a structured public alternative to secret denunciations.

Finally, the *circatores* and the chapter meetings freed the abbot from much petty disciplinary work and from the need to listen to brothers complaining about the observance of other brothers. By explicitly excluding the abbot from making the rounds, the *Liber ordinis* of St. Victor helped highlight other aspects of the abbot's role by limiting his involvement in monitoring the daily observance of the brethren. Although the abbot was very much the superior, in this matter at least fraternal interaction seems to have been furthered, rather than hindered by his role.

Caroline Bynum has offered evidence that fraternal example was a more important value among canons regular than among monks.[28] It may also be that fraternal, as opposed to abbatial, correction loomed larger in the canonical *ordines* than in monastic usages. This will require further study. Meanwhile, it certainly is clear that what differences, if any, there were between monastic and canonical *circatores* were counterbalanced by a substantial shared tradition. The canons of St. Victor, who followed the *Rule of St. Augustine*, saw nothing incongruous in adopting the customs of earlier monks who lived under the *Rule of St. Benedict*.

Notes

1 Luc Jocqué and Ludo Milis, eds. *Liber ordinis Sancti Victoris Parisiensis, Corpus Christianorum Continuatio Medievalis*, vol. 61 (Turnholt: Brepols, 1984), ix. Hereafter cited as LO.

2 LO, pp. 194-196. Unless otherwise indicated, translations are mine.

3 *RB 1980: The Rule of St. Benedict in Latin and English with Notes*, ed. Timothy Fry (Collegeville, MN: Liturgical Press, 1981), pp. 250-251. Some of the rules collated by Benedict of Aniane in his *Concordia regularum* as commentaries on chapter 48 of the *Rule of St. Benedict* assign the supervision to deans. The editors of the *Concordia* note that these officials were called *circatores* in medieval monastic legislation: J.P. Migne, ed. *Patrologia Latina*, 103:1178.

4 *Rule of St. Benedict* 27.t(2x), 1; 7.18; 28.5. Adalbert de Vogüé and Jean Neufville, eds. *La règle de saint Benoît, Sources Chrétiennes* 182 (Paris: Cerf, 1972), p. 701.

5 Frontinus, *Les aqueducs de la ville de Rome*, ed. and

trans. Pierre Grimal (Paris: Les Belles Lettres, 1944), p. 56.

6 Vegetius, *Epitome rei militaris* 3, quoted in *Lexicon totius latinitatis*, ed. J. Facciolati, Ag. Forcellini, J. Furlanetti, and Francesco Corradini (Patavii: Typis Seminarii, 1864), II, 619. Vegetius' work was very popular in the Middle Ages; see Bernard S. Bachrach, "The Practical Use of Vegetius' *De Re Militari* during the Early Middle Ages," *The Historian* 47 (1985), pp. 239-255.

7 See the texts cited in du Cange, *Glossarium mediae et infimae latinitatis*, rev. Léopold Favre et al., (Paris: Librairie des Sciences et des Arts, 1937), II, 335-336.

8 Gregory the Great, *Dialogues*, ed. Adalbert de Vogüé, trans. Paul Antin, SC 260 (Paris: Cerf, 1979) II, 428.

9 Alcuin, *Ep.* 114, ed. E. Duemmler, *Monumenta Germaniae Historica Ep. caroini aevi* 2 (1985), 167, lines 17-18.

10 Mattaei Parisiensis, Monachi Sancti Albani, *Chronica majora*, ed. Henry Richards Luard, Rolls Series 57 (1880), V, 226.

11 *Ordo Casinensis I dictus Ordo regularis*, ed. T. Leccisotti, in *Initia consuetudinis benedictinae*, Corpus Consuetudinum Monasticarum 1 (Siegburg: Fr. Schmitt, 1963), pp. 102-104. Hereafter cited as CCM 1.

12 *Capitula notitiarum* XIV, ed. D.H. Frank, CCM 1, 343, lines 5-13. In other Carolingian legislation this task is assigned to seniors: *Synodi primae Aquisgranensis decreta authentica* 32, ed. J. Semmler, CCM 1, 446, lines 5-7; *Regula Sancti Benedicti abbatis Anianensis sive Collectio capitularis* 27, ed. J. Semmler, CCM 1, 523, lines 2-4; *Collectio capitularis Benedicti levitae* 33, ed. J. Semmler, CCM 1, 549, lines 5-7; *Legislationis monasticae Aquisgranensis collectio Sancti Martialis Lemovicensis*, ed. J. Semmler, CCM 1, 559, lines 3-5.

13 *Capitula notitiarum* 13, ed. D.H. Frank, CCM 1, 344, lines 1-4.

14 See the comments and references in Sr. M. Alfred Schroll, *Benedictine Monasticism as Reflected in the Winefrid-Hildemar Commentaries on the Rule* (NY: Columbia University Press, 1941), pp. 61, 83, 146-147. Scholars now attribute these commentaries to Hildemar, whose commentary is available in several recensions. For the literature see Mayke de Jong, "Growing up in a Carolingian Monastery: Magister Hildemar and His Oblates," *Journal of Medieval History* 9/2 (1983), 99-128.

15 Ekkehardus Sangallensis IV, *Casus S. Galli*, MGH SS (1829), II, 111-112, 94-97, 98-99. The first incident is translated in J.M. Clark, *The Abbey of St. Gall as a Centre of Literature and Art* (Cambridge: Cambridge University Press, 1926), p. 12; the second is translated in G.G. Coulton, *Life in the Middle Ages* (NY: Macmillan, 1930), IV, 50-55.

16 *Escape of a Certain Captive Told in a Figurative Manner*, ed. and trans. Edwin H. Zeydel, University of North Carolina Studies in the Germanic Languages

and Literatures 46 (1964; NY: AMS, 1966), pp. 48-49, lines 468-470.

17 *Consuetudines Floriacenses antiquiores* 10, ed. Anselm Davril and Linus Donnat, in *Consuetudinum saeculi X/XI/XII monumenta non-Cluniacensia*, ed. Kassius Hallinger, CCM 7/3 (Siegburg: Fr. Schmitt, 1984), pp. 17-19.

18 *Regularis concordia anglicae nationis*, ed. Thomas Symons, et al., CCM 7/3, 132-133, 87.

19 *Redactio sancti Emmerammi dicta Einsidlensis* 7-8, ed. Maria Wegener and Candida Elvert, CCM 7/3, 251-252. These procedures for the confession of faults at chapter resemble closely those followed in the weekly chapter of faults in the Swiss-American Benedictine Congregation: *Declarationes in Sacram Regulam et Constitutiones Helveto-Americanae Ordinis Sancti Benedicti* (St. Benedict, OR: Mount Angel Abbey, 1950), Nos. 69-70.

20 *Redactio Fuldensis-Trevirensis*, ed. Maria Wegener, Candida Elvert and Kassius Hallinger, CCM 7/3, 276-278, 291-292.

21 *Redactio Virdunensis*, ed. Maria Wegener and Kassius Hallinger (following the text of E. Martene, *Antiquis ecclesiae ritibus* [1738] 4:847-860), CCM 7/3, 419.

22 Bernard, *Ordo Cluniacensis sive consuetudines*, Pars 1, chs. 3, 4, 18, ed. M. Hergott, *Vetus disciplina monastica* (Paris: Carolus Osment, 1726), pp. 141-144, 176-177.

23 Ulrich, *Consuetudines Cluniacensis* 3.7 (PL 149.741CD); William of Hirsau, *Constitutiones Hirsaugienses* 2.21 (PL 150.1067-1068); *Redactio Wirzeburgensis*, ed. Rudolf Grunewald, Kassius Hallinger and Candida Elvert, in *Consuetudines Cluniacensium antiquiores cum redactionibus derivatis*, ed. Kassius Hallinger, CCM 7/2 (Siegburg: Fr. Schmitt, 1983), pp. 272-274, 277.

24 LO 33, pp. 157-163.

25 Pierre de Calon, *Cosmas or the Love of God*, trans. Peter Hebblethwaite (London: Collins, 1980), pp. 68-69.

26 Robert of Bridlington, *The Bridlington Dialogue. An Exposition of the Rule of St. Augustine for the Life of the Clergy*, ed. and trans. by a Religious of the C.S.M.V. (London: Mowbray, 1960), pp. 139-145.

27 Achard of Saint Victor, *Sermons inédits* 13.25, ed. Jean Chatillon (Paris: J. Vrin, 1970), pp. 156-158; Richard of St. Victor, *Sermones centum* 44 (PL 177: 1018A-1019C).

28 Caroline Bynum, "The Spirituality of Regular Canons in the Twelfth Century: A New Approach," *Medievalia et Humanistica* 4 (1973), 3-24; *Docere verbo et exemplo. An Aspect of Twelfth-Century Spirituality*, Harvard Theological Studies 31 (Missoula, MT: Scholars Press, 1979). In another study I will examine the *circatores* in some of the new religious groups of the twelfth and thirteenth centuries.

Monastic Medicine in Pre-Crusade Europe: The Care of Sick Children

Bernard Bachrach and Jerome Kroll

A study of the care given to sick children in monasteries can shed light on two separate but related controversies in early medieval studies. Monasteries in early medieval Europe were the most intensely Christianized enclaves in an otherwise indifferently Christianized world *and* were the centers of learning for both secular and sacred education. This role in education included the transcription, annotation, revision, and utilization of medical tracts and herbals from classical and late antiquity. A study of the care of sick children can provide evidence about the degree and ease with which theological and naturalistic theories and practices were accommodated to each other. One focused question that may be asked concerns the textual evidence which supports a particular operational definition of theological reasoning about illnesses, namely, whether it was believed that sin caused illness.[1] An examination of the responses to children's illnesses can be thought of as testing the depth of such a causal relationship between sin and illness, since young children tended to be viewed generally as free of the most venial sins, except for the rather abstract notion of original sin, and not responsible for their actions in secular law.[2] Ostensibly children were not capable of the types of sin (stealing monastic property; attacking an influential saint; adultery) which we have demonstrated in our previous research were viewed in the early Middle Ages as deserving divine punishment in the form of disease.[3]

Second, a study of monastic responses to children's illnesses provides evidence regarding the value of Aries' thesis that, prior to the Renaissance, the special nature and needs of children were not recognized, and of DeMause's thesis that the principle mode of relating to children in the Middle Ages was one of neglect, abandonment and abuse.[4] Thus the manner in which the monastic community regarded and treated ill children may be seen to reflect a view by an important segment of early medieval society concerning the value of children and the efforts one should make on their behalf.

Method

During the past several years we have been collecting descriptions of medical cases in pre-Crusade Europe from a variety of narrative sources, but mostly from chronicles and saints' lives. Our data base is now over 600 cases. We decided to use nonmedical sources because we are interested in the lay description of cases of illnesses and the popular responses to illnesses rather than in the transmission and transmutation of medical manuscripts. Underlying our use of hagiography and, in general, religiously oriented chronicles as sources of medical information is the confidence that, in large part, the very casualness with which illnesses appear in the periphery of the texts lends to them a fair degree of credibility as descriptions of the types of illnesses from which people suffered and sought help.[5] One need not endorse *completely* either the miracle cures or the occasional etiological references, but neither should such additional bits of information be discarded as irrelevancies.

The basic descriptions of illnesses in the sources that we have used range from brief statements that someone became ill to full descriptions of symptoms and course that even permit some reasonable hypotheses about the nature of the disease process. Our focus, however, has not been to demonstrate how many illnesses we can diagnose, although this is of general interest and considerable importance. Rather, our aim in the overall research, of which this is a small but integral part, has been to work toward a comprehensive picture of attitudes and behavior concerning illness in pre-Crusade England and the Frankish kingdoms.

Results and Discussion

In a previous study we reported on seventy-six cases

of illnesses in children from twenty-two sources.[6] Thirty of the seventy-six cases were treated at a monastic complex for illnesses ranging from spirit possession to plague.[7] Twenty-four of the thirty are reported to have been permanently healed. Twenty-three of the children treated are clearly indicated to have been brought from the outside and were not resident within the monastic complex broadly defined. In seven of the thirty cases (23%) there is unambiguous evidence of physical or naturalistic methods of treatment employed. These include routine bleeding, surgical procedures, nursing back to health, and general physical care.

Several of the monasteries are singled out as the place to go because they are known to have "skilled physicians" working there.[8] In one case at Poitiers, a doctor who is said to have trained in Byzantium as a surgeon is reported to have operated successfully by removing the testicles of a youth with severe groin pain.[9] One would hope that the lad had a strangulated hernia or torsion of the spermatic cord in order to justify such a procedure. In another case a visiting bishop demonstrates his medical knowledge by reprimanding a young girl in a monastery for having been bled on the fourth day of the moon, when the light of the moon and the pull of the tide are increasing. It is clear that the bishop understood the medical practice, and its attendant literature, that indicated the proper conditions for phlebotomy. Whereas one could also read this example as demonstrating the healing power of the bishop's blessing, the fact remains that prophylactic bleeding was a routine medical procedure at the monastery. Its purpose was not to let the devils out, but to restore proper balance to the humors.[10]

In a particularly illuminating case referred to in the text as a miracle, Saint Genovefa brings back to life a very young boy who lay submerged in a well for three hours. When the unconscious boy is brought to Genovefa, she wisely covers him with her cloak.[11] We can assume that the boy was suffering from exposure and hypothermia rather than drowning, and that the proper treatment, as applied by Genovefa, was to bring his body temperature back to normal. The text does not even mention that Genovefa added prayers to her pragmatic treatment. It is reasonable to inquire why Genovefa was able to appreciate that the boy could be resuscitated when his mother and the townspeople thought that he was dead. We can only hypothesize that Genovefa had both a certain degree of practical medical knowledge that led her to recognize the effects of hypothermia (shallow breathing, faint pulse, cyanosis) and an ability to act decisively. Peter Brown has

commented, in regard to healing of illnesses, that "we get a very wrong impression if we look only at the miraculous element in the holy man's relations with his clients. In his relation to contemporary medical science, for instance, the holy man appears far more often than we might at first sight suppose in a merely supporting role."[12] As Brown suggests, people such as Genovefa earned their reputations as holy men and women by being effective and hard working and providing a real community service. Finally, in the context of naturalistic treatment and service, St. Romaricus is said to have built a special facility for the care of girls suffering from leprosy.[13] No mention is made here of miracle cures, but simply a clear-cut recognition that young girls with this illness required long-term protective care.

It is also worth noting that several children were reported to have died from plague and dysentery in the monasteries. There are no apologies, no blaming of the devil or the sin of humans; it was accepted as a fact of life that certain illnesses, such as plague and dysentery, entail a high lethality, especially among children.[14]

As we turn to those children cured by supernatural means, an analysis of the maladies from which they suffered is instructive. We are particularly wary of the *post hoc* reasoning that if an illness was cured by prayer, laying on of hands, annointing with holy oil, or drinking a potion of tomb dust and water, then it must have been an hysterical condition. Nevertheless, there are certain descriptions of illness that lend themselves to this hypothesis. Cases that most likely fall into this category include those with blindness, certain types of paralysis, and demon possession or epilepsy. We are not suggesting that all such cases are hysterical, but only that some must have been and others very likely were. We say this for several reasons. First of all, throughout the ages temporary blindness has been a fairly common hysterical symptom and lends itself particularly well to sudden onsets and recoveries.[15] The same is true of temporary paralysis of limbs, a syndrome well described in the nineteenth-century neurological literature. We also know from modern EEG studies of persons with epilepsy that a certain percentage of epileptics, especially young women, exhibit seizure behavior in the *absence* of a cerebral epileptic discharge, i.e., some of the seizures are simulated. Without simultaneous EEG monitoring, it is at times very difficult even for physicians to ascertain whether the seizure is *bona fide* or simulated.[16] Second, in the case of persons allegedly blind from birth who are suddenly cured, we know from modern cases of congenital cataracts that when the cataracts are removed and corrective lenses used, the person is functionally blind in terms of recognizing visually objects and shapes that are well-known by touch.[17] One suspects, but cannot know, that the incidence of hysterical conditions was greater in the early Middle Ages than now.

An example in which we suspect a psychogenic condition is that of a young blind girl who is brought to the tomb of Saint Benedict at the monastery of Fleury.[18] She recovers her sight and promises to become a serf of the saint. Later she breaks her promise and subsequently becomes blind. A rather straightforward explanation is one of hysterical blindness or conversion reaction ameliorated by the anticipation and psychological impact of the holy shrine. Later, either her guilt or fear engendered by breaking her promise precipitates the return of the symptom. Yet even here one cannot easily resort to a psychological explanation. There are medical conditions which can cause the onset and remission of blindness, the most notable one being multiple sclerosis. This condition typically has its onset in young women, and visual symptoms are frequently the first heralding of the disease.[19]

Similarly the case of a youth with ascending paralysis whose condition worsened while the skilled physicians at the monastery of Lindesfarne were unable to reverse it might be readily ascribed to hysteria.[20] His cure was occasioned when he put on Saint Cuthbert's sandals. However, the description of the illness—the youth asked to place Cuthbert's shoes on his feet because his paralysis began there—taken together with its time course suggest that the condition might have been Guillain-Barré Syndrome, a neurological illness probably of viral etiology with a time-limited course of ascending paralysis and a gradual spontaneous recovery.[21]

We note that in none of our thirty cases is the primary cause of the disease attributed to sin. This fits with our earlier study of over 600 cases in which sin was noted as the etiology of disease only when there was propaganda value to be derived from such an ascription. While we found that, on the average, about 20% of all cases of illness were attributed to sin, we find no mention of sin at all in our thirty children's cases, except perhaps by inference in the case in which the young girl's blindness returned when she broke her promise to serve Saint Benedict. It would seem that, despite recent suggestions that children in the Middle Ages were viewed as sinful and evil little creatures,[22] the medieval writers of our sources well realized that children were not responsible for their own illnesses, especially since they were powerless to offend a saint or threaten monastic holdings.

Finally we point out the considerable trouble and cost which parents and guardians expended in seeking care for their sick children. The prevailing picture here is not one of neglect, abandonment, and indifference, but of costly and risky (even if local) pilgrimages to shrines, incurrment of worldly and spiritual debt, and great devotion and attachment to the sick children who occasionally find their way into the chronicles and saints' lives.

Conclusion

In the process of examining medicine in the monasteries of early medieval Europe it becomes clear that the monks subscribed at least in part to a naturalistic model. For example, it was common, following the rule of St. Benedict, that sick monks be given special considerations including a diminished work load and a special diet.[23] Also, children in the monastery were to follow special health rules. When conditions required, the inhabitants of the monastery who were ill were placed in the infirmary. Indeed, the existence of an infirmary or hospital was basic to the monastic complex of buildings.[24] There is also considerable evidence that bleeding as a medical procedure was a routine practice in most monasteries.[25] In addition, the monks maintained herbal gardens in which special plants were cultivated and these were boiled, ground, dried and treated in a variety of other ways according to recipes which were concocted in order to be efficacious in the treatment of various maladies.[26] In short it is clear that within the monastery a naturalistic medical model existed and indeed flourished side by side with whatever religious explanations the monks may have had with regard to the etiology and treatment of disease. Children were clearly the beneficiaries of this aspect of monastic medicine.

Notes

1   E.H. Ackerknecht, in *A Short History of Medicine* (Baltimore: Johns Hopkins University Press, 1982) summarizes the concensus regarding supernatural causation and illness as follows: "Christianity originally held its own theory of disease; disease was either punishment for sins, possession by the devil, or the result of witchcraft" (p. 81). Laudatory reviews of Ackerknecht's book are: G.A. Lundeboom, *Janus*, 65 (1978), 218; *Journal of the History of Medicine*, 38 (1983), 236; A.S. Lyons, *Clio Medica*, 18 (1983), 271-273; *Journal of the History of the Behavioral Sciences*, 20 (1984), 255-256. In a similar vein, Ell summarizes the theological writings on this subject as follows: "Writers in the Early Middle Ages lost the distinction between physical disease and sin." S.R. Ell, "Concepts of disease and the physician in the Early Middle Ages," *Janus*, 65 (1978), 153-165 (p. 161). For descriptions of the influence of the naturalistic concept of disease in early medieval Europe, see: H. Sigerist, *Studien und Texte Zur frühmittelalterlichen Rezeptliteratur* (Leipzig, 1923); J. Joerimann, *Frühmittelalterliche Rezeptarien* (Zurich, 1925); L. MacKinney, "Bishop Fulbert: Teacher, administrator, humanist," *Isis*, 14 (1930), 285-300; "Tenth-century medicine as seen in the *Historia* of Richer of Rheims," *Bulletin of the Institute of the History of Medicine*, 2 (1934), 347-375; S.W. Jackson, "Unusual mental state in medieval Europe," *Journal of the History of Medicine*, 27 (1972), 262-297; C.H. Talbot, *Medicine in Medieval England* (London: Oldbourne, 1967); Stanley Rubin, *Medieval English Medicine* (New York: Barnes and Noble, 1974).

2   F. Pollack and F. Maitland, *The History of English Law* (Cambridge: Cambridge University Press, 1911); W.S. Holdsworth, *A History of English Law, Volume 3* (Boston: Little, Brown, 1927); K.F. Drew, ed. and trans., *The Burgundian Code* (Philadelphia: University of Pennsylvania Press, 1973); E.H. Freshfield, ed. and trans., *The Procheiros Nomos* (Cambridge: Cambridge University Press, 1928). See also A.M. Platt and B.L. Diamond, "The origins and development of the 'wild beast' concept of mental illness and its relation to theories of criminal responsibility," *Journal of the History of the Behavioral Sciences*, 1 (1965), 355-367.

3   J. Kroll and B. Bachrach, "Sin and the etiology of disease in Pre-Crusade Europe," *Journal of the History of Medicine*, in press.

4   There is considerable hyperbole written about the plight of children in the Middle Ages, much of it stemming from Phillippe Aries, *Centuries of Childhood* (New York: Vintage, 1982) and Lloyd DeMause, "The evolution of childhood," in *History of Childhood*, ed. by Lloyd DeMause (New York: Harper and Row, 1974). For more balanced views of children, see J. Kroll, "The concept of childhood in the Middle Ages," *Journal of the History of the Behavioral Sciences*, 13 (1977), 384-393; Luke Demaitre, "The idea of childhood and child care in medical writings of the Middle Ages," *Journal of Psychohistory*, 4 (1977), 461-490; Mary Martin McLaughlin, "Survivors and surrogates: Children and parents from the ninth to the thirteenth centuries," in *History of Childhood*; Ilene Forsyth, "Children in early medieval art: Ninth through twelfth centuries," *Journal of Psychohistory*, 4 (1976), 31-70; David Herlihy, "Medieval children," in *Essays on Medieval Civilization*, ed. by B.K. Lackner and K.R. Philip (Austin: University of Texas Press, 1978).

5   See Michel Rouche, "Miracles, maladies et psychologie de la foi à l'époque carolingienne en France," *Hagiographie, Cultures et Sociétés: IVe-XIIe siècles* (Paris: Etudes Augustiniennes, 1981), pp. 319-337, for some useful methodological observations on the problems of using hagiographical sources and the value of a quantitative approach. For a discussion and critique of recent works which apply statistical analyses to hagiographical works see John Howe, "Saintly statistics: Review article," *Catholic Historical Review*, 70 (1984), 74-82.

6   J. Kroll and B. Bachrach, "Child care and child abuse in early medieval Europe," *Journal of the American Academy of Child Psychiatry*, in press. There were an additional seventeen sources reviewed which described illnesses in adults, but not in children.

7   Bede, *Historia ecclesiastica gentis Anglorum*, ed. B. Colgrave and R.A.B. Mynors (Oxford, 1969), Bk. III, ch. 12; Bk. IV, chs. 8, 14; Bk. V, ch. 3; Gregory, *Historia Francorum*, ed. B. Krusch and W. Levison, in *MGH, SRM* (Hannover, 1951), vol. I.1: Bk. VI, ch. 29; Bk. X, ch. 15; *Vita Sanctae Aldegundis*, chs. 13, 17 (*AASS*, Jan.); *Vita Sanctae Waldetrudis* (*AASS*, Apr.), ch. 14; *Miracula Genovefae*, chs. 31, 42, 48, and *post obit.* ch. 4 (*AASS*, Jan.); Andre, *Miracula Sancti Benedicti*, Bk. IV, ch. 3; Bk. V, ch. 14; Bk. VII, ch. 5 (*Les miracles de Saint Benoît*, ed. E. de Certain [Paris, 1958]); Bede, *Historia abbatum monasterii in Wiremutha*, ed. C. Plummer (Oxford, 1896), chs. 41, 45; Walahfridus Strabo, *Vita tertia Galli*, ed. B. Krusch, in *MGH, SRM* (Hannover, 1902), vol. IV, Bk. II, chs. 13, 36, 37, 38, 39, 42, 43; *Vita Romarici*, ed. B. Krusch, in *MGH, SRM* (Hannover, 1902), vol. IV, ch. 7; Flodoardus, *Annales*, ed. Ph. Lauer (Paris, 1905), *an.* 919; and *anon. Vita Cuthberti*, ed. B. Colgrave in *Two lives of S. Cuthbert* (Cambridge, 1940), chs. 15, 17. All abbreviations and other *sigila* follow the form set out in *Mediae Latinitatis Lexicon Minus*, eds. J.F. Niermeyer, *et al.* (Leiden, 1984).

8   Skilled physicians, Bede, *Hist. Abbat*, ch. 45; Strabo,

Vita tertia Galli, Bk. II, ch. 36.

9   Anon, *V. Cuth.*, ch. 17; and Gregory, *Hist.*, Bk. X, ch. 15, for surgery on testicles.

10 Bede, *Historia*, Bk. V, ch. 3. See C.H. Talbot, pp. 127-131, for a discussion of the importance of astrology in determining the timing and location for blood-letting. See also L.E. Voights and M.R. McVaugh, *A Latin Technical Phlebotomy and Its Middle English Translation* (Philadephia: American Philosophical Society, 1984).

11 *Mirac. Genov.*, ch. 31.

12 Peter Brown, "The rise and function of the holy man in late antiquity," in Peter Brown, *Society and the Holy in Late Antiquity* (Berkeley: University of California Press, 1982), p. 147.

13 *V. Romarici*, ch. 7.

14 Bede, *Historia*, Bk. III, ch. 12; Bk. IV, chs. 8, 14, are good examples.

15 In his 1906 Harvard lectures, Pierre Janet said the following in regard to hysterical blindness and other hysterical visual symptoms: "But there is a [perceptual] sense so interesting from the point of view of hysteria, and the alterations of which are so characteristic for the comprehension of this neurosis that I want to devote to it as much time as possible, and it is the reason why our study on the hysterical disturbances of the perceptions must be, above all, a study on the diseases of vision." Pierre Janet, *The Major Symptoms of Hysteria* (New York: Macmillan, 1907).

16 E.H. Reynolds and M.R. Trimble, *Epilepsy and Psychiatry* (New York: Churchill Livingstone, 1981); T.L. Riley and A. Roy, *Pseudoseizures* (Baltimore: Williams and Wilkins, 1982); S.V. Ramani, L.F. Quesney, D. Olson, and R.J. Gumnit, "Diagnoses of hysterical seizures in epileptic patients," *American Journal of Psychiatry*, 137 (1980), 705-709.

17 R.L. Fantz, "Pattern vision in young infants," *Psychological Record*, 8 (1958), 43-47; M.S. Banks, R.N. Aslin, and R.D. Letson, "Sensitive period for the development of human binocular vision," *Science*, 190 (1976), 675-677; C.M. Mistretta and R.M. Bradley, "Effects of early sensory experience on brain and behavioral development," in *Studies on the Development of Behavior and the Nervous System*, Volume 4, ed. by G. Gottlieb (New York: Academic Press, 1978), pp. 215-248; M. Hofer, *The Roots of Human Behavior* (San Francisco: W.A. Freeman, 1981).

18 Andre, *Mirac. S. Benedicti*, Bk. IV, ch. 3.

19 C. Kennedy and F.D. Carroll, "Optic neuritis in children," *Transactions of the American Academy of Ophthalmology and Otolaryngology*, 64 (1960), 700; M.M. Cohen, S. Lessell, P.A. Wolf, "A prospective study of the risk of developing multiple sclerosis in uncomplicated optic neuritis," *Neurology*, 2 (1979), 208; A.B. Baker and L.H. Baker, eds., *Clinical Neurology*, Volume 4 (Philadelphia: Harper and Row,

1984), Chapter 66, pp. 42-55.

20 Bede, *Hist. abbat.*, ch. 45.

21 F. Leneman, "The Guillain-Barré syndrome: Definition, etiology, and review of 1100 cases," *Archives of Internal Medicine*, 118 (1966), 139; S.C. Melnick and T.H. Flewett, "Role of infection in the Guillain-Barré syndrome," *Journal of Neurology, Neurosurgery, and Psychiatry*, 17 (1964), 395; R.D. Adams and M. Victor, *Principles of Neurology* (New York: McGraw-Hill, 1981).

22 See Carl Haffter, "The changeling: History and psychodynamics of attitudes to handicapped children in European folklore," *Journal of the History of the Behavioral Sciences*, 4 (1968), 55-61.

23 Benedictus de Nursia, *Regula monachorum*, ed. Ph. Schmitz (Maredsous, 1946), chs. 34, 35, 36, 37, 39. For a very useful guide to the regulations concerning life in the monastery as well as concerning what actually occurred with regard to children, see the section on Rules and Customs (pp. 119-122) and the section on Life and Activities (pp. 137, 139-141) in Giles Constable, *Medieval Monasticism, a Select Bibliography* (Toronto: University of Toronto Press, 1976).

24 Percy Flemming, "The medical aspects of the medieval monastery in England," *Proceedings of the Royal Society of Medicine*, Section of the History of Medicine, (1928), 25-36. See also Stanley Rubin, especially the chapter on Monastic Medicine (pp. 172-188). For the elaborate infirmary at Saint Gall, see W. Horn, *The Plan of St. Gall* (Berkeley, 1979), 3 vols. and for more easily accessible copy of the plan of the infirmary facilities, see MacKinney, *Early Medieval Medicine*, pl. I.

25 See C.H. Talbot, and Edward Kealey, *Medieval Medicus* (Baltimore: Johns Hopkins, 1981) for discussions of blood-letting. Lynn Thorndike, *A History of Magic and Experimental Science*, Volumes I and II (New York: Columbia University Press, 1923) also provides more than twenty references to bleeding in the late classical and medieval literature.

26 Teresa McLean, *Medieval English Gardens* (New York, 1981), begins her study with a chapter on "The Monastic Garden" and observes (p. 28), "Infirmarers were the first specialist gardeners, growing the herbs needed to keep the community healthy..." She goes on to conclude that "Benedictine nuns earned themselves widespread acclaim for their teaching and dispensing of medicine to all who needed it." For a source of great importance, see Walahfridus Strabo, *De cultura hortorum carmen*, ed. E. Dummler, in MGH, *Poet. lat.* (Berlin, 1884), II, pp. 335-350. See also L.E. Voights, "Anglo-Saxon plant remedies and the Anglo-Saxons," *Isis*, 70 (1979), 250-268, (p. 254); J. Riddle, "Theory and practice in medieval medicine," *Viator*, 5 (1974), 157-184; and J. Riddle, "Ancient and medieval chemotherapy for cancer," *Isis*, 76 (1985), 319-330.

Monastic Minting in the Middle Ages

Alan M. Stahl

As in other periods of history, coinage in the Middle Ages was a governmental right and function. In many parts of medieval Europe, however, minting was carried out by a variety of individuals and groups other than the monarch, claiming rights to this activity by royal privilege or feudal tenure. Among such minters was a sizeable number of monasteries, especially in France and in the Empire. While most of this monastic minting was based on a claim of royal privilege, charters are not extant for all cases, and some that exist appear to have been forged.[1] The nature of this monastic involvement in coining varied with time and place, but in no instance does it appear that monks or nuns actually worked in the mint.[2]

Since the meaning of mint names on Merovingian coins is the subject of debate, the appearance of the names of monasteries on gold tremisses is of uncertain significance.[3] In the Carolingian period, the names of monasteries appear in the position generally used for the names of urban mints. This apparently indicates that imperial mints were located at certain monasteries, probably to take advantage of a periodic market there.[4] The earliest extant minting privilege to a monastery is from Louis the Pious to Corvey in 833. It authorized a *moneta publica nostrae auctoritatis* there because of the lack of a market; however, no coinage is known with the mint name of Corvey for the next century and a half.[5] In 861 Lothar granted the monastery of Prum minting rights, also citing the need there for a market.[6] In 889 Odo granted minting rights to the monastery of Saint Philibert in Tournus; a charter of Charles the Simple to the same house in 915 specified that the coins bear the royal name and type and be in accordance with royal standards.[7] On later coins, the name of the king was dropped and the original patron of the monastery, Valerian, replaced Philibert, to whom the house had been rededicated in the Carolingian period.[8]

Monasteries frequently profited from the minting of coinage, even of mints removed from their locality. In 965 the monastery of Saint Michael in Luneberg was granted a tithe of the tolls of Bardowick, including the profits of the mint operated there by the archbishops of Bremen.[9] The origin of the rights of Cluny to operate a mint is unclear; tenth- and eleventh-century grants are of doubtful authenticity. In any case, the coinage of Cluny in her own name is rare and was probably of little importance. Of more profit to the monastery, no doubt, was the tithe it received to important coinages of Aquitaine and of Bearn.[10]

The abbots of Bury Saint Edmunds maintained a mint under their own control from the reign of Edward the Confessor until the fourteenth century. Though the monastery retained all the profits from the coinage and was identified as the mint, the coins followed the general appearance and standard of royal coinage, with the king's portrait and name on the obverse; though occasionally the minting practices at Bury failed to keep pace with those of the rest of the kingdom.[11]

In the early tenth century, the abbey of Saint Martin of Tours was granted the right to mint coins *percussam proprii*, that is with their own images rather than in accordance with royal types. The pennies of Tours, with their punning tower obverse type, became among the most widely respected in eleventh- and twelfth-century France; they appear commonly in hoards throughout the kingdom. When Philip Augustus extended his royal coinage in the lands won from England at the beginning of the thirteenth century, he based his issues for the region on the types of the Abbey of Saint Martin, thus creating the *denier tournois*, which was to stand as a base of the French monetary system until the Revolution.[12]

The Cluniac priory of Souvigny was another French monastery with a significant coinage; it appears to have been the principal mint for Cluny and the other houses of the order. The documentation for this minting is very sparse, but the height of independent coinage by Souvigny appears to have been in the twelfth century. In the thirteenth century, local lay lords shared in the minting, and by the fourteenth century this coinage, like most other French seigneurial issues, gave way in the face of the efforts of Capetian kings to establish monetary hegemony throughout the realm.[13]

Though many of the monasteries of the Empire with Merovingian and Carolingian foundations acquired minting rights and minted through the Middle Ages, those which were to develop the most important coinages were chiefly the Imperial abbeys founded in the tenth and eleventh centuries, which received minting rights along with markets and tolls at or soon after the time of their foundation.[14] The histories of the dozens of monastic mints in present-day Germany, Austria, Switzerland, Belgium and the Netherlands is complex and, in many cases, obscure, but a review of the coinage of Quedlinburg, a convent on a branch of the Elbe in Saxony, can illustrate many of the vicissitudes of monastic minting in the Empire. Quedlinburg was founded in 936 by Otto I, the first of a series of imperial houses in the diocese of Halberstadt; within the next century fourteen convents and seven monasteries were established in the region.[15] In 994 Otto III gave the convent the right to market, to tolls and to coinage.[16] Five other Saxon monasteries received minting rights with markets in the late tenth century, after which period such new privileges become rare.[17] While other Saxon convents later lost their direct imperial status, and hence many of their rights and lands, those like Quedlinburg which had daughters of emperors as their abbesses were able to keep their status.[18] The earliest coins attributed to the mint of Quedlinburg are from the reign of Otto III and from the abbacy of his sister Adelheid, just after the turn of the millenium (Ill. 1).[19] Coins with the name of Otto appear in hoards from around the year 1000, while those of Adelheid are found in

deposits made a few decades later. Though Quedlinburg coins appear in at least thirty-six hoards of the eleventh century, they do not seem to have been a major currency; they never appear as more than two percent of a hoard, and are usually less than one percent.[20] In the later eleventh century Quedlinburg maintained its strong imperial ties in the persons of two daughters of Henry III, who successively ruled the house for a total of five decades; it was one of only three Saxon houses which remained loyal to Henry IV through the Investiture Contest.[21]

The twelfth century appears to have been prosperous and peaceful for Quedlinburg. Its coinage in the first half of the century gained a bit of ground in comparison with that of its neighbors, though few hoards date from the period (Ill. 2).[22] In the middle of the century, like other mints of the region, Quedlinburg began producing bracteates: large, thin, single-sided coins, with complicated scenes. One such coin of the abbess Beatrice II depicts her seated between towers, with two female figures beneath (Ill. 3).[23] Another bracteate of Beatrice shows four

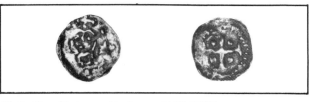

Ill. 2. Quedlinburg, Gerburg, 1113-1137.

Ill. 3. Quedlinburg, Beatrice II, 1138-1160.

Ill. 1. Quedlinburg, Adelheid I, 999-1044.

Ill. 4. Quedlinburg, Beatrice II, 1138-1160.

figures surrounding the abbess; details on these coins are seldom clear enough to distinguish attributes of these figures, but they are usually assumed to be women of the convent (Ill. 4).[24] A bracteate showing an abbess alone in an architectural framework has been variously attributed to Beatrice and her successor Adelheid III (Ill. 5).[25] Another bracteate of about the same period shows an abbess seated next to a male figure with sword and standard. It is likely that the male figure represents the lay advocate of the monastery, who may have taken charge of the minting during the *sede vacante* between Beatrice and Adelheid.[26] The question of

the rights of an advocate over a convent was settled by Frederick Barbarossa in 1188, when he determined that the abbess of Eschenwege had all rights over the coinage itself, while her advocate had only the bann over legal questions arising out of coinage and one third of fines.[27] A document of the period of Agnes II at the end of the century has a witness identified as Henricus *"monetarius"*; it was probably drawn up at a daughter house of the convent within the same town (Ill. 6).[28]

The abbacy of Sophia of Brehna in the early thirteenth century was a stormy one. Sophia was of a family committed to the Welfish cause, while the advocates of the abbey were of the Hohenstaufen party. In 1206 the abbess received a charter from Innocent III supporting her in all of her rights, including the striking of coinage (Ill. 7). In the following two decades Sophia attempted to install an advocate of her choice, while the opposing advocate supported a rival claimant for the title of abbess. After several attempted settlements, Sophia was removed and was replaced by Bertrade Krosigk, favorite of the Hohenstaufen.[29]

The coinage of the abbesses of Quedlinburg was

Ill. 5. Quedlinburg, Beatrice II, 1138-1160 or Adelheid III, 1162-1184.

Ill. 6. Quedlinburg, Agnes II, 1184-1203.

Ill. 7. Quedlinburg, Sophia, 1203-1224.

Ill. 8. Quedlinburg, Bertradis I, 1225-1229, Gera mint.

Ill. 9. Quedlinburg, advocates, fourteenth century, Weida mint.

not limited to the mint in that town. They had received land in Gera in Thuringia from Otto III, and by the end of the twelfth century were receiving profit from a mint there. Their Thuringian coins have two large branches added to the usual attributes of the figure of the abbess (Ill. 8). By 1237 the rights to this minting had been granted to their advocates in Gera, presumably in exchange for a payment.[30] Such purchase of coinage rights as a monastic advocate was one of the few ways that a lay noble could become a minter; in the Hohenstaufen period new minting rights were granted chiefly to Imperial free cities and a few court officials.[31] In the course of the fourteenth century the advocates of Gera minted coins with no reference to the abbess of Quedlinburg and transferred the minting right of Gera within their family (Ill. 9).[32]

By the end of the thirteenth century the bracteates of Quedlinburg had decreased both in size and in complexity of image; they came to resemble the seal used by the abbesses through the Middle Ages: a seated woman holding a lily and book (Ill. 10).[33] In two charters of this period benefitting a male

Ill. 10. Quedlinburg, Gertrude, 1233-1270.

Ill. 11. Quedlinburg, fifteenth century.

Ill. 12. Quedlinburg, Hedwig, 1458-1511.

house in Quedlinburg dependent on the convent, a layman identified as a *monetarius* appears as a witness; it seems that the actual coining for the abbesses was done away from the convent, as the minters do not appear in charters drawn up there. In 1300 the abbess transferred the revenues of the mint to the chapter itself for fifty-and-a-half marks; an idea of the value of this can be inferred from the fact that in the same document she transferred the rights to a mill for forty-seven marks. By this period, the possessions of the abbess were apparently separate from those of the chapter of the house, and coinage was one of her personal rights. Later in the year 1300 the convent sold the new town of Quedlinburg to a lay lord but specifically reserved the right of coinage. When the new town was transferred in 1330 to the town council of the old town, the burghers had to pledge to the abbess not to issue coinage.[34]

By the late fourteenth century, the coins of Quedlinburg were small bracteates with only a crude female head to identify them (Ill. 11). No coins are attributed to the first half of the fifteenth century, nor do documents attest to the mint's activity.[35] In 1451 the abbess of Quedlinburg finally granted minting rights to the burghers of the town for a period of five years only; this contract was renewed for another five years and confirmed by the Bishop of Halberstadt. However, no coins have been attributed to this civic minting.[36] That the abbesses regained their minting rights is demonstrated by the groschen minted under the next abbess, Hedwig of Saxony, some of which copy the issues of her father Frederick II of Saxony, and others of which bear the heraldic arms of the convent (Ill. 12). The coinage of the convent of Quedlinburg continued into the modern period, finally giving way to the coinages of its lay neighbors in the eighteenth century.[37]

For some medieval monastic houses, coinage represented a source of income to supplement that derived from agricultural exploitation, tithes, tolls and other revenues. It was also a sign of the political status which these houses held in the temporal sphere. While the physical participation of a monk or nun in the minting process might have been considered unacceptable, the institutional activity of the monastery in coinage was firmly established in law and jealously guarded against encroachment.

Notes

1 E.G. Eschwege, Essen, Nivelles, Zurich, and Remiremont, whose privileges are unknown, and Lindau, whose purportedly Carolingian privilege appears to be a twelfth-century forgery: Dorothea Menadier, "Das Münzwesen der Reichsäbtissen," *Zeitschrift für Numismatik*, 32 (1915), 194.

2 The four stage evolution of minting privileges set forth by Soetbeer and widely repeated is useful for categorization, but should not be considered a fixed chronological sequence: Adolf Soetbeer, "Beiträge zur Geschichte des Geld- und Münzwesens in Deutschland," *Forschungen zur deutschen Geschichte*, 6 (1866), 31-37; cf. Karl Theodor Eheberg, "Über das ältere deutsche Münzwesen und die Hausgenossenschaften," in *Staats- und socialwissenschaftliche Forschungen*, ed. G. Schmoller, Bd. II, Heft 5 (Leipzig, 1879), 7-9.

3 My conclusion that Merovingian coins were under royal control goes against most of the literature on the subject: Alan M. Stahl, *The Merovingian Coinage of the Region of Metz*, Numismatica Lovaniensia 5 (Louvain-la-Neuve, 1982), 131-35.

4 Jean Lafaurie, "La surveillance des ateliers monétaires au IXe siècle" in *Histoire comparée de l'administration, IVe-XVIIIe siècles*, ed. W. Paravicini and K.F. Werner, Beihefte der Francia 9 (Munich, 1980), 486-96.

5 Wilhelm Jesse, *Quellenbuch zur Münz- und Geldgeschichte des Mittelalters* (Halle, 1924), pp. 14-15, #44; Philip Grierson, "Money and Coinage under Charlemagne," in *Karl der Grosse, I Persönlichkeit und Geschichte* (Dusseldorf, 1965), p. 535.

6 Jesse, *Quellenbuch*, p. 15, #45.

7 Traute Endemann, *Markturkunde und Markt in Frankreich und Burgund vom 9. bis 11. Jahrhundert* (Constance, 1964), p. 102; Reinhold Kaiser, "Münzprivilegien und bischöfliche Münzprägung in Frankreich, Deutschland und Burgund im 9. - 12. Jahrhundert," *Vierteljahrschrift für Sozial- und Wirtschaftsgeschichte*, 63 (1976), 303.

8 Faustin Poey d'Avant, *Monnaies féodales de France*, 3 vols. (Paris, 1958-62), III, 181-84.

9 Vera Jammer, *Die Anfänge der Münzprägung im Herzogtum Sachsen (10. und 11. Jahrhundert)*, Numismatische Studien 3, 4 (Hamburg, 1952), 37.

10 Adrien Blanchet, "La monnaie et l'église," *Revue Numismatique*, Ser. 5, 12 (1950), 63-4. Poey d'Avant, *Monnaies féodales*, III, 179-81.

11 John Craig, *The Mint* (Cambridge, 1953), pp. 13 and 41.

12 Eheberg, *Münzwesen*, pp. 19-20; A. Dieudonné, *Monnaies féodales francaises*, Manuel de numisma-

tique française 4 (Paris, 1936), pp. 365-67.

13 Dieudonné, *Monnaies féodales*, pp. 104-06; Etienne Fournial, *Histoire monétaire de l'occident médiéval* (Paris, 1970), pp. 148-57.

14 Jammer, *Anfänge der Münzprägung*, pp. 27-33; Leo Santifaller, *Zur Geschichte des ottonisch-salischen Reichskirchensystems*, Österreichische Akademie der Wissenschaften, Philosophisch-historische Klasse, Sitzungsberichte 229, Abhandlung 1 (Vienna, 1954), pp. 63-65.

15 Anton Ulrich von Erath, ed., *Codex Diplomaticus Quedlinburgensis* (Frankfurt am Main, 1764), p. 3, #5; Karl Leyser, *Rule and Conflict in an Early Medieval Society: Ottonian Saxony* (London, 1979), p. 65.

16 Erath, p. 25, #33; MGH, DD II.2, #155.

17 Jammer, *Anfänge der Münzprägung*, pp. 28-30.

18 Theodor Mayer, *Fürsten und Staat; Studien zur Verfassungsgeschichte des deutschen Mittelalters* (Weimar, 1950), p. 38.

19 Hermann Dannenberg, *Die deutschen Münzen der sächsischen und fränkischen Kaiserzeit*, 4 vols. (Berlin, 1876-1905), I, 241-2.

20 Jammer, *Anfänge der Münzprägung*, p. 69; pp. 122-69.

21 Hans-Erich Weirauch, *Die Güterpolitik unter der Grundbesitz des Stiftes Quedlinburg im Mittlelalter* (Halle, 1937), 133.

22 Jammer, *Anfänge der Münzprägung*, p. 122 (Aschen II), 152 (Prague), 157 (Santersleben), and 167 (Weddewarden).

23 Ulrich Klein, "Münzen der Stauferzeit" in *Die Zeit der Staufer*, ed. Reiner Haussherr, 4 vols. (Stuttgart, 1977), I, 143, #189.28.

24 Klein, "Münzen," I, 143, 189.29.

25 Adalbert Düning, *Übersicht über die Münzgeschichte des Kaiserlichen freien weltlichen Stifts Quedlinburg* (Quedlinburg, 1886), p. 16; Klein, "Münzen," I, 143, 189.34.

26 D. Menadier, "Münzwesen," 246-55. A bracteate in the Berlin collection in the name of Beatrice with five figures, the center and one other of whom has a sword, is probably also from this interregnum: Arthur Suhle, *Hohenstauferzeit im Münzbild* (Munich, 1963), p. 15.

27 Von Graba, "Münzen der Benedictiner-Frauabtei in Eschwege," *Archiv für Bracteatenkunde*, 4 (1898-1906), 106-7.

28 Erath, *Codex Diplomaticus*, 110-11, #41.

29 Erath, p. 124, #6; Weirauch, *Güterpolitik*, pp. 145-53.

30 Berthold Schmidt and Carl Knab, *Reussische Münzgeschichte* (Dresden, 1907), pp. 1-14.

31 Richard Scholz, *Beiträge zur Geschichte der Hoheitsrechte des deutschen Königs zur Zeit der ersten Staufer (1138-1197)*, Leipziger Studien aus dem Gebiet der Geschichte 2, 4 (Leipzig, 1896), pp. 105-07; Richard Gaettens, "Die Münzrechtsverhältnisse der Hohen-

stauferzeit und des nachfolgenden Jahrhunderts," *Blätter fur Münzfreunde und Münzforschung,* 23 (1959), 1-28.

32 Schmidt and Knab, *Reussische Münzgeschichte,* pp. 102-06.

33 H. Ph. Cappe, *Beschreibung der Münzen des vormaligen Kaiserlichen freien weltlichen Stifts Quedlinburg* (Dresden, 1851), pp. 52-61; Erath, *Codex Diplomaticus,* pl. XVII-XXXVIII.

34 Erath, *Codex Diplomaticus,* p. 222, #178; p. 237, #215; p. 320, #393; p. 323, #399; pp. 416-7, #165-6.

35 J. Menadier, "Quedlinburger Pfennige des vierzehnten Jahrhunderts," *Berliner Münzblätter,* 102 (February, 1889), cc. 921-23; rpt. in *Deutsche Münzen; Gesammelte Aufsätze,* 4 vols. (Berlin, 1891-1922), I, 56-59.

36 Erath, *Codex Diplomaticus,* p. 759, #197; p. 766, #208; Düning, *Übersicht,* pp. 23-4.

37 Düning, *Übersicht,* pp. 25-35.

Photographs courtesy of the American Numismatic Society, New York.

The Monastic Idea of Justice in the Eleventh Century

Geoffrey Koziol

The antipathy of twelfth-century monastic reformers towards litigation is well known. Norbert of Xanten, for example, condemned all litigation wholesale; and his attitude would have been unhesitatingly seconded by all contemporary reformers, including, of course, the monks of Cîteaux.

> It is our intent [wrote Norbert] never to sue for what belongs to another, to make no claim through litigation, pleas, or secular judges, over that which has been taken from us; nor will we bind anyone with anathema for bringing any injury or damage upon us.[1]

Dereine explained this attitude by saying that the reformers hoped to avoid all worldly entanglements and, in particular, the pursuit of landed wealth which had typified earlier Benedictine monasticism.[2] Cistercians and Premonstratensians did not seek lands, or tithes, or privileges. They would therefore not need to litigate in order to uphold property rights and defend privileges. Hence, the attitude towards litigation was determined by the twin urges of the reformed orders: their flight from the world and their rejection of wealth. This interpretation is certainly correct, and finds direct corroboration in early Cistercian statutes. But one suspects that something else is at work too. The reformed orders did not simply oppose litigation because it inevitably resulted from the pursuit of wealth and required worldly involvement. They also tried to replace one idea of social order with another. That is, they were not simply reacting negatively against abuses. They were also expressing a more positive vision of social relations, one in which men would be governed not by law but by love.[3] Early Cistercian houses, for example, fell into many disputes with neighboring families and with other houses of the order.[4] The Cistercians were not distinctive because they avoided disputes. What was special about them is that they rejected formal litigation as a way of settling disputes. Instead of going to court they preferred to negotiate pacts or concords with their rivals, sub-

stituting the concord of peace for order imposed by judgment.[5] In so doing they claimed only to be following the precept of Paul, given to the Ephesians (4:3), to maintain "the unity of the spirit in the bond of peace."[6]

Given this emphasis on love rather than law, one can perhaps understand that the reformed orders were not simply reacting against earlier Benedictines' worldly involvement or pursuit of wealth through litigation. I say "not simply" because these were surely considerations. But they were also reacting against earlier monastic attitudes towards social order in which the idea of love played little role, unless, perhaps, it was that love which builds the community by cutting off diseased members. Contrast, for example, the Cistercian emphasis on love and concord with the attitudes expressed in a prayer called the "clamor to God."[7] This was a prayer said by monks when they sought God's aid against their enemies. First the monks humiliated their relics. That is, they set them rudely on the ground in front of the altar—humiliated, because the saints' enemies had desecrated their lands; humbled, because one could address a just petition to God only in the guise of a prostrate suppliant requesting the Lord's mercy. Candles on the altar were extinguished. The monks chanted without removing their cowls, intoning psalms which beseeched God's mercy. And then the monks, prostrate like their relics, made their petition. This version is taken from the *Liber Tramitis* of Cluny.

> In the spirit of humility and with contrite soul we come before your sacred altar, before your most holy Body and Blood, Lord Jesus, Savior of the world, and we render ourselves guilty against you because of our sins, for which we are justly afflicted. To you, Lord Jesus, we come. To you, prostrate, we clamor because proud and iniquitous men, made audacious by others, have risen against us on all sides. They seize the lands of this, your sanctuary, and of other

churches subject to it, plundering them and laying waste to them. They force your poor cultivators of these lands to live in grief and hunger and nakedness. They kill with swords and instruments of terror; and even our property, which blessed souls have bequeathed to this place for their salvation and by which we are supposed to live in your holy service— even this they have seized and taken away from us with violence. O Lord, this your holy church, which you founded in ancient times and raised to the honor of the always blessed Virgin Mary, resides in sadness; and there is no one who can console it and free it, if not you, our God. Rise up then, Lord Jesus, in our aid. Comfort us and aid us. Battle those who battle against us and break the pride of those who afflict us and your place. O Lord, you know who they are and what their names, and their bodies and their hearts were known to you before they were born. Therefore, God, by your strength teach them justice. Make them know their misdeeds. Free us by your mercy. Do not turn away from us, O God, who clamor unto you in affliction; but because of the glory of your Name and the mercy by which you founded this place and raised it in honor of your Mother, send us peace and deliver us from our present danger.[8]

Nothing could be farther from the Cistercian idea of order founded on love. Here the monks voice no love. What they are interested in is vengeance against their enemies. "By your strength teach them justice." *Justifica in virtute tua.* This is perfectly proportional justice—a kind of talion in which the avenger is God rather than the victim. God shall rise up against those who have risen up against him and battle against those who battle against him. He shall humble those who are proud and raise those who are humble. And though the monks end their prayer with a plea for peace, this is not a "bond of peace" between men but a peace which is deliverance from evil men.

Monks and canons clamored to God, but they also clamored to earthly lords. To make clamor to a lord was, in fact, one of the ordinary ways of demanding that he do justice.[9] In at least one case, which involves the abbey of St.-Eloi of Noyon, the monks made the parallels between the two types of clamor explicit.[10] First they clamored to the bishop of Noyon. Then they humiliated the relics of St.-Eloi, an early bishop of the see, and made clamor to God. In this way joining clamor to the current bishop with the humiliation of his predecessor's relics, the monks in some sense constrained the bishop by humiliating his own patron.[11]

As this incident shows, the monks did not believe that the divine vengeance sought of God was qualitatively different from the kind of justice sought of an earthly lord. Far from it, God's justice was

regarded as a model for earthly princes. What monks sought from God was protection for the humble and vengeance against the proud who oppressed them. And throughout the early Middle Ages monks told God's earthly vicars that for them, too, true justice lay in protecting the humble and vanquishing the proud.[12] Alcuin, for example, had told Charlemagne that his praise, glory, eternal reward lay in his zeal to correct the people.[13] Three centuries later, Abbot Suger praised Louis VI for exacting vengeance against those who oppressed the poor—the poor meaning the powerless and unarmed, who of course included monks and clerics.[14] Nor was vengeance the prerogative and duty of kings alone, since William of Poitiers extolled the same twin virtues in the duke of Normandy: To the poor he showed mercy; to their oppressors, vengeance.[15]

Underlying this identification of justice with vengeance was the assumption that monastic property was inviolate. The clamor itself stated the justification for this assumption: "Our property, which blessed souls have bequeathed to this place for their salvation and by which we are supposed to live in your holy service—even this they have seized and taken away from us. . . ." In other words, monastic lands had been set aside to support the monks intercessory prayers to God and the saints on behalf of the donors. Loss of lands affronted the piety of the donors and made the task impossible. The violation of monastic property was therefore a violation of the cult. Furthermore, to attack monastic property was also to attack the heavenly powers directly, for monks regarded their lands as the property of God and his saints. Those who usurped or abused the property of monasteries therefore abused God directly and committed sacrilege.[16] From all these perspectives, threats to property were threats to religion. Given these assumptions, disputes over property could not be compromised. The rivals of monks were the enemies of God whose claims had to be suppressed entirely.

The monks' intransigent attitude towards their rivals was also reinforced by conservative political values. The great political change of the eleventh century was the emergence of independent castellans. In some cases they may have received their jurisdictional and military powers by the express delegation of kings, counts, and bishops; in other cases they had perhaps simply usurped them. But whether or not their powers were legitimate, they used those powers to increase the revenues or labor services they received from merchants or peasants.[17] Monks opposed these claims partly because their own dependents and revenues were affected. They also opposed them because they believed that the castellans were undermining legitimate political authority. Kings, counts, and bishops—these lords derived their authority from God. And their authority was a ministry to protect the humble. But castellans had no authority, no ministry, only power; and that power derived solely from their military and economic superiority. There was nothing divine about it.[18] When castellans maintained their power at the expense of monastic lands and peasants, monks easily came to regard their enemies as the enemies of a political order authorized by God.

And they treated them as such, particularly the monks of northern France, where the wealth and influence of monasteries greatly depended on kings and counts. Whether one reads *vitae*, or chronicles, or charters from this region, one is consistently struck by the hostility of monks towards those castellans and knights who dared dispute their lands and revenues. Their own accounts of disputes reveal no effort to understand the motivations of their rivals. Or rather, they reveal that monks understood their enemies' motivations in simplistic and dichotomous terms. Their antagonists were quite simply "proud," "presumptuous," "insolent," "iniquitous," "malicious," "greedy," "deceitful," "full of hate," "raging," "depraved," "avaricious," "malicious," and just plain "evil."[19] That is why they taxed peasants, imposed labor services on them, extended their jurisdictions at the monks' expense, and committed a host of other sins at the expense of monastic privileges and property.

These epithets were more than just random slurs. They served to place disputes within a time-honored iconography that divided the world into antagonistic forces. The clamor itself cast the parties into their proper iconographic roles. By clamoring to one of God's ministers, abbot and monks identified themselves with the figure of the humble and prostrate petitioner who recognized the lord's divinely ordained authority and deserved his mercy. At the same time the monks' clamor identified their enemy as an enemy of God and of those who ruled in place of God. Such a man deserved not mercy but vengeance. The monks' clamor is again the best statement of the idea: Where the prostrate suppliant deserved protection, the enemy of God deserved to be broken, to be prostrated in turn. The psalms which monks chanted daily told the story with its familiar ending: God would have mercy on his miserable ones. He and his vicars would exalt the humble and cast down the proud. That was the justice for which monks clamored to God and to those who ruled by the grace of God.

On the one hand the powerful, on the other the poor. The corrupt against the pure. The worldly against the naive. This dichotomous interpretation of conflict saw ordinary disputes as part of a providential battle. All history was nothing more than the working out of a ceaseless contest between the two Cities.[20] Disputes were part of that larger contest.[21]

As an example, take one of the more frequent sets of epithets—that which derided lords and knights as mad or insane. The idea was imbued with cosmological overtones. According to Raoul Glaber, "the gift of reason" is what placed man above the beasts; and it was in his reason that man most especially assumed the image of God. Conversely, to act unreasonably was to descend to the level of the raging beasts of the wild. As Raoul explained:

> Just as moderation and love of its author—in other words, true humility and perfect charity—maintain the good of man's reason, so concupiscence and madness destroy its usefulness and render it worthless. By not repelling these evils man is made like the beasts, whereas by not serving them he is made conformable to the image of the Savior.[22]

The author of the *Gesta Episcoporum Cameracensum* reached back to an ancient tradition to make the same point: In the early days of the human race, men wandered about like wild beasts, without the benefit of reason and knowing neither human nor divine laws. Only when they gathered together in cities, wrote the chronicler, "did they learn to cultivate faith and to hold to justice and grow accustomed to obey others willingly."[23]

Reason was therefore bound up with devotion to God, because reason was the faculty that made men like God. But as usually happened with religious attributes in the early Middle Ages, reason was also treated as a social attribute, since reason taught men to subordinate their own desires to social norms. As the social norms of the early Middle Ages reinforced the traditional order, so reason led men and women to be loyal to lords and to honor servants of God. Conversely, to live according to one's own desires—and this is what Raoul meant by *concupiscentia*—this was to abandon the rules of society, clouding one's reason and returning to the level of the beasts.

Those who rebelled against kings and princes were frequently accused of madness.[24] So too were heretics, rebels against God's church.[25] By extension, any action against any part of the divine order was proof of insanity. Since monastic lands and privileges were part of that order, the enemies of monks were also enemies of God, who forfeited the image of God, which was reason. The cartulary of St.-Bertin, for example, tells the story of one Bodora, a lowly "subminister" who oppressed St.-Bertin's peasants at Chaumont. He was warned to desist. He did not. Far from it, he extended his abuses by seizing the peasants' cattle as they grazed in the fields and using them for his own lord's work. He had been warned once by the abbot's representative. Now he was told that he was about to suffer "the rod of heavenly wrath." And in fact, Bodora immediately underwent a metamorphosis. His head was turned around, so that his face was where his hair should have been and his hair was where his face should have been. His neck swelled and so did his lips. "What greater wonder could be seen or written about?" wrote the abbey's chronicler. "There was nothing human in him that remained to be looked upon." And to complete Bodora's descent into unreasoning bestiality, the wretch began to bellow like a bull. Again, note the proportionate justice. Bodora was punished by being transformed into what he really was: a beast without language, without reason, without the image of God.[26]

Given these presuppositions, it will come as no surprise that eleventh-century litigation was perceived as the restoration of reason. King Henry I, in a charter for St.-Médard, called society "an order of reason."[27] The purpose of litigation was to gain the triumph of the *ordo rationis*. The entire judicial process was, in fact, nothing more than a forum in which reason could be manifested. The enemies of monks were challenged to make "reasonable contradiction" of the monks' claims or to "show reason" for their own exactions.[28] Conversely, a court would justify its condemnation of one of the parties by claiming that "his response was void of all just reason."[29] Finally, a defeated party might approach the abbot whose claims he had opposed and beg absolution, "having listened to saner counsel."[30]

As this last example shows, the end of a dispute also sometimes required the defeated party to beg absolution from the abbot and monks. This was probably always the case when he had been excommunicated during the course of a dispute.[31] It was also often enough the case when no excommunication is otherwise mentioned.[32] Take the example of Baldwin, the eldest son of Lord Raoul of Baxincourt, in the Vexin. His father had given St.-Martin of Pontoise a small parcel of land. Baldwin later reneged on the gift, even though the monks claimed that he had explicitly consented to the donation. But at last he came to recognize that he had acted unjustly, and he went to St.-Martin to renounce his claim.

> When the brothers had been convened, Baldwin himself went before the altar of the blessed confessors, Martin and Germain; and falling at the feet of the Lord Abbot Theobald, with many tears he begged to be absolved.[33]

With or without explicit mention of prostration, this type of ending is common in eleventh-century disputes. Henry I forced Robert of Choisy to do penance for his oppression of St.-Médard of Soissons.[34] Dodo of Heudicourt and his brother confessed that they had sinned in unjustly claiming an allod from Mont-St.-Quentin.[35] A man who had made excessive exactions on an estate of St.-Germain-des-Prés was said to have sinned.[36] The oppressor of a monastery is a sinner and must therefore do penance, a public penance which is, in fact, a public humiliation. Those who oppressed the humble have been humbled in turn, forced to prostrate themselves at the feet of their victims. The godly have triumphed over the godless. This is how order was restored in eleventh-century litigation.

There was, of course, a role for mercy in this idea of justice. After all, mercy was the necessary corollary of strict judgment, as political theorists never tired of reminding kings and princes.[37] But even so, mercy was due only to those who showed themselves humble, reasonable, and submissive. As the Frankish coronation orders said, the proud deserve to be cast down. They merit judgment. Only the humble deserve to be exalted. They alone merit mercy. As an example of how this might work in litigation, take a dispute between the abbot of Mont-St.-Quentin and one Nicholas, son of Albuin. Nicholas had claimed the revenues of a church possessed by Mont-St.-Quentin. The abbot recognized Nicholas' right to half of those revenues, but not to the entirety. Nicholas and the abbot were equally convinced of their right; and so the dispute dragged out, until the lord of Peronne negotiated a compromise, a compromise enunciated in terms of Nicholas' humility towards his rightful lord.

> Recently having accepted the counsel of Lord R[obert] of Peronne and his wife, Lady A[delide], and that of several clerics and laymen, Nicholas entered the presence of the Lord Abbot H[enry] and his monks; and all that he had claimed . . . he set aside entirely, without any [right of] revindication; and he relinquished it into their power. After this was done, the aforesaid lords and also the clerics and laymen, taking into consideration the humility of that young man, asked on his behalf that the Lord Abbot show him some mercy for his life. The Lord Abbot, receptive to their entreaties, with the assent of his monks con-

ceded that he might hold for his life those two parts which . . . he had relinquished.[37]

The pattern was not uncommon. Monks did allow mercy to be shown to their enemies, but only after their enemies had submitted, had shown themselves obedient, submissive, and humble.[38]

Perhaps we can see now how truly important was the new monastic attitude towards justice in the early twelfth century. Cistercians and Premonstratensians were consciously trying to create a new idea of social harmony in which consensus replaced deference, and love between men replaced judgment against sinners. Hence, Cistercian monks negotiated their disputes with local lords and knights, as each party compromised its rights in order to achieve peace. And though I have said quite enough, I would like to close with one coincidence: It is well known that Cistercians, and many of the reformed orders generally, received their strongest support from among the lesser nobility and knights.[39] In other words, the monks who popularized a new vision of concord between monks and laity came from the very social classes that the old Benedictines had regarded as the embodiment of evil. If we knew nothing more, this would go a long way towards explaining their rejection of the old Benedictine idea of justice.

Notes

1 Cited by Charles Dereine, "La spiritualité 'apostolique' des premiers fondateurs d'Affligem (1083-1100)," Revue d'histoire ecclésiastique, 54 (1959), 49.

2 Loc. cit.

3 On the importance of "love" in twelfth- and thirteenth-century dispute-settlement see Michael Clanchy, "Law and Love in the Middle Ages," in Disputes and Settlements: Law and Human Relations in the West, ed. John Bossy (New York: Cambridge University, 1983), pp. 47-68. It is surprising, however, that Clanchy does not make more of the Cistercian emphasis on love and concord, which is discussed by Jean Leclercq, Monks and Love in Twelfth-century France: Psychohistorical Essays (New York: Oxford University, 1979).

4 A glance at any Cistercian cartulary will show this, as that of Notre-Dame d'Ourscamp, ed. A. Peigné-Delacourt (Amiens: Société des Antiquaires de Picardie, 1865). See also Giles Constable, Monastic Tithes from their Origins to the Twelfth Century (Cam-

bridge: Cambridge University, 1964) for Cistercian litigation over tithes. Dereine, loc. cit., noted the same phenomenon with respect to Affligem, as did Ludo Milis with respect to Arrouaise: L'ordre des chanoines réguliers d'Arrouaise: son histoire et son organisation (Bruges: De Tempel, 1969), I, 101 and n. 3.

5 Again evident from the cartulary of monasteries such as Ourscamp. But the Cistercian emphasis on concord emerges equally clearly from the order's early statutes. See Statuta capitulorum generalium ordinis Cisterciensis, ed. J-M Canivez (Louvain: Bibliothèque de la Revue d'histoire écclésiastique, 1933), IX (1116-1220), xxviii (bonum pacis et caritatis inter se reforment), pp. 13 (indissolubili inter se pace custodienda diligentissime tractent), 20 (communi assensu omnium abbatum, si possit concorditer fieri, definiatur), 26 (non debent abbates vel monachi aut conversi nostri ordinis interesse placitis, nisi suis aut aliorum de ordine nostro), 29 (convocent vicinos abbates ordinis nostri, et eorum consilio pacem ineant), and 36, where mediation of disputes is counselled (Si... inter eos familiariter per aliquos religiosos mediatores componi non poterit.).

6 See Peigné-Delacourt, p. 11; The Letters of Bernard of Clairvaux, trans. Bruno Scott James (Chicago: Regnery, 1953), p. 26; Bernard of Clairvaux, Tractatus et opuscula, vol. III of Sancti Bernardi Opera, ed. J. Leclercq and H-M Rochais (Rome: Editiones Cistercienses, 1963), p. 87.

7 Discussed by Patrick Geary, "L'humiliation des saints," Annales, E.S.C., 34 (1979), 27-42.

8 Liber Tramitis Aevi Odilonis Abbatis, ed. Petrus Dinter, Corpus Consuetudinum Monasticarum, 10 (Siegburg: Schmitt, 1980), pp. 244-47.

9 Cartulaire de Notre-Dame de Noyon (Beauvais, Arch. départ. de l'Oise, G 1984), ff. 60-62; Cartulaire de Notre-Dame d'Homblières (Paris, B.N. lat. 13911), ff. 64-67; Recueil des actes de Philippe Ier, roi de France, ed. Maurice Prou (Paris, 1908), nos. 27, 75; Chartes de coutume en Picardie, ed. Robert Fossier, (Paris: Bibliothèque nationale, 1974), no. 2; Cartulaire de l'abbaye de Saint-Corneille de Compiègne, ed. E-E Morel, I (Montdidier, 1904), no. 15; William Mendel Newman, Le domaine royal sous les premiers capétiens (Paris: Sirey, 1937), p.j. 2, pp. 226-228; Léon Levillain, Examen critique des chartes merovingiennes et carolingiennes de l'abbaye de Corbie (Paris, 1902), no. 40; Hariulf, Chronique de l'abbaye de Saint-Riquier, ed. F. Lot (Paris, 1894), 4.22; Recueil des chartes de l'abbaye de St.-Germain-des-Prés, ed. René Poupardin (Paris, 1909), I, no. 52; Cartulaire du chapitre de la cathédrale d'Amiens, ed. J. Roux (Amiens, 1897), no. 9. Alongside the clamor there were many expressions which spoke of the judicial lord as monks spoke of God in their liturgies. See for example Cartulaire de l'abbaye de St.-Vaast d'Arras rédigé au XIIe siècle par Guimann, ed. Van Drival (Arras, 1875), pp. 45-46: idem rustici ad abbatem recurrebant . . . cum querela deplorantes;

Miraculi Sancti Adalhardi, II.1 (M.G.H. SS, 15.2, p. 863): *quaerimoniam lacrimabilem coram regis praesentia fuderunt et super hoc eius consilium et auxilium imploraverunt;* and especially the plaint of Abbot Fulk of Corbie to Pope Alexander II (*Gallia Christiana*, 10, instr. 286-7): *ad te spes nostra, in te defensio nostra, patiente membro compati debet et caput.*

10 *Cartulaire de St.-Eloi de Noyon* (Paris, B.N. lat. 12669), f. 109v.

11 See Bernard Meehan, "Outsiders, insiders, and property in Durham around 1100," *Studies in Church History*, 12 (1975), 50 for another case in which a bishop was regarded as occupying the see of a saint and therefore responsible to the saint.

12 As kings were told at their coronations that it was their responsibility to "scatter the proud and raise the humble": See the coronation orders of Edgar, Fulrad, and Stavelot printed in P.E. Schramm, *Kaiser, Könige und Päpste* (Stuttgart: Hiersemann, 1968), II, 237-8, 247, III, 90-93, 100, no. 21. See also Abbo of Fleury's warning to Kings Hugh and Robert to keep in mind their duty to "spare the subject and cast down the proud" (PL 139.473).

13 J.M. Wallace-Hadrill, *Early Germanic Kingship in England and on the Continent* (Oxford: Clarendon, 1971), pp. 105-108; Schramm, II, 219, 237, 246.

14 Claude Aboucaya, "Politique et répression criminelle dans l'œuvre de Suger," *Mélanges Roger Aubenas* (Montdidier: Faculté du droit et des sciences économiques de Montpellier, 1974), pp. 9-24; Gabrielle M. Spiegel, "Defense of the realm: evolution of a Capetian propaganda slogan," *Journal of Medieval History*, 3 (1977), 117-118.

15 Raymond Foréville, "Aux origines de la renaissance juridique," *Moyen Age*, 58 (1952), 57-8.

16 Among many possible examples see the *Miracula Sancti Adalhardi* II.1 (M.G.H. SS, 15.2, p. 863): *quicquid erga sanctum Petrum et sanctum Adalardum deliquerat, emendavit; Miracula Sancti Walarici* (A.A.S.S. Apr., I), p. 29: *suum contra sanctum Dei Walaricum forisfactum recognoscens; Cartulary of Mont-St.-Quentin*, ed. William M. Newman, no. 4: *idem alodium martyris . . . cepit usurpare.* (A typescript of this last work was provided to me by Prof. John Benton of the California Institute of Technology. The work has not been published, and I am indebted to Prof. Benton for allowing me to use it.)

17 Georges Duby, *Rural Economy and Country Life in the Medieval West*, translated by Cynthia Postan (Columbia, South Carolina: University of South Carolina, 1968), pp. 182-231; idem, *The Early Growth of the European Economy: Warriors and Peasants from the Seventh to the Twelfth Century* (Ithaca: Cornell University, 1974), pp. 172-76; Robert Boutruche, *Seigneurie et féodalité*, 2 ed. (Paris: Aubier, 1968-1970), I, 126, II, 125-40; Robert Fossier, *La terre et les hommes en Picardie* (Paris: Béatrice-Nauwelaerts, 1968), II, 495-6, 510-18, 560.

18 A good example is one Godefrid, described as *vir potens et fortis et tanto superbior, quanto potentior, nec hominem metuens nec Deum: Vita Arnulfi* II.23-24 (A.A.S.S. Aug., III, pp. 23-24).

19 *Vita Arnulfi*, pp. 234-5; Hariulf, 4.6 (proud and faithless), 4.9 (proud and rapacious), 4.21 (malicious, avaricious, cupidinous), 4.22 (unjust and impious); *Herimanni Liber de Restauratione monasterii Sancti Martini Tornacensis* (M.G.H. SS, 14), pp. 236-7 (savage); *Cartulaire de Notre-Dame d'Homblières* (Paris, B.N. lat. 13911), F. 41 (malicious); *Recueil des chartes de . . . St.-Germain-des-Prés*, I, no. 51, p. 80 (rapacious); Jules Tardif, *Monuments historiques: cartons des rois* (Paris, 1866), no. 243, p. 152 (malicious); G. Bourgin, *La commune de Soissons et le groupe communal soissonais* (Paris, 1908), p.j. 8 (malicious); C.V. Langlois, *Textes relatifs à l'histoire du Parlement depuis les origines jusqu'en 1314* (Paris, 1888), no. 1 (evil and treacherous); *Recueil des actes de Philippe Ier*, nos. 75 (bearing hate) and 125 (perverse, mad, raging); *Cartulary of Mont-St.-Quentin*, no. 44 (*acer in animo*); *Vita Arnulfi*, p. 241 (*vituperabilem vitam*); Hugh of Flavigny, II.11, p. 377 (insolent). For denunciations of the accused as mad or insane see the following: Hariulf, 4.7, 4.21; *Recueil des actes de Philippe Ier*, no. 125; *Chartes de l'abbaye de Jumièges*, ed. J-J Vernier (Paris, 1916), I, no. 11; *Cartulaire de Notre-Dame d'Homblières*, f. 41. Cf. also *Les miracles de saint Benoît*, ed. E. de Certain (Paris, 1858), pp. 181, 225, 281, 296; *Vita Arnulfi*, pp. 77-79; *Miracula Sancti Adalhardi* (M.G.H. SS, 15.2), p. 86.

20 Jean Leclercq, "Monastic historiography from Leo IX to Callistus II," *Studia monastica*, 12 (1970), 76-86; R.W. Southern, "Aspects of the European Tradition of Historical Writing: The Classical Tradition from Einhard to Geoffrey of Monmouth," *Transactions of the Royal Historical Society*, series 5, vol. 20 (1970), 182-84; Jacques Chaurand, "La conception de l'histoire de Guibert de Nogent," *Cahiers de Civilisation Médiévale*, 8 (1965), 382-84.

21 For other examples of this combative attitude towards disputes see Cantin's remarks on public disputation in the late eleventh century in *Etudes de civilisation médiévale (IXe-XIIe ss.) Mélanges offerts à Edmond-René Labande* (Poitiers: Centre d'Etudes Supérieures de Civilisation Médiévale, 1974), pp. 91-103.

22 Raoul Glaber, *Les cinq livres de ses histoires*, ed. Maurice Prou (Paris, 1886), III.viii.29, p. 78.

23 Cited by R.W. and A.J. Carlyle, *A History of Medieval Political Theory in the West* (Edinburgh: Blackwood, 1903-1936), III, 107 n. 3.

24 Raoul Glaber, III.ix.31 (p. 80), III.ix.36 (p. 85); Guillaume de Jumièges, *Gesta normannorum ducum*, ed. J. Marx (Paris, 1914), 7.1 (p. 116), 7.2 (p. 117), 7.4 (p. 119).

25 Raoul Glaber, II.xi.22 (pp. 49-50), III.viii.26 (pp. 74-75).

26 *Cartulaire de l'abbaye de Saint-Bertin*, ed. B. Guérard

(Paris, 1841), c. xviii (pp. 190ff.)

27 *Cartulaire de St.-Médard de Soissons* (Laon, Arch. départ de l'Aisne, H 477), ff. 66v-67. Cf. also RHF 11.580-82: *tam jussu potentissimi Principis, quam praesentium ratione firmissima nobilium victus.*

28 *Recueil des chartes . . . de St.-Germain-des-Prés*, I, no. 49, p. 78 (*propter rationabilem contradictionem*); RHF 14.624 (*rationem diceretis*); *Cartulaire de Notre-Dame de Noyon* (Beauvais, Arch. départ. de l'Oise, G 1984), ff. 60-62 (*redderet rationem*).

29 Hariulf, 4.7.

30 Cf. *Miracles de saint Benoît*, p. 307; Raoul Glaber, III.viii.30.

31 Hariulf, 4.21; *Cartulaire de l'abbaye de Saint-Vaast*, pp. 381-2.

32 *Cartulaire de l'abbaye de Saint-Martin de Pontoise*, ed. J. Depoin (Pontoise, 1895-1909), no. 21; *Cartulaire de l'abbaye de Saint Vaast*, pp. 277-8; *Miracula Sancti Walarici* (A.A.S.S., Apr., I), p. 29.

33 *Cartulaire de St.-Martin of Pontoise*, no. 21.

34 RHF 11.580-82.

35 *Cartulary of Mont-St.-Quentin*, no. 15.

36 *Recueil des chartes . . . de St.-Germain-des-Prés*, I, no. 49, p. 78.

37 *Cartulary of Mont-St.-Quentin*, no. 22.

38 See the case translated in *Sources for the History of Medieval Europe*, ed. Brian Pullen, (Oxford: Basil Blackwell, 1971), pp. 32-33; also Hariulf, 3.32 and 4.7, 4.21; Léon Levillain, "Jugement d'un pape Jean en faveur de Corbie," *Moyen Age*, vol. 19, pp. 33-4; *Cartulaire de Notre-Dame de Noyon* (Beauvais, Arch. départ. de l'Oise, G 1984), ff. 60-62.

39 Leclercq, *Monks and Love*. On the ways in which the chivalric background of the Cistercians permeated their organization and ethos, see Southern, *Western Society and the Church in the Middle Ages* (Harmondsworth, England: Penguin Books, 1970), pp. 250-59.

Deconstructing the Monastery
in Umberto Eco's *The Name of the Rose*

Helen T. Bennett

Umberto Eco in *The Name of the Rose* addresses the relationships among language, structure, meaning, and truth, and undermines those relationships to invite a deconstructionist reading of the work. Eco creates a structure which appears to generate meaning just when it is not doing so, and Eco appears to be accurately re-creating an outside reality just when he is not doing so. Initially, I will relate the novel's overall plot and strategy to the aims and methods of deconstruction and then demonstrate the suitability of a medieval setting for that endeavor. Having established those connections, I will argue that Eco's primary image for the meanings of the novel and for how the text comes to have meaning (if it does) is the monastery, a constant force, presence, and symbolic signifier in the work.

To understand the novel's movement on at least one level, the reader must understand some basic tenets of deconstruction. As its name implies, deconstruction is defined by what it does not intend to be or to do: it is not a systematic method for generating interpretations of texts. Developed in answer to structuralism, its post-structuralist aims are to undermine structuralist beliefs and strategies. Jonathan Culler in the introduction to *On Deconstruction* sums up the opposition:

> Structuralists take linguistics as a model and attempt to develop 'grammars'—systematic inventories of elements and their possibilities of combination—that would account for the form and meaning of literary works; post-structuralists investigate the way in which this project is subverted by the workings of the texts themselves. Structuralists are convinced that systematic knowledge is possible; post-structuralists claim to know only the impossibility of this knowledge; ... structuralists ... optimistically elaborate theoretical metalanguages to account for textual phenomena; post-structuralists skeptically explore the paradoxes that arise in the pursuit of such projects and stress that their own work is not science but more text.[1]

Deconstructionists see the fundamental quality of all language, literary and otherwise, as metaphoricity. Eco himself calls deconstruction a "metaphysics" which "argues that neither philosophy nor science is able to give us truths, only texts. Deconstructionism is the interpretation of text without regard to any hypothetical outside reality it might be assumed to describe."[2] Instead, texts acquire meaning in relation to other texts, a concept called "intertextuality." Deconstructionists subject texts to rhetorical questioning to find paradoxes or tensions between meanings of words, between what a text says and how it says it, between literal and figurative meanings. They do not seek to resolve the tensions, only to expose them. As Eco says, "Inside the text, there is not one immutable meaning or truth, intended or otherwise, but many."[3]

Eco's novel *The Name of the Rose* is presented as an exercise in deconstruction. The novel gives us texts the validity of which is immediately called into question—by the presence or absence of other texts. The page before the preface contains the words "Naturally, a Manuscript," drawing us towards a shared set of associations: an accidental discovery, obscure origins, a text removed from us in time and space, a doubtful authenticity. These associations all prove accurate, and the text continues to be self-conscious and self-questioning as the fictional modern translator 1) questions the existence of an original fourteenth-century manuscript for the French version of the seventeenth-century edition that has come into his hands, and 2) questions the point of publishing his Italian rendering of the French version. His only evidence that the original manuscript existed consists of passages quoted in a translation of a translation of another work. Both the original manuscript and the original of the work containing the quotations are now "impossible to find."[4] Furthermore, once the translator has completed his translation, even the version he was working with disappears from his grasp. This is a clear case of the truth of a text being determined by other texts. Full of doubts about authenticity, the translator decides to publish his work for "sheer narrative pleasure" (p. xviii), as if a text could exist for some other purpose.

Adso, the fourteenth-century German novice who as an old man is the author of the translated manuscript, begins his narration believing in the truth of texts, at least of a text created by God. Adso's first words are, "In the beginning was the Word and the Word was with God, and the Word was God," which constitutes the one "never-changing event whose incontrovertible truth can be asserted." This one truth is contrasted with human faulty vision of it: "we see in fragments (alas, how illegible) in the error of the world, so we must spell out its faithful signals even when they seem obscure to us" (p. 3). Here the text is true, but the human reader is unequal to the reading. As he tells his story, Adso struggles to tell the whole truth, to recount events faithfully, even when he would rather avoid the telling. Yet, by the end of the novel, he too is questioning language, meaning, and truth. Addressing the unknown reader, he says, "it is a hard thing for this old monk, on the threshold of death not to know whether the letter he has written contains some hidden meaning, or more than one, or many, or none at all" (p. 610).

Linguistic structures (texts) are set up as vehicles for containing meaning and then subverted or destroyed. The plot structure follows a similar course. Among other things, the novel is a detective story. Conventionally, this genre contains a detective who is a masterful reader of a text of clues which lead to the solution of the crime and the apprehension of the villain. Implicit in this format is the assumption that clues form a pattern, and with multiple crimes, that the acts themselves occur in a pattern. Red herrings notwithstanding, all a mystery should require is the right mind to decipher the clues. William of Baskerville, the English monk-detective, has a wonderfully rational mind filled with the entire spectrum of medieval learning and a humane spirit to handle that knowledge. The first moment we meet him, he is figuring out patterns of clues: he discerns that the abbey horse Brunellus has disappeared. Throughout the novel, he deciphers codes—in the manuscript of Venantius, in the floorplan and inscriptions of the library—and clues to crimes, figuring out that victims were not murdered where their bodies were found, for example. And throughout the novel, he is proud of what he can decipher and clarify. We come to trust

him and believe that minor setbacks are just conventional devices for prolonging the suspense, that William will figure out the meaning of it all by the last page. Yet, while William does ultimately unravel the mystery, he has been given the key clue to penetrating the library by Adso's dream (a non-rational activity), has come upon the murderer's method by accident, and has discovered that the answer to all the murders is that there is no pattern, that, in fact, the murderer imposed an erroneous pattern only after he heard that William was looking for that particular one. In the end, William is unable to save any lives or manuscripts or the monastery itself.

All along, however, part of William's temperament has been unsuited to detective work. He repeatedly argues against factionalism when it comes to truth. He sees Jorge as the Antichrist because of Jorge's excessive love for his own truth. William, sounding very like a deconstructionist, concludes that "the only truth lies in learning to free ourselves from insane passion for the truth" (p. 598). He refuses to subscribe to absolute dichotomies of right and wrong, truth and falsehood, orthodoxy and heresy, always promoting the relativity of truth, a position that has led him to resign his post as inquisitor. The roles of inquisitor and detective share some characteristics, but it is only at the end of the novel that William has become equally disillusioned with both occupations and equally suspicious of the structures that supposedly lead both practitioners to the truth.

Eco thus sets up a text which questions its own authenticity and a reader of texts who tries to impose rational patterns where none exist in order to give meaning to events. The Middle Ages is a very appropriate period in which to locate the process of setting up structures to create meaning only to subvert or destroy the structures or their validity. When Adso says "the universe is surely like a book written by the finger of God, in which everything speaks to us of the immense goodness of its Creator, in which the humblest rose becomes a gloss of our terrestrial progress" (p. 333), he is expressing the medieval neoplatonists' view on the metaphoricity of the world. But as Eco points out in *Semiotics and the Philosophy of Language*, different choices of metaphorical correspondences can lead to contradictory interpretations, as in the lion standing for Christ or the mouth of Hell, an example that also appears in the novel (p. 285). Medieval scholars chose among the interpretations the one confirmed by some authoritative text. Thus, they were guided in their reading of God's text (Creation) by human texts, and right and wrong reading becomes a question of intertextuality or "cultural networks, not ontological realities."[5] And medieval rationalists even questioned the relationship between signs and things, how humans make connections and give meaning.[6] When Adso speaks of "a great theophanic design that sustains the universe, arranged like a lyre, miracle of consonance and harmony"(p. 334), he is articulating the medieval emphasis on structure and order.[7] Yet, during the Middle Ages, a dominant image and imminent reality was the Apocalypse, the ultimate destruction of order.[8] The paradoxical nature of human thought and belief in the Middle Ages is congenial to Eco's purposes in the novel.

Eco's strategy in creating structures and re-creating realities that invalidate themselves or that are accurate in entirely other and contradictory ways than they at first seem to be is most apparent in his treatment of the monastery. He is adamant about trying to close the gap between sign and thing and to re-create with accuracy. In his *Postscript to The Name of the Rose*, Eco says he spent a year working on "the construction of the world."[9] He describes his research on the monastery:

> I conducted long architectural investigations, studying photographs and floor plans in the encyclopedia of architecture, to establish the arrangement of the abbey, the distance, even the numbers of steps in a spiral staircase. . . . When two of my characters spoke while walking from the refectory to the cloister, I wrote with the plan before my eyes; and when they reached their destination, they stopped talking.[10]

He includes in the introductory material a diagram of the abbey to enhance the reader's belief in its structure and its reality. The modern translator finally believes in the existence of an original manuscript because he finds accurate descriptions of the labyrinthine library in another text. Both instances represent textual proofs of external realities and therefore deserve to be regarded with suspicion. Furthermore, the seeming order and harmony that the monastery represents—Adso sees in it a reproduction of the order of the universe—is continuously being violated. Monks are consistently sneaking into parts of the monastery at times when those parts are officially off limits. Doors that are supposed to be locked are repeatedly opened; secret passageways with coded entrances are used to get to forbidden places and to indulge sacriligious desires—lust, greed, thirst for power, pursuit of knowledge out of intellectual pride. What is supposed to be an international group of monastic scholars is actually a group of men struggling for various kinds of control and power.

Just as Eco gives us a historically accurate spatial structure that masks a disorder, so he utilizes the monastic structuring of time to simulate stability: the text is divided into seven days (an appropriate duration for constructing a world); within each day, time and text are measured by canonical hours. Paralleling the diagram of the abbey, readers are given a guide to the canonical hours, this time by the fictional narrator. But this temporal order is also illusory. The canonical hours are never used twice in exactly the same way to organize the text, leading up to the seventh day, when the only two chapters are both called "Night," not a canonical designation of time. And the narrator providing the guide admits to being "puzzled" because the names of the canonical hours vary in meaning "according to the place and the season" (p. xx). Thus, another structural principle is rendered unreliable.

The dominant part of the monastery, physically, thematically, and allegorically, is the Aedificium, housing from bottom to top the kitchen, the scriptorium, and the library. The Aedificium is the building Adso first notices when he and William approach the abbey. None of the monasteries Adso has seen before have anything to compare with it. To him it represents order and harmony, but the description consistently implies delusion due to a limited perspective. The octagonal structure "from a distance seemed a tetragon (a perfect form which expresses the sturdiness and impregnability of the City of God)" (p. 15). It is the apparent and not the actual shape that has the first positive allegorical significance. The northern side of the Aedificium *seems* to grow out of the mountain from an abyss; the cliff *seems* to reach to heaven. As Adso and William get closer, their more accurate vision consists of a recognition of what is invisible. Although the embodiment of God's glory should inspire serenity, Adso speaks of its frightening appearance, particularly on stormy days. Therefore, the appearance changes as well as deceives.

Within the Aedificium, the historical accuracy is also deceptive. Eco places his story between the period when libraries were little more than storage vaults and the time when the library rivaled the church as architectural focus of the monastery.[11] Only certain monasteries were designated for producing manuscripts, but those that were usually had a common scriptorium. The scriptorium might well have been placed over the kitchen—as it is in the novel—to solve the very real problem of heating it.[12] Historical precedents exist for the library over the scriptorium, and in general the library was situated on an upper floor to protect it from flooding, dampness, and fire. One Cistercian monastery even has a spiral staircase connecting the scriptorium and the library.[13] Eco's version of the library's administration is also fact-based. Various monastic orders had elaborate library regulations governing the acquisition of books by the monastery, the ownership of books by the monks, and the supervision of the library and the scribes.[14] Libraries often had two different book collections: the reference collection, housed in the library and fastened by chains to reading desks; and a collection to be distributed for separate reading.[15] At S. Francesco in Assisi, the Mother House of the Franciscan Order erected after the death of the founder, these two collections were named *libreria publica* and *libreria secreta*, respectively. Both the chaining of the reference collection and the name of the lending collection attest to an unwillingness to share the library's holdings freely and openly. This protectiveness is historically evident as well between scribes and their manuscripts. The practice of scraping and reusing vellum, combined with the belief that copying a pious book gave the scribe protection from the devil, often led scribes to end their manuscript with an anathema against anyone who would erase or scrape it.[16]

While Eco begins constructing his library with historical accuracy, the secretiveness is exaggerated to become the dominant characteristic. The catalog of holdings is a chained volume, but all other books are in a library to which only the librarian and his assistant have access. Books are arranged there according to a complex and secret code known only to the librarian and the assistant. Furthermore, the librarian only gets a requested book for a monk if the request is "justified and devout" (p. 81). The library is described as "full of secrets, and especially of books that had never been given to the monks to read" (p. 155).

Solving the mystery of the library becomes synonymous with solving the mystery of the murders and solving the mystery of the novel's meaning. The representation of all the mysteries is the physical form of the library—the labyrinth. Again, Eco plays with historical accuracy and truth. In the *Postscript*, he says that all the labyrinths he found in his research were outdoor labyrinths whereas he needed an indoor labyrinth that was not too complicated to let in the air necessary to spread the fire at the end; he also says he worked for months constructing his labyrinth.[17] Eco fails to mention actual medieval church labyrinths painted on walls and floors in France and Italy, primarily during

the twelfth century.[18] Their exact significance is unknown, but various metaphorical and allegorical significances have been attributed to them: the confusions and snares in the Christian's path, the "entangling nature of sin"; or the path from the house of Pilate to Calvary. One theory posits that those unable to undertake actual pilgrimages could enact a miniature pilgrimage by tracing on their knees the path of the labyrinth on the church floor; wall labyrinths served for pilgrimages performed by the penitent's index finger.[19] In the text of the *Postscript*, Eco also neglects to mention that he takes the very unusual shape of the Aedificium from a pavement labyrinth in the cathedral at Rheims, though a picture of that labyrinth does appear in the book some thirty pages after Eco's discussion on medieval labyrinths.

In addition to actual church labyrinths, literary labyrinths were also popular in the Middle Ages. Together with their religious symbolism, labyrinths were used as a principle of narrative structure; as an image of artistic creation and the suffering that accompanied that work; and as the representation of a place where signs (directional and narrative) lose their meaning. According to critic Piero Boitani, the labyrinth in Chaucer's *The Hous of Fame*, for example, is a place where reality is "fragmented and transformed into its narrative sign, inextricably composed of true and false."[20]

The labyrinth in the novel acquires the medieval significances and others Eco himself describes in his theoretical works. It provides a model for interpreting texts (*The Role of the Reader*) and for structuring knowledge (*Semiotics and the Philosophy of Language*). In both *Semiotics and the Philosophy of Language* and the *Postscript*, Eco identifies several types of labyrinths. One type can be unraveled but contains many blind alleys; this labyrinth represents the process of trial and error.[21] Another type, the rhizome, is a net with every point connected to every other point. It does not have an outside, so it cannot be seen as a whole; in addition, its structure changes through time. For these two reasons, a "global description" is not possible.[22] This type of labyrinth offers the model for structuring knowledge, which can only be structured locally and temporarily.[23]

While Eco says that the library labyrinth in the novel is of the trial and error type,[24] the labyrinth of the novel's meaning turns out to be rhizomatic. William, believing that figuring out the library's labyrinth will bring him to the murderer, must decipher a code just to gain access to the library. The first time he and Adso enter the library, William thinks he understands its layout and gets lost as a result. The next time William and Adso are able to plot out the structure by decoding the inscriptions above the entranceway to each room, and they discover a walled-up room. Although William can interpret clues and figure out circumstances of individual murders, he cannot put together the whole picture until he has penetrated the heart of the labyrinth, the walled-up room. And there he does find the murderer. However, this simultaneous penetration of mysteries does not provide pat solutions. By the time William enters the *finis Africae*, he already knows the non-answers he will receive. Blind, old Jorge has devoted his life to perverting the ends of the library, to suppressing learning, and his efforts have culminated in his turning a text he wanted to conceal into a murder weapon. William already knows that the apparent apocalyptic pattern in the murders was a diversionary tactic, and yet it turns out to be prophetic. The innermost secrets of the abbey's structure having been discovered, the abbey virtually self-destructs by fire, and chaos prevails. The fire begins in the most disorderly room of the library and exposes the weaknesses in the library's structure that have up to now gone undetected. Monks scurry about, haphazardly and ineffectually trying to save the monastery.

According to Eco, William understands that the world "has a rhizomatic structure; that is, it can be structured but is never structured definitively."[25] At the end he is shown once more that figuring out everything can mean figuring out nothing. He has simultaneously succeeded and failed. The paradoxical view of William parallels the contradictions in Jorge's role. A blind man preventing a library from spreading learning, willing to murder to achieve his ends, must clearly be a moral and intellectual villain. Yet, in *Semiotics and the Philosophy of Language*, Eco says "in a rhizome blindness is the only way of seeing (locally), and thinking means to *grope one's way*.[26] The traditional associations with blindness are here reversed and challenge our analysis of Jorge. Interpretation of Jorge must also take into account Argentine writer Jorge Luis Borges, who in life was blind and was director of the National Library of Argentina. Borges uses the image of the labyrinthine library in his story "The Library of Babel," but his consistently provisional position on everything including language and reality is antithetical to Jorge of Burgos' deadly certainty. So how are the final confrontation and conflagration in the novel to be interpreted?

The problem of interpretation is confronted by the old Adso in his writing. He records how, returning to the monastery years after the fire, he finds the Aedificium still standing and scraps of manuscripts scattered in and around the library. Out of these he tries to construct—first he acts as if trying "to piece together the torn pages of a book"; later, after more comprehensive work, he reconstructs "a lesser library, a symbol of the greater, vanished one: a library made up of fragments, quotations, unfinished sentences, amputated stumps of books" (p. 609). It is a structure composed of elements lacking meaning. In these fragments Adso tries to see a message, attribute a meaning, and he fluctuates between seeing clear signs from heaven and seeing no message and no design.

In his prologue, Adso expresses the hope that the reader will find the design where he cannot, but Eco tricks *his* reader into believing in a design that does not exist and would not make any difference if it did. All we have left is the text, and the text is not one thing. The modern translator calls the manuscript "a tale of books" (p. xix), and Eco says "books always speak of other books"[27]—intertextuality. Depending on which parts of which books the reader brings to the novel, readings will differ. In its uncertainty and irridescence, the text can stand. In its declaration of order and meaning created through rigid structure, the monastery, with its false assurances, destroys itself.

Notes

1 Jonathan Culler, *On Deconstruction: Theory and Practice after Structuralism* (Ithaca: Cornell University Press, 1982), pp. 22, 24-25.

2 Melik Kaylan, "Umberto Eco...Man of the World," *Vogue*, April 1984, p. 393.

3 Kaylan, p. 393. For a good introduction to deconstruction, see Christopher Norris, *Deconstruction: Theory and Practice* (New York: Methuen & Co. Ltd., 1982), and Vincent B. Leitch, *Deconstructive Criticism: An Advanced Introduction* (New York: Columbia University Press, 1983).

4 Umberto Eco, *The Name of the Rose*, trans. William Weaver (New York: Warner Books, Inc., 1984), p. xvi. All subsequent references to this work appear parenthetically in the text.

5 Umberto Eco, *Semiotics and the Philosophy of Language* (Bloomington: Indiana University Press, 1984), p. 104.

6 Gordon Leff, *Medieval Thought: St. Augustine to Ockham* (Chicago: Quadrangle Books, Inc., 1958),

pp. 279-290.

7   Discussions of divine versus human text and of the "panmetaphorical attitude" of the Middle Ages appear in Norris, p. 66, *Semiotics and the Philosophy of Language*, pp. 103-105, and Jacques Derrida, *Of Grammatology*, trans. Gayatri Chakravorty Spivak (Baltimore: The Johns Hopkins University Press, 1976), pp. 15-16.

8   In "Umberto Eco's Revelation: *The Name of the Rose*," *Humanities of the South*, No. 61 (1985), pp. 3-5, Lois Zamora analyzes the role of the apocalyptic vision in the novel's meaning and structure.

9   Umberto Eco, *Postscript to The Name of the Rose*, trans. William Weaver (New York: Harcourt Brace Jovanovich, 1983), p. 24.

10 Eco, *Postscript*, p. 25.

11 James F. O'Gorman, *The Architecture of the Monastic Library in Italy 1300-1600* (New York: New York University Press, 1972), pp. 3-4, 9, 17.

12 George Haven Putnam, *Books and Their Makers During the Middle Ages, I 476-1600* (New York: Hillary House Publishers Ltd., 1962), p. 76.

13 Putnam, p. 150.

14 K.W. Humphreys, *The Book Provisions of the Medieval Friars 1215-1400* (Amsterdam: Erasmus Booksellers, 1964).

15 Putnam, p. 152.

16 Putnam, p. 73.

17 Eco, *Postscript*, pp. 28-29.

18 W.H. Matthews, *Mazes and Labyrinths: Their History and Development* (New York: Dover Publications, Inc., 1970), p. 54.

19 Matthews, pp. 67-68.

20 Piero Boitani, "Chaucer's Labyrinth: Fourteenth-Century Literature and Language," *The Chaucer Review*, 17 (1983), 209.

21 Eco, *Postscript*, p. 37.

22 Eco, *Semiotics*, pp. 81-82.

23 Eco, *Semiotics*, p. 83.

24 Eco, *Postscript*, p. 57.

25 Eco, *Postscript*, p. 58.

26 Eco, *Semiotics*, p. 82.

27 Eco, *Postscript*, p. 20.

Fideli famae adscribendam iudicantes
Four Monks in Search of a
Hagiographic Method, 980-1125

Thomas Head

Through the course of the eleventh and early twelfth centuries many monks and canons felt compelled to recompose the sacred history of their foundations.[1] The ravages of the age of invasions had destroyed many of their links to that past. A canon of Meung-sur-Loire, in the Orléanais, expressed typical regret over the hard times which had befallen his foundation. There were few extant written records about its patron saint and the canon compared the loss of such texts to the dispersion of the monastery's property. Charters showed the former wealth of his house, and hagiographic texts would have demonstrated the *virtutes* of its patron. He attributed the absence of antique records either to the lack of a *scriptorium* or to the unrest caused by war. He concluded, "Since we are unable to restore completely these lost properties . . . let us try to restore, which we can, the praises of God in his saint, lest we seem ungrateful."[2] He and his fellow hagiographers moved to fill the void, drawing on the oral and written traditions available to them.

In much of this hagiography, monastic writers pieced together traditions about the long dead saints of their own foundations without employing a conscious critical method. Sometimes, however, a foundation would commission such a work from a hagiographic specialist. Such specialists were more explicitly concerned with the truth of their written sources.[3] I wish to focus on three writers of commissioned works and a fourth who commented on the enterprise of hagiography: Letaldus of Micy and Theodoric of Fleury, both active in the decades around the year 1000, and Hugh of Fleury and Guibert of Nogent, who flourished in the early twelfth century. These writers were hardly unique. Similar examples abound throughout Europe: Two other writers from Fleury, Isembard and Vitalis, also composed commissioned hagiographic works in Neustria.[4] Adso of Montier-en-Der wrote several

hagiographic texts for Austrasian monasteries.[5] A number of foreign hagiographers, including Folcard and Jocelyn, were active in England in the decades after the Conquest.[6]

Letaldus, a monk of Micy near Orléans, composed at least five hagiographic works.[7] The *Miracles of Saint Maximinus,* the earliest, recounted the stories of the founder and patron of Micy, of the monastery itself, and of the veneration of the saint's relics there.[8] Letaldus explicitly wished to reestablish the links of his community with its own past. In the prologue he expressly outlined the principles of his research, principles which would govern his future work at the request of other communities. Letaldus accepted only those stories for which he had eyewitnesses, or which had been handed down by trustworthy written (*literae*) or oral (*traditio vivae vocis*) traditions. "And where there is neither of these things, and there is some question as to whether (an event) happened or not, all men will be silent with me."[9] At various points in the narrative he emphasized the reliability of his sources.[10]

Letaldus' services as a hagiographer came to be in high demand. In the following three decades he wrote four works: for the council of Charroux (on the procession of the relics of St. Junianus to this meeting instrumental in the development of the peace movement), for Bishop Avesgaud of Le Mans (on the life of Julian, the first bishop of that city), for Jouin-sur-Marne (on St. Martin of Vertou whose relics had been translated there), and for Celles-sur-Cher (on St. Eusicius, patron of that monastery).[11]

How did such a man receive and perform these commissions? The *Miracles of Saint Martin* reveals a scholarly monk wandering the French countryside in search of sources:

> Moreover we are going to say scarcely anything about the man of God, Martin, since the book of his life once in the city of Thouars has been burned, and

with it the almost incomparable ornaments of his life also perished. Another small volume, however, remained in which various poems were contained, among which is found an abbreviated life of the holy man himself, told in sweet and pleasing rhymes. And so after I had come unworthy and a monk in habit only to the monastery where the body of the same holy man now rests, I was compelled by the brothers of the place . . . to compose an account in prose from the same poem. Since I was not able to refuse, I wrote, in as much as God permitted it, in prose all those things which the (poem) revealed, with the exception of those things which were said in poetic language; and I expressed (them) in the way of a translator, not word for word, but sense for sense; and I expanded it a bit upon the request of the brothers. But, since a group of older men had lived up to our time, who had committed to memory many things from the (lost) *Life* of the blessed man . . . we thought it right to put down separately whatever we discovered in their account which had not been included in the above mentioned book, making, as it were, another *corpus* of the volume, beginning with those things which Martin did while living in the body and extending on to those things which he accomplished, with Christ working through him, after his death.[12]

Thus he composed two related works for the monastery of Jouin: a new life based on the old *libellus*, and a collection of the saint's miracles, which had occurred both during the saint's life and posthumously.

Similarly at Celles he used an *antiquus schedulus* as a source for the life of Eusicius and interviews with the monks to write the collection of posthumous miracles:

> On the urging of Odulfus . . . we turned the *Tract on the Life of the Blessed Confessor of Christ Eusicius* into prose, (a book) which we did not choose ourselves, but which was taken from ancient codices, not word for word, but sense for sense, in the wary manner of a translator. We followed faithfully those things which were said, not by ourselves, but by an ancient speaker, judging it to be written down from a faithful report (*fideli famae adscribendam iudicantes*). Since many and unnumbered miracles occur almost daily around the venerated tomb of Blessed Eusicius, (Odulfus also) requested that I touch lightly upon these very miracles . . . and commit something to writing . . . for the future use of those who would hear or see it.[13]

In both works Letaldus followed the distinction between written and oral tradition (*litterae* and *tradition vivae vocis*) first drawn in the *Miracles of St. Maximinus*.

Neither the *libellus* nor the *antiquus schedulus*

survives, but Letaldus' source for the *Life of St. Julian* is extant. Goffart has shown that this life was the work of the so-called "Le Mans forger" in the early ninth century, an author who composed a history of that diocese to support the property claims of its cathedral chapter by weaving together passages from earlier hagiographic texts.[14] Letaldus himself realized that the author of the earlier *Life* had contradicted the accounts of Gregory of Tours. More remarkably, Letaldus also recognized that large sections of his source were adapted almost verbatim from the *Passion of St. Denis*, the *Virtues of St. Fursaeus*, and the *Passion of St. Clement*.[15]

Letaldus explained that he sought to see through his corrupt source to an authentic antique tradition: "We therefore have confirmed, as much as we could from the authority of preceding fathers, what we have written about St. Julian, and we have related some things simply according to ancient tradition, but others, which seemed to us less probable, we have omitted."[16] He likened these traditions to the pleasing rhythms of old songs; to add anything new would be jarring and discordant.[17] Letaldus wished to find the kernel of truth which stood behind his source and to write down only those things which were verifiable about the saints: "They ought to be recited in the presence of truth . . . For nothing is pleasing to God, except that which is true. Moreover, there are some who, when they seek to exalt the deeds of the saints, offend against the light of truth."[18] In composing his new *Life* Letaldus omitted virtually every story which his predecessor had borrowed.

Letaldus was interested both in searching out factual error which had entered into the traditions about the saints and in correcting that error. He was remarkably successful, in that his new *Life of St. Julian* was written with the approval of the bishop of Le Mans and became the most commonly used text about the saint in that region, despite the fact that it denied the apostolicity of the diocese's first bishop. A contemporary of Letaldus, Benedict of La Chiusa, fared rather less well when he tried to debunk the similar claim adduced for St. Martial of Limoges. Adhemar of Chabannes, who himself had written some of the crucial texts asserting Martial's apostolicity, publicly accused Benedict of heresy for his failure to accept this tradition of relatively recent invention.[19]

Letaldus was certainly atypical in his ability to discover how his predecessors had factually embroidered upon tradition. More commonly, when monastic authors of this era spoke of a corrupt tradition, they referred to stylistic error. In the tenth century Regino of Prüm had corrected a source "According to the rules of Latin grammar."[20] About the same time Bishop Stephan of Liège had rewritten the *Life of Saint Lambert* because people laughed when they heard the outmoded style of the old work as it was recited in church.[21] In the early eleventh century, Vitalis of Fleury excused the composition of a new *Life of St. Paul of Léon* both because the old one was tediously lengthy and because the Latin of its author (the Breton Wormonoc of Landévennec) was so wretched that reading it became "an onerous burden."[22]

A contemporary, and at one time near neighbor, of Letaldus, Theodoric of Fleury, wrote about the need to expunge corruption from hagiographic texts, focusing on such stylistic matters.[23] Theodoric, a monk of Fleury who was German by birth, left that monastery in the first decade of the eleventh century on pilgrimage for Rome. He never returned. Between 1002 and 1010 he wrote at least seven hagiographic works for Italian communities, of which three survive.[24]

Theodoric composed all three by reworking earlier sources. In the *Life of Pope Martin* he wrote:

> For they (the canons of St. Peter) claimed, and the truth bore them out, to have certain *gesta* of the saint, but *gesta* lied about and falsified in such a rustic style that they frightened rather than soothed educated ears. They ascribed the fault for this lying to the scribe rather than to the author. For what illiterate man untutored in the grammatical arts would have presumed to undertake the great task of declaring the merits of such a great man?[25]

Complaints about the style of antique sources were also voiced by the clerics who commissioned Theodoric's other extant works. One requested the *Life of Ss. Tryphonius and Respicius* because he wished Theodoric, whom he called a "doctor," to improve the style of an older work ". . . so that just as unlearned writers have made bad from good, so too we strive to make good from bad."[26] Similarly, the monks of Monte Cassino attacked ". . . a certain very well-known *grammaticus* of that province who, having been led by supercilious arrogance, was thought to have distorted rather than embellished the story of the life of Firmanus in his prolix and shameless telling."[27]

In the *Life of Pope Martin*, Theodoric treated one incident from the saint's life, the controversy with the Byzantine emperor over Monotheletism, during which Martin was brought to Constantinople for trial. Theodoric used three sources: the chapter on Martin from the *Liber Pontificalis*; Theodore Spudeus' collection of letters concerning Martin; and the same author's *Commemoration of Pope Martin*

(these latter in the translation of Anastasius the Librarian, to whom Theodoric referred as "scribe" in the above-quoted passage).[28] Theodoric claimed to subject his sources to "literary discipline," altering their style, but leaving the factual account intact. He combined them into one continuous narrative, making numerous grammatical changes.[29] Poncelet's analysis of Theodoric's use of sources in the other two extant works shows that he followed a similar course there.[30] For Theodoric, a story's truth was intimately linked to its style. The claims of Theodoric and those who commissioned his works, that the older sources had lost their versimilitude, show how important the question of style was and how relatively small changes in language could affect a work's audience.

Letaldus and Theodoric felt that the traditions of the past had been corrupted, and tried to redress that situation for various religious communities by rewriting those corrupt traditions. Letaldus altered whole stories; Theodoric, their language. Letaldus said that it was impious to falsify the deeds of the saints; Theodoric implied that it was impious to compose those deeds in a bad style. Both authors were concerned with the purity of a textual tradition. Over the course of the following century a sense of a critical or historical method developed, paralleling the growth of "textual communities" chronicled by Brian Stock.[31] One of the best places to look for the flowering of these ideas is in the work of Hugh of Fleury.[32]

A prolific historian, Hugh wrote only one piece of commissioned hagiography, the *Life, Translation, and Miracles of St. Sacerdos*, composed around 1106 at the request of the monks of Sarlat in the Limousin.[33] Like his predecessors, he reworked and criticized an earlier source (an *antiqua series vitae* which is no longer extant):

> . . . in which there are many superfluous things. Moreover, noticing certain details distorted by the fault of the scribes, I have decided to correct it in the modern time; and to describe more decorously and clearly the text of the same story, transformed and improved in its succinct brevity.[34]

Abbot Arnaldus of Sarlat had himself realized the factual corruption of the old *series*, and "forced" Hugh to undertake the task of rewriting it, so that the truth which had been obscured by the earlier text would again be revealed.[35]

For Hugh, as for Letaldus, the truth of the narrative was all important:

> My poor love for Sacerdos was enriched by God's help, to the praise of the confessor, but to add anything in the manner of the *series* is not worthy praise,

but a nefarious deed. For true sanctity and pure religion are not dependent on human lies, and they are on the contrary obscured when wrapped up in a scheme of falsity.[36]

While Hugh thought that the addition of anything false was impious, he deemed it proper to add new stories. The truth of a saint's life was determined not simply by reaching back to the pure antique tradition through the meditation of a corrupted intermediary, as Letaldus had done, but by doing research in other sources: "It is right for the wise man, as I think, to construct the truthful story about an ancient thing, and to replace uncultivated words with more decorous ones."[37]

In his researches, presumably those which resulted in his later *Ecclesiastical History*, Hugh had come across a number of stories relating both to Sacerdos personally and to his times; not only did Hugh add these episodes to his narrative, but he arranged the sources in the margins of his new work.[38] Thus the text which he sent to the monks of Sarlat was not simply a narrative work, but a manuscript arranged much in the manner of a glossed Bible or copy of Gratian.[39] He used the same *topos* as Letaldus to describe how he adapted these new sources into his narrative, "But I am not eager to transcribe word for word, nor to hammer out something entirely in place of the old; but I am eager to bring out sense for sense by improving it, according to the poverty of my literary talent, such as it is. Thus the skill of the reader will be able, by investigating each *series* carefully, easily to accept (mine) as true."[40]

Letaldus and Hugh both realized that the received written tradition about the saints was frequently full of factual error. They differed in one important respect. Letaldus supplemented his one faulty source with oral tradition about both past and contemporary events. Hugh supplemented his source by using other written sources for past events, and oral tradition only for contemporary posthumous miracle stories, an interesting corollary of Stock's thesis about the growing "textualization" of intellectual discourse.

Although Letaldus, Theodoric, and Hugh criticized the written hagiographic record, they did so in the context of continuing the veneration of saints' relics. In 1125 Abbot Guibert of Nogent wrote a large scale investigation into the many possible problems associated with the veneration of relics.[41] He introduced the work as an attempt to solve problems which had arisen with respect to saints' relics because of "vulgar," that is primarily oral, traditions.

The first book of the treatise was a handbook of fraudulent stories. In some cases alleged relics were associated with people who were not truly saints. A boy of a knightly family who died on Holy Friday was venerated as a saint simply because of the time of his death. Many "rustics desirous of novel things" (*rustici rerum novarum cupidi*) came as pilgrims to the tomb and its cult supported by "poisoned" (*infectus*) miracles.[42] In other cases bones were falsely associated with real saints. Bishop Odo of Bayeux had paid much money to the *custos* of the church of Corbeil to obtain the relics of St. Exupery. The man substituted the body of a peasant who shared the name of the saint, and provided a vaguely worded guarantee. Thus Odo had the satisfaction of thinking he had the relics, while Corbeil retained them.[43]

To solve these problems with received tradition, Guibert developed an explicit theory of the relationship of saints' relics to the saints themselves and the role played by written texts in that relationship:

(Relics) are reverenced and honored for their example and their protection. For my part the only authentication which has validity in such matters as determining whether someone (i.e., relic) is to be called a saint is not popular opinion (*opinio*), but the firm tradition of verified ancient sources. For how can you think that someone, as I say, is a saint, if no memory of his authority is known, still less any texts or experience of miraculous signs? I say that even texts are questionable in their efficacy, for there are many tales about these saints whose publication it would be better to defile among the infidels than to use in any way as an example. And even when (these tales) are true, they can be written in such ragged, pedestrian or poetic language . . . that they are believed to be false.[44]

In Guibert's eyes, error, both stylistic and factual, was rampant in the traditions supporting the cult of the saints. He went on to say that not only the falsification of evidence, but even the veneration of dubiously authenticated relics was sinful. Almost grudgingly he admitted that the pious veneration of inauthentic relics, when done in good faith, was meritorious.[45]

Guibert cannot simply be understood as a medieval skeptic, critical of the veneration of relics. For him, the combination of antique texts and contemporary miracles were the only trustworthy guarantee for the *auctoritas* of a saint. Many traditional cults (he specifically mentioned that of St. Martin of Tours) met his criteria.[46] He also believed in miracles, some of which he had witnessed.[47] In general, however, the abbot of Nogent wished to turn the faithful to the cult of the Eucharist, the subject of the following three books. That veneration was fully guaranteed by scripture, open to intellectual discussion, backed by true textual evidence, and controlled by the clergy. His inclinations in this matter were simply the first glimmerings of a massive change in piety toward the veneration of the Eucharist, Marian images, and the relics of recently deceased saints, a change which would culminate in the institution of new standards for the proof of sanctity at the Fourth Lateran Council.

Notes

1   This article comes in part from my study of the long-term growth of hagiography and the cult of the saints in the Orléanais in my unpublished doctoral dissertation, "The Holy Dead and Christian Society: The Cult of the Saints in the Orléanais, 750-1215," Diss. Harvard University, 1985. In the Orléanais, the first half of the eleventh century saw more hagiography composed than in all the rest of the Middle Ages.

2   *Miracula s. Lifardi*, chap. 2; Luc d'Archery and Jean Mabillon, eds., *Acta sanctorum ordinis s. Benedicti*, 1st ed., 9 vols. (Paris: 1669-1701), I, 160. (Hereafter abbreviated as *AASSOSB*.)

3   For a more general consideration of the analysis of the accuracy of sources in medieval hagiography, see Klaus Schreiner "'Discrimen veri et falsi.' Ansatze und Formen der Kritik in dem Heiligen- und Reliquienverehrung des Mittelalters," *Archiv für Kulturgeschichte*, 48 (1696), pp. 1-53; and "Zum Wahrheitsverständnis im Heiligen- und Reliquienwesen des Mittelalters," *Saeculum*, 17 (1966), pp. 131-169. Schreiner primarily considers evidence from the twelfth century and later.

4   Head, "The Holy Dead and Christian and Society," p. 263.

5   On the works of Adso, see Adso Dervensis, *De ortu et tempore antichristi, necnon et tractatus qui ab eo dependunt*, D. Verhelst, ed. (Corpus Christianorum Continuatio Medievalis, Vol. 45; Turnholt: 1976), pp. vi-ix.

6   Antonia Gransden, *Historical Writing in England c. 550 - c. 1307* (London: 1974), pp. 107-111. Jocelyn particularly displayed his critical ability in the *Libellus contra inanes sanctae uirginis Mildrethae usurpatores*, which was edited and discussed by Marvin Colker, "A Hagiographic Polemic," *Medieval Studies*, 39 (1977), pp. 60-108.

7   On Letaldus, see *Histoire littéraire de la France*, 41 vols. (Paris: 1733-1875), VI, 528-537; Barthélemy Hauréau, *Histoire littéraire du Maine*, 4 vols. (Le Mans: 1843-1852), II, 1-10; Ambroise Ledru, "Origines de Lethald, moine de Micy (fin du Xe siècle)," *Le province du Maine*, 16 (1908), pp. 326-328; Max Manitius, *Geschichte der lateinischen Literatur des Mittelalters*, 3 vols. (Handbuch der Altertumswissenschaft, IX, 2; Munich: 1911-1931), II, 426-432; Jean-Paul Bonnes, "Un lettré du Xe siècle. Introduction au poème de Letald," *Revue Mabillon*, 33 (1943), pp. 23-47; and Cora Lutz, "Letaldus, a Wit of the Tenth Century," *Viator*, 1 (1971), pp. 97-106. For some revisions of the earlier accounts, see my discussion of Letaldus, "The Holy Dead and Christian Society," pp. 130-134.

8   *Miracula s. Maximini (Bibliotheca hagiograhica latinorum 5820)*; *AASSOSB*, I, 598-613. (Hereafter abbreviated as *BHL*.) From internal evidence this work was written in 986-987.

9   *Miracula s. Maximini*, chap. 1; *ASSOSB*, I, 598.

10   See, for example, *Miracula s. Maximini*, chaps. 16 and 28; *AASSOSB*, I, 602 and 605.

11   (1) *Delatio corporis s. Juniani ad synodem Karoffensem (BHL 4564)*; *AASSOSB*, IV, part 1, 434-435. This work was composed in 988/989. (2) *Vita s. Juliani (BHL 4544)*; J.-P. Migne, ed., *Patrologia Latina*, 221 vols. (Paris: 1844-1864), CXXXVII, 781-796 (hereafter abbreviated as *PL*). This work was composed after 1000, the year of Avesgaud's consecration. (3) *Vita et Miracula s. Martini Vertavensis (BHL 5667-5668)*; *Acta sanctorum*, Jean Bolland, et al., eds., (Antwerp and Brussels: 1643-present, October X, 805-817. (Hereafter abbreviated as *AASS*.) Portions of this text were reedited by Bruno Krusch, *Monumenta Germaniae historica, Scriptores rerum merovingicarum*, Vol. 3 (Hannover: 1896), pp. 567-575. (Hereafter abbreviated as *MGH, SRM*). Krusch first attributed this text to Letaldus; *MGH, SRM*, Vol. 4 (Hannover: 1902), p. 771 (4) *Vita et Miracula s. Eusicii (BHL 2754-2756)*; Phillippe Labbe, ed., *Novae bibliothecae manuscriptorum librorum . . . . , tomi I and II* (Paris: 1683), II, pp. 372-376 and 463-466. I have edited the preface to the *Vita* and demonstrated reasons for attributing the entire work to Letaldus, "The Holy Dead and Christian Society," pp. 415-425. Letaldus also wrote a mock epic poem, *De quodam piscatore quem ballena absorbuit*. For the critical edition of this work, see Bonnes, "Introduction au poème de Létald," 37-45. Jan Ziolkowski has shown how Letaldus there adapted folkloric tradition, "Folklore and Learned Lore in Letaldus' Whale Poem," *Viator*, 15 (1984), pp. 107-118.

12   *Miracula s. Martini Vertavensis*, prologue; *MGH, SRM*, III, 567.

13   *Miracula s. Eusicii*, prologue; Labbe, *Nova bibliotheca manuscriptorum*, II, 463.

14   Walter Goffart, *The Le Mans Forgeries. A Chapter in the History of Church Property in the Ninth Century*

(Harvard Historical Studies, Vol. 76; Cambridge, Mass.: 1966), pp. 50-55. *BHL* 4546 has never been published, but it consists of parts of two other works by the same author: the *Vita s. Juliani* (*BHL* 4545) and the first chapter of the *Actus pontificum Cenomannis in urbe degentium* (*BHL* 4543). These two works have been published, although in an edition which has been made partially obsolete by the work of Goffart: G. Busson and A. Ledru, eds., *Actus pontificum Cenomannis in urbe degentium*, Vol. 2 of *Archives historiques du Maine* (Le Mans: 1901), pp. 10-27 (*BHL* 4545) and pp. 28-39 (*BHL* 4543). The text of *BHL* 4546, Letaldus' source, occurs in two manuscripts, both from Fleury: Vatican, Reginensis latinus 318, ff. 235-249v and Paris, Bibliothèque nationale latin 12606, ff. 13-15. I have compared both manuscripts to the printed version with the aid of Goffart's study. *BHL* 4546 begins with the text of *BHL* 4543 (Busson and Ledru, p. 28, line 1 to p. 35, line 13) and continues with the text of *BHL* 4546 (Busson and Ledru, p. 14, line 9 to p. 27, *explicit*). There are certain minor variations from the two printed texts: (1) *BHL* 4546 substitutes general statements for the list of specific church properties contained in *BHL* 4543, (2) the sentence in *BHL* 4546 connecting the two printed versions differs from the text *BHL* 4545, (3) *BHL* 4546 also omits two cross references from *BHL* 4545.

15 "For many things are written in (this *Life of St. Julian*) which are also found in the same sense and sometimes even in the same words in the *Lives* of either Blessed Clement or Blessed Denis the martyrs, or the *Life* of St. Furcaeus the confessor." *Vita s. Juliani*, chap. 3; *PL*, CXXXVII, col. 783A. For editions of these other texts: *Passio s. Dionysii* (*BHL* 2171); *MGH, Auctores antiquissimi*, Vol. 4, (Berlin: 1881), pp. 101-105. *Virtutes s. Fursaei* (*BHL* 3213); *MGH, SRM*, Vol. 4 (Hannover: 1902), pp. 440-449. *Passio s. Clementi* (*BHL* 1848); Bonino Mombrizio, ed., *Sanctuarium, seu Vitae sanctorum*, 2 vols. (Milan: 1479?), I, 193-195.

16 *Vita s. Juliani*, chap. 4; *PL*, CXXXVII, col. 784A.

17 *Vita s. Juliani*, chap. 4; *PL*, CXXXVII, col. 784B.

18 *Vita s. Juliani*, chap. 1; *PL*, CXXXVII, cols. 781D-782B.

19 For Adhemar's description of the confrontation, see his *Epistola de apostolatu s. Martialis*, *PL*, CXLI, cols. 89-112, particularly cols. 90A-91D and cols. 95C-96A. For discussions of this dispute, see Louis Saltet, "Une discussion sur Saint Martial entre un Lombard et un Limousin en 1029," *Bulletin de littérature ecclésiastique*, 26 (1925), pp. 165-186 and 279-302; and Daniel Callahan, "The Sermons of Adémar of Chabannes and the Cult of St. Martial of Limoges," *Revue bénédictine*, 86 (1976), pp. 251-295, particularly pp. 256-258.

20 *Chronicon*, entry for 813; *PL*, CXXXII, col. 76A.

21 *Vita s. Lamberti*, prologue; *MGH, SRM*, Vol. 6 (Han-

nover: 1913), p. 385. On this text, see Baudouin de Gaiffier, "L'hagiographie dans le marquisat de Flandre et le duché de Basse-Lotharingie au XIe siècle," *Etudes critiques d'hagiographie et d'iconologie* (Subsidia hagiographica, Vol. 43; Brussels: 1967), p. 444.

22 *Vita s. Pauli Aureliani*, chap. 1; *AASS*, March 2, 112. True to his word, Vitalis excised much material from the earlier *Life*. Andrew of Fleury later remarked: "Another man, Vitalis, both in name and deed. corrected with the judgment of his provident incisiveness the *Life* of the excellent Paul, the celebrated eremitical bishop of the Bretons." *Vita Gauzlini abbatis Floriacensis monasterii*, chap. 2; *Vie de Gauzlin, abbé de Fleury*, Robert-Henri Bautier and Gillette Labory, eds. and trans. (Sources d'histoire médiévale publiées par l'IRHT, Vol. 2; Paris: 1969), pp. 34-36.

23 On Theodoric, see Albert Poncelet, "La vie et les œuvres de Thierry de Fleury," *Analecta Bollandiana*, 27 (1908), pp. 5-27; Manitius, *Geschichte der lateinischen Literatur*, II, 449-455; and Anselme Davril, "Un moine de Fleury aux environs de l'an mil: Thierry, dit d'Amorbach," in René Louis, ed., *Etudes ligériennes d'histoire et d'archéologie médiévales. Mémoires et exposés présentés à la Semaine d'études médiévales de Saint-Benoît-sur-Loire du 3 au 10 juillet, 1969* (Auxerre: 1975), pp. 97-104.

24 (1) *Vita s. Martini papae* (*BHL* 5596); Angelo Mai, ed., *Spicilegium romanum*, 10 vols. (Rome: 1839-1844), IV, 293-295 (prologue only), and Laurentius Surius (Laurence Suhr), ed., *Historiae seu Vitae sanctorum...*, 13 vols., 5th ed. (Marieta: 1875-1880), XI, 421-440 (text). (2) *Passio ss. Tryphonii et Respicii* (*BHL* 8340); Mai, ed., *Spicilegium romanum*, IV, 291-293. (3) *Vita s. Firmani* (*BHL* 3001); Albert Poncelet, "La vie de s. Firmanus, abbé au diocèse de Fermo par Thierry d'Amorbach," *Analecta Bollandiana*, 28 (1899), pp. 22-33 (which contains only sections of Theodoric's work). The four lost works were a sermon on the forty martyrs of Sebaste, a passion of St. Anthimus and his companions, and two *Translations*, for the coming of the head of St. Damian and of the relics of St. Basilidus and his companions to Rome. The list is found in the prologue to the *Passio ss. Tryphonii et Respicii*. Later in his life, while residing at the monastery of Amorbach in Franconia, Theodoric also composed a work on the cult of St. Benedict at Fleury (the *Illatio s. Benedicti*, *BHL* 1122) and several non-hagiographic works.

25 *Vita s. Martini Papae*, prologue; Angelo Mai, ed., *Spicilegium romanum*, 10 vols. (Rome: 1839-1844), IV, 294.

26 *Passio ss. Tryphonii et Respicii*, prologue; Mai, ed., *Spicilegium romanun* IV, 293.

27 *Vita s. Firmani*, prologue; Poncelet, "La vie de s. Firmanus," p. 25.

28 *Liber Pontificalis*, chap. 76 (*BHL* 5595); Th. Momm-

sen, ed., MGH, *Gesta pontificum romanorum*, Vol. 1 (Berlin: 1898). For the latter two sources Theodoric used the translations of Anastasius Bibliothecarius (*BHL* 5592), the same man who was probably responsible for first collecting the *Liber Pontificalis*; *PL*, CXXIX, 584-609.

29 Theodoric's *Vita s. Martini papae* consisted of five sections: (1) An original passage on the saint's birth and virtues, *Vita s. Martini papae*, 1-5; Surius, *Vitae sanctorum*, XI, 421-424. (2) Material from the *Liber Pontificalis* to which Theodoric added one original passage, *Vita s. Martini Papae* chaps. 6-9; Surius, *Vitae sanctorum*, XI, 424-425. (The original passage begins "O praeclara Dei pietas . . ." and continues to the end of the chapter.) (3) Two letters of Martin, which Anastasius had translated in the first person narrative, *Vita s. Martini Papae* chaps. 9-12; Surius, *Vitae sanctorum*, XI, 427-430. (Compare *PL*, CXXIX, cols. 587B-589C. Theodoric's passage does not include the entire text of the letters.) (4) A transcription of almost all of Anastasius' translation of Theodore's *Commemoratio*, *Vita s. Martini Papae*, chaps. 15-23; Surius, *Vitae sanctorum*, XI, 431-438. (Compare *PL*, CXXIX, cols. 591A-599A.) (5) A largely original concluding section, *Vita s. Martini Papae*, chaps. 24-26; Surius, *Vitae sanctorum*, XI, 438-440. (One passage of chap. 26 is adapted from the *Commemoratio; PL*, CXXIX, 599D-600A.) There are also brief original connecting passages.

30 The sources of both the *Passio ss. Respicii et Tryphonii* and the *Vita s. Firmani* exist only in incomplete manuscripts, which I have been unable to consult. Poncelet describes Theodoric's use of the *Passiones ss. Respicii et Tryphonii* (*BHL* 8336 and 8339), "Thierry de Fleury," pp. 14-19; and his use of the earlier *Vita s. Firmani* (no *BHL* listing), "La vie de s. Firmanus," pp. 24-26, n. 1.

31 *The Implications of Literacy. Written Language and Models of Interpretation in the Eleventh and Twelfth Centuries* (Princeton: 1983). Stock particularly considers the cult of the saints during the eleventh century on pp. 64-78, but without reference to the writers discussed here.

32 On Hugh of Fleury, see Manitius, *Geschichte der lateinischen Literatur*, III, 518-521; and Nico Lethink, "Pour une édition critique de l'*Historia Ecclesiastica* de Hugues de Fleury," *Revue bénédictine*, 91 (1981), pp. 386-397.

33 *Vita, Translatio, et Miracula s. Sacerdotis* (*BHL* 7456); *PL*, CLXIII, 979-1004.

34 *Vita, Translatio, et Miracula s. Sacerdotis*, prologue; *PL*, CLXIII, col. 979D.

35 *Vita, Translatio, et Miracula s. Sacerdotis*, prologue; *PL*, CLXIII, cols. 980D-983A.

36 *Vita, Translatio, et Miracula s. Sacerdotis*, prologue; *PL*, CLXIII, col. 983A.

37 *Vita, Translatio, et Miracula s. Sacerdotis*, prologue;

PL, CLXIII, col. 983C.

38 *Vita, Translatio, et Miracula s. Sacerdotis*, prologue; *PL*, CLXIII, cols. 979D-980D.

39 The manuscript itself has been lost, but Couderc edited a test concerning St. Saderdos and Sarlat which may represent a medieval transcription of these marginalia; C. Couderc, "Notes sur une compilation inédit de Hugues de Sainte-Marie et sa vie de saint Sacerdos évêque de Limoges," *Bibliothèque de l'Ecole des Chartes*, 54 (1893), pp. 468-474. This text reveals that Hugh used a wide variety of hagiographic and chronicle sources in his researches.

40 *Vita, Translatio, et Miracula s. Sacerdotis*, prologue; *PL*, CLXIII, cols. 980D-981A.

41 *De pignoribus sanctorum*, *PL*, CLVI, cols. 607-680. On the date of the text, see John Benton, *Self and Society in Medieval France. The Memoirs of Abbot Guibert of Nogent* (New York: 1970), pp. 238-239. Klaus Guth has extensively analyzed the work, *Guibert von Nogent und die hochmittelalterliche Kritik an der Reliquienverehrung* (Studien und Mitteilungen zur Geschichte des Benediktiner-Ordens und seiner Zweige, Vol. 21; Ottobeuron: 1970). Stock considers the work in terms of twelfth-century developments in both piety and the "textualization" of culture, *The Implications of Literacy*, pp. 244-252.

42 *De pignoribus sanctorum* I, 2; *PL*, CLVI, col. 621.

43 *De pignoribus sanctorum*, I, 3; *PL*, CLVI, cols. 625C-626A.

44 *De pignoribus sanctorum*, I, 1; *PL*, CLVI, cols. 613D-614A.

45 *De pignoribus sanctorum*, I, 1; *PL*, CLVI, col. 615A.

46 *De pignoribus sanctorum*, I, 3; *PL*, CLVI, col. 622C.

47 *De pignoribus sanctorum*, I, 1; *PL*, CLVI, col. 616A.

English Cathedral Monasteries and the Reformation

Stanford E. Lehmberg

Everyone who has traveled in England, or even dreamed of doing so, is aware of the marvelous cathedrals which form the country's greatest legacy of medieval architecture. Canterbury, York, Durham, Winchester, Salisbury, Lincoln, Wells: who has not seen glamorous pictures of these buildings, perhaps in advertisements of the British travel board, and yearned to visit them?

Although the glories of English cathedrals are well known, several aspects of cathedral history deserve further study.[1] Even students of medieval monasticism, for instance, may not have realized that more than half of the English cathedrals were also monasteries, staffed by monks rather than by secular priests. Of the nineteen cathedrals established in England at the end of the Middle Ages, ten were monastic in organization. Canterbury, Winchester, Worcester, Rochester, Durham, Ely, Norwich, Coventry, and Bath were Benedictine priories, while the cathedral at Carlisle was a house of Augustinian canons. The older of these monastic cathedrals owed their structure to Lanfranc, who brought the monastic rule to bishops' sees which antedated the Norman conquest. In all of these houses the duties of a cathedral were grafted onto the normal monastic arrangements; the monks' common life centered around the choir services, the refectory, the library, and the dormitory. Secular cathedrals followed a different pattern, also established in Normandy before 1066. At York, Salisbury, Lincoln, Exeter, Hereford, Lichfield, Chichester, Wells, and St. Paul's in London, services were maintained by secular canons who lived in separate houses and enjoyed individual incomes derived from landed estates.[2]

The life of the monastic cathedral priories came to an end between 1538 and 1540, when these religious houses were suppressed as part of Henry VIII's general dissolution of the monasteries. Evidence collected by the King's commissioners, working under the direction of his great minister Thomas Cromwell, suggested that gross disorders and immorality existed in the religious houses and that even God would be pleased by their dissolution. Modern historians of the suppression have discounted some of the more ludicrous tales of sexual scandals but have generally agreed that monasticism was no longer the vital force it had been in earlier centuries and that the men in religious orders had become secular in outlook, more interested in a comfortable, easy life than in spirituality and scholarship.

Some evidence from the cathedral monasteries, however, suggests that this judgment may be too harsh and that some of the houses, at least, continued in good form to the very end. At Durham, where records are unusually full and unusually accessible, the situation appears to have been very positive. While some other houses had experienced a decline in numbers, associated with a diminished appeal of monastic professions, the population of the Durham priory remained stable: here the number of monks had held to a constant figure of about seventy since 1360, when the house recovered from the effects of the Black Death. There were 69 monks at Durham in 1535, 72 in 1538, and 66 at the time of dissolution in 1540. The age structure of this monastic population had not changed much either. At the beginning of the sixteenth century members of the community had been in the priory for an average of fifteen years, while at the dissolution the average tenure had risen to about eighteen years, perhaps indicating increased longevity as much as a decline in the intake of young men. Nor had revenues declined. For years Durham had been able to anticipate an annual income of about £1,500, principally from landed estates which the house had acquired over the centuries, and the revenues had been rising, in part because of increased profits from salt pans.[3] The cathedral maintained two schools, the almonry school for poor children and the song school for choristers. It possessed the largest library in northern England (the holdings can be traced in the great catalogs of medieval libraries in England compiled by N.R. Kerr and can still be viewed by the visitor to Durham since most of them, quite remarkably, remain *in situ*).[4] The number of monks with a university education was surprisingly high. Since the fourteenth century Durham had maintained a cell, Durham College, at Oxford; at the time of the dissolution twenty-one of the monks had studied there, five held bachelor's degrees in theology, and a further five had attained the doctorate. One could hardly argue that such an establishment had fallen on evil times.

There were, of course, some signs of secularism. The Prior of Durham held an attractive manor just outside the city, usually called Bearpark though the name is a corruption of French (Beaurepaire) which referred to the beauty of the site rather than the keeping of a zoo, and monks were invited there on a rotating basis for what we would now call rest and rehabilitation.[5] The rigors of monastic diet were allayed by invitations to join the prior in his separate hall, where guests were entertained and meat was served, even on fish days. Similar privileges were available in other houses; at Canterbury, for instance, annual holidays were the rule, feasts became very elaborate, and sick monks who entered the infirmary were regaled with sugar cordials, lozenges, and a host of similar luxuries. Troops of wandering players occasionally brought their entertainments to Canterbury, if not to the more remote Durham. And these admittedly two of the best Cathedral priories. Norwich, as far as we can make out, was about the worst. Even histories predisposed to be favorable have found it hard to say anything good about the status of the Norwich house just before the dissolution, or about the bishop and prior of this period.[6]

Whatever their condition, the monasteries were dissolved, the smaller houses beginning in 1536 and the greater ones, including most of the cathedral priories, shortly after a second act of dissolution was passed by Parliament in 1539.[7] But Henry VIII and Cromwell had no intention of closing the cathedrals totally; they were to be given new constitutions and refounded with a staff of secular priests.

A number of surviving documents enable us to trace the development of the government's plans. One set of papers, dating from 1539, gives specific proposals in minute detail, with salaries designated for all officials, from the dean down to bellringers, vergers, and groups of poor men to be supported on the foundation.[8] In every case these proposals

would have returned most of the old endowments of the monastic cathedrals to their secular successors. Canterbury, for instance, was valued at £2388, and the proposed new establishment was to be allocated £1963. Durham was given £1593 out of the previous income of £1688. Rochester, always a small, poor see, was to retain £702 of its former £849. The monks at Carlisle had received a mere £418 a year before the dissolution, but the new cathedral was to have £603, the difference being made up out of lands which had belonged to another religious house. Norwich is not included in this list; it was handled, as we shall see momentarily, as a special case. Nor are the houses at Bath and Coventry. These two were unusual cases, for in each instance they served a diocese which had another cathedral already staffed by secular priests. So they were simply dissolved, the diocese of Bath and Wells now being served by Wells alone and Coventry and Lichfield by Lichfield.[9]

Refoundation schemes went beyond this, however; they proposed the erection of a number of new bishoprics, each with a cathedral which would take over the buildings of a large monastery which had not previously enjoyed cathedral status. As many as sixteen new cathedrals were originally proposed. Had they all been founded there might now be a functioning cathedral rather than the gloriously picturesque ruins at Fountains in Yorkshire, and St. Albans might have been spared its centuries of decay followed by over-zealous Victorian restoration at the hands of Lord Grimthorpe. But in the end only six new sees were established. Westminster Abbey functioned as a cathedral only briefly, for Bloody Mary restored its monks in 1556 and when Elizabeth turned them out finally in 1559, the Abbey became a "royal peculiar" rather than the mother church of a diocese. (What with St. Paul's, London did not need another cathedral or another bishop.) The cathedrals established at Gloucester, Peterborough, Chester, and Bristol have survived as planned in 1539, and the new diocese of Oxford has remained as well, although its cathedral was originally to have been the dissolved monastery at Oseney, in the countryside outside Oxford, rather than the house associated with the new college of Christ Church. Endowments in these cases were less generous. Westminster, it is true, was given £1687, but that was little more than half of its former revenues. Oxford was supposed to operate on £577 a year, and Chester on a mere £471.[10]

The first monastic cathedral to be converted into secular foundation had already received a new charter when these proposals were drafted. In May 1538 Norwich was transformed. Its last prior became the first dean. Five monks were named prebends, and sixteen more were made canons. The dean and chapter were given power to make their own statutes (they did not get around to doing so until the seventeenth century!) and to allocate revenues for the support of the clergy and choristers.[11] The other monastic cathedrals, as well as the new foundations, had their regulations imposed from without, in the form of statutes compiled by two bishops and a Cambridge don who later obtained the bishopric of Ely. Although there were a few local variations—special provision for preachers at Canterbury and for a grammar school at Worcester—these statutes have a basic common text. Appointments to the deanery and canonries were placed in the gift of the Crown, an important difference from the arrangements in the old secular cathedrals, where the bishop appointed the canons and the chapter itself elected the dean. Canons of the new cathedrals had no individual rights or revenues but rather became part of a corporation, styled the dean and chapter. Minor canons and lay clerks—the men who sang in the cathedral choirs—were provided for, as were boy choristers; the statutes mention skill in singing as an essential qualification but provide no mechanism for dismissal if vocal abilities faltered. Constitutionally the position of these musical establishments differed markedly from that of the so-called vicars choral of the secular cathedrals, since the colleges of vicars choral formed separate legal corporations with property and revenues of their own, apart from the endowments of the dean and chapter.

The new statutes for the former monastic cathedrals appoint the first deans and prebendaries by name. It was common for the prior of the former monastery to remain as dean of the new foundation; this arrangement was followed at Durham, Ely, Rochester, Winchester, and Worcester. At most of the new cathedrals—Westminster, Chester, Gloucester, Bristol, and Peterborough—the deans had also been heads of the dissolved monasteries. Only at Oxford and Canterbury were secular priests appointed to the new offices.

Many of the lower-ranking monks retained similar positions as well. In general, the new cathedral establishments were about half the size of the monastic communities; those monks who could not be accommodated with cathedral appointments were pensioned off, generally at the standard allowance of £6 a year. In some cathedrals the groups of ex-monks remaining at the cathedral were substantial:

at Durham twenty-six out of fifty-four monks stayed on; at Canterbury twenty-eight of the fifty-three monks joined the collegiate establishment; at Norwich more than twenty remained; and at Gloucester fourteen were "dispatched" and fourteen stayed.[12]

And so the monastic cathedrals were gone well before the end of Henry VIII's reign, early victims of the English Reformation. But, as Dom David Knowles once commented, "the change-over was effected with a minimum of dislocation. The monks who remained, the most intelligent and generally useful members of the old community, found themselves living a life that differed little from that in the monastery, save that they gradually came to dwell in separate lodgings carved out of the old buildings."[13] Within a generation their successors would be allowed to marry and have families, and communal life would disappear. But much of the work of the monastery remained, and indeed remains today. The liturgy, though eventually simplified and turned into English, continued. The musical traditions lingered. Libraries were often preserved. Education was fostered, alms were given, and some sort of hospitality remained. It is perhaps no exaggeration to say that the English cathedrals kept what was finest from the medieval monastic tradition and enabled it to live on, in an altered form, within a new, more secular environment.

Notes

1   This paper forms part of a larger study, which will describe the role of cathedrals in English society during the sixteenth century, with particular attention to the changes associated with the Reformation.

2   See Stanford E. Lehmberg, "The Reformation of Choirs: Cathedral Musical Establishments in Tudor England," in DeLloyd J. Guth and John W. McKenna, eds., *Tudor Rule and Revolution: Essays for G.R. Elton from his American Friends* (Cambridge: Cambridge University Press, 1982), pp. 45-67, esp. p. 46.

3   Information drawn from manuscript sources preserved in the Prior's Kitchen, Durham, and from analysis of these sources by Alan Piper of the Department of Palaeography and Diplomatic, University of Durham. I am grateful to Mr. Piper and to Patrick Mussett for their kind assistance when I was studying materials in the Durham archives.

4   N.R. Kerr, *Medieval Libraries of Great Britain: A List*

of Surviving Books (London: Royal Historical Society, 2nd ed., 1964), pp. 62-72, and Kerr, *Medieval Manuscripts in British Libraries* (2 vols., Oxford: Clarendon Press, 1977), II, 483-511.

5   See R.B. Dobson, *Durham Priory, 1400-1450* (Cambridge: Cambridge University Press, 1973), pp. 97-99.

6   Cf. Dom David Knowles, *The Religious Orders in England, Vol. III: The Tudor Age* (Cambridge: Cambridge University Press, 1959), pp. 73-74.

7   Lehmberg, *The Later Parliaments of Henry VIII, 1536-1547* (Cambridge: Cambridge University Press, 1977), pp. 61-64.

8   E 315/24, Public Record Office, London, calendared in *Letters and Papers, Foreign and Domestic, Henry VIII,* 21 vols., (London: H.M.S.O., 1862-1932), XIV, pt. II, no. 429.

9   Knowles, p. 389; A. Hamilton Thompson, ed., *Durham Cathedral Statutes* (Durham: Surtees Soc., Vol. 143, 1929), p. xxv.

10   E 315/24, P.R.O.; Lehmberg, "Reformation of Choirs," pp. 52-54.

11   Thompson, pp. xxvi-xxxi.

12   Ibid., pp. xxxi-lii; Knowles, pp. 389-392.

13   Knowles, p. 392.